# LIDDELL'S RECORD

St. John Richardson Liddell

# LIDDELL'S RECORD

## St. John Richardson Liddell
### Brigadier General, CSA

*Staff Officer and Brigade Commander*

*Army of Tennessee*

Edited by Nathaniel C. Hughes

MORNINGSIDE

1985

ISBN No. 089029-314-7

Published by Morningside House, Inc.
260 Oak Street, Dayton, Ohio 45410
P. O. Box 1087, Dayton, Ohio 45401

# FOR MY FRIENDS

The Teachers and Students
of
Webb School, 1959-1962
Bell Buckle, Tennessee

St. Mary's School, 1962-1973
Memphis, Tennessee

GPS, 1973-1985
Chattanooga, Tennessee

# CONTENTS

# PREFACE

Twenty-seven years ago I began gathering information on William J. Hardee. As a graduate student I went through a multitude of sources like a vacuum cleaner. I took far too many notes and strayed into many coves, but enjoyed the chase.

One day, at the Southern Historical Collection, I came across a manuscript fragment, written in longhand, in ink, on ruled 8½ x 14 inch legal sheets. The slightly water-stained sheets were bradded together and marked, "Section Four." Reading a portion, I realized that the document was important.

The manuscript belonged to the General Daniel Govan Papers. Who had written it? By using Fletcher Green's method of internal criticism, I proved to the satisfaction of James W. Patten, Director of the Southern Historical Collection, that Govan was not the author. Soon I proved that St. John Richardson Liddell was.

Where was the rest of the manuscript? Had it been completed? Did it still exist? Luckily, Hardee nuggets and Liddell nuggets are often found in the same strata. In addition to the four sections at Chapel Hill, twenty-two, twenty-eight, twenty-four, and twenty-one pages in length, I found three sections in the archives at L.S.U., and the remainder at Tulane. Two sections had been published by Basil Duke in the *Southern Bivouac* (December, 1885, and February, 1886).

When I had assembled the whole manuscript, "Liddell's Record and Impressions of the Civil War," I felt not a little smug, just like fitting in the last piece of a frustrating puzzle.

*Hardee* demanded, however, and *Liddell's Record* began to gather coffee stains. When *Hardee* came out in 1965, I returned to Liddell.

What was I to do with *Liddell's Record?* It couldn't stand by itself. No one but a galley slave or a Confederate scholar would read it through.

Liddell's sentences are endless and aimless. His paragraphs

7

stop only at the bottom of the page. The order is chronological, with great gaps and digressions. Errors abound. Liddell seems to have raced through certain sections, leaving places and dates for a subsequent draft. Writing from memory caused errors in detail.

A massive and indiscriminate use of semicolons and dashes, misspelling and inconsistencies of spelling, redundancies, doubled-back descriptions, lack of proportion, and batches of improperly located discourses clogged the flow of the narrative. Entire blocks of the manuscript were incoherent.

I found three versions of the manuscript. Portions had been copied and redrafted by his children. The ability to recognize Liddell's handwriting helped greatly. Corrections, information, and observations had been inserted in the second and third drafts. Some of the changes, however, Liddell made himself. He had also bits of paper here and there in the manuscript with additional information.

To preserve this valuable historical document, I felt it should be published. Publication, however, required radical surgery.

I cut and cut. I integrated many of the marginal notes and loose scraps. Some of these ran several paragraphs, but all were in Liddell's hand. I broke up the interminable sentences, and inserted verbs and prepositions, deleted clauses, paragraphs, and even pages. I corrected spelling; I rearranged both sentences and paragraphs.

I chose to ignore many deletions made by Liddell and his helpers. I reinserted them where they were located originally or moved them to a more appropriate location.

*Liddell's Record* is the writing of a participator, a doer, a fully engaged human being. Liddell was a violent man. He killed. He was tried for murder. He was murdered.

Liddell believed in the Southern cause; he supported slavery and he blamed the Yankees for the war. Liddell hated well, and never apologized for it. No one ever considered him to be an objective, reflective type with the insight of a Pepys. In fact, I find it remarkable that this emotional man of action wrote at all.

This is why Liddell's protective friends, aware of his astonishing candor, urged Basil Duke to delete passages from the chapters he published. Liddell goes too far. He says too much and says it intemperately. But this is the man who would toss a glass filled for a toast out the dining room window and precipitate a feud.

I wish Liddell had spent more time observing and reporting,

rather than moralizing and justifying his own actions. The *Record* is descriptive, but its subjectivity dilutes its credibility. I wish Liddell had not allowed his narrative to degenerate into fault-finding. I wish he had avoided the "I told you so" syndrome that smears the ink of his sincere intentions. But he didn't.

Greater insight into the personalities and relationships surrounding him would have made this a far more valuable document. The reader can surmise readily how many remarks and situations Liddell misconstrued. Prejudice distorted his judgment. Perhaps the gripping gloom of 1866 in the swamps of Louisiana blinded him. Where is the humor of the Arkansas boys? You know they were laughing and embarrassed rushing pell-mell (and not in time) from a huge picnic to defend Liberty Gap.

I am sorry Liddell's writing is dark and labored and biased and disproportioned. As his editor, I have tried to help because I admire this brave brigade commander who lies forgotten and unappreciated.

I like St. John Liddell's elemental humanity. He is brash and he is unfair. He suffers and he carps and he frets and he envies and he hates and he loves.

*Liddell's Record* contributes to Civil War historiography because it is the work of a man involved in the making of history. He took care to relate a conversation, trying hard to capture, if not the exact words spoken, then the manner and mood of the person with whom it was held. He provides fresh information and insight for some of the questions that nag historians. He moved about with unusual freedom, having been "admitted to the councils" and possessing "in very full measure the confidence of Generals Albert Sidney Johnston and Braxton Bragg." Basil Duke noted "no officer of his rank in the Confederate army, perhaps, saw more constant and important service, or witnessed or became personally familiar with events of real historic value."

His experiences indeed range widely. He pored over Beauregard's battle maps prior to the Battle of Bull Run; he saw action in Missouri in 1861; he fought with the Army of Tennessee through 1862 and 1863; he operated in the Trans-Mississippi Department in 1864; and he ended the war defending Mobile. As a consequence of his broad service, his familiarity with the old army establishment, and his social contacts, Liddell knew or had entree to the Confederate military and political high command. He himself was not an important historical figure, but he was well placed.

Liddell wrote fast. In July, 1866, he completed the first chapter. By mid-October, 1866, he was through. Writing in the summer of 1866, of course, lends value to his work. Anger, despair, frustration, sadness, jump out from the print. Liddell was blinded by the immediacy of his experience, but he was not blinded by the fog of time.

Unlike many Civil War memoirs, Liddell's views are often blunt, even harsh. Virtually no one is spared. "I am not going to protect my friends in making a faithful record." He felt an obligation to history and refers to "the truth of history" several times. He knew that many of his friends and acquaintances had already become historical figures. He realized that he had experienced important historical events. He believed that he was fortunate to be spared and he owed it to his dead comrades and to his beloved brigade to put down his memories and his impressions.

Constrained by several considerations, this editor faced the dilemma of how to provide sufficient biographical material without disturbing the continuity of the *Record*. As the reader will observe, I have used content footnotes to supply bits of information. A biographical essay is chunked before and behind Liddell's narrative.

The *Liddell Papers* at L.S.U. and the complementary holdings there and at Chapel Hill yielded over nine thousand documents touching Liddell's life. I wish that I had been able to weave more of this material, particularly personal correspondence, into the text. I thought of doing a biography itself, but lacked the desire.

Several short attempts at Liddell's biography have been made: one in the Louisiana volume of Evans' *Confederate History;* an incomplete two-page effort written by his nephew Frank Liddell Richardson in 1887; and a talk given by his adjutant general, George A. Williams, in 1902.

The Jones-Liddell Feud complicated my work greatly, but it lent intrigue and adventure to introverted scholarship.

I hope I have been fair.

I am indebted to several individuals for their generous and thoughtful assistance: Bill Meneary, Tulane Library; M. Stone Miller, LSU Archives; Wilma McCarver, Catahoula Parish Library; Mrs. Nell Broders, Baton Rouge; Mercedes King; the late Dr. James W. Patten; Louise Werner, GPS; Elizabeth Lansing, St. Mary's School; Lt. Gail Petty, U.S.A.; Bill Hughes, who did leg work for me; Christine Cureton, who checked out the missing towns of Georgia; Stuart Butler, National Archives; the late Dr. Sidney Foreman, U.S.M.A.; the late Thomas Robson Hay; Dr. Carolyn Wallace, Southern Historical Collection; Katherine R. Ramsey, Catahoula Parish Court Clerk's Office; Sam Hughes, who tried to perfect the imperfect; Betty Webster, GPS; Kenneth W. Rapp, U.S.M.A. Archives; and Pat Eynard, Louisiana Historical Association's Confederate Museum.

# THE YEARS BEFORE THE WAR

St. John Richardson Liddell was born September 6, 1815, at Elmsley, a plantation near Woodville, Mississippi, where his parents had just made their "first crop in the woods."

His mother, Bethia Frances Richardson (1788-1824) had come west with her parents from Sumter County, South Carolina. She was the youngest daughter of William and Magdaline Richardson. The Richardsons were a propertied family of South Carolina, long prominent in the political and military affairs of that state.

Moses Liddell (1785-1856) had also come west from South Carolina as a young man in 1805. He moved about among the Mississippi River communities until 1812, when he settled in Wilkinson County at Woodville. He married Bethia Richardson on October 20, 1814, and they set about establishing Elmsley.

Moses Liddell's father, Andrew Liddell, was born in Ireland, emigrated to America and settled in South Carolina. A Revolutionary soldier, he married Jane Johnson. Jane's father was burned to death by Tories and Cherokees in his home during the Revolution. Jane, Moses' mother, was left destitute, "literally stripped of everything." St. John was told this story many times.

St. John, or as he was commonly called, "John," had three younger sisters: Ann Caroline (Nancy), who married William Smith Griffin, Emily Jane, who married John Hampton Randolph, and Bethia Frances, who married Francis DuBose Richardson. The two latter families became well-known and well-off in Louisiana. They kept in close contact with St. John and his family.

11

William Griffin died in 1835 and Nancy in 1844, leaving an orphan, Carolina, to be raised by St. John.

Moses Liddell became a prosperous Mississippi planter, a "model probate judge," and acquired many slaves and many acres. He gave his children the best education available in Mississippi, and enabled them to mix socially with the leading families of western Mississippi and eastern Louisiana. Moses saw to it that St. John became accustomed to New Orleans as well as Natchez.[1]

St. John Liddell entered the University of Virginia in 1832. Scarcely enrolled, he became dissatisfied and applied for admission to West Point. He wrote several letters to the most influential men he had met in Mississippi and asked them to help him to gain admission. He even wrote to Lewis Cass, Secretary of War. The letter that clinched the appointment, however, was that of Franklin E. Plummer, Congressman from Mississippi and friend of Moses.

St. John Liddell entered the United States Military Academy in the summer of 1833. Among his classmates (class of 1837) were Braxton Bragg, John C. Pemberton, Joseph Hooker, Jubal Early, W. H. T. Walker, and W. W. Mackall. By December, 1833, Liddell was miserable and pleaded to come home. Finally, but reluctantly, Moses gave his permission for John to resign.[2]

John did not resign, however; he stayed on, although his academic record promised little. Abruptly on February 19, 1834,

1. Frank Liddell Richardson, "St. John R. Liddell," Liddell Family Papers, Louisiana State University Archives, Baton Rouge, Louisiana (hereinafter cited as LSU); Marcellin Gillis Papers, Southern Historical Collection, University of North Carolina, Chapel Hill, North Carolina (hereinafter cited as SHC); Weston A. Goodspeed, *The Province and the State; a History of the Province of Louisiana* (Madison, 1904), p. 251; 1850 Adams County, Mississippi, Census; 1850 Catahoula Parish, Louisiana, Census; Liddell Family Cemetery, Wilkinson County, Mississippi; Genealogical Record, in J. H. Randolph Papers, LSU; *Biographical and Historical Memoirs of Louisiana*, 2 vols. (Chicago, 1892), II, 329 et passim; Moses Liddell's Elmsley Plantation Notebook, Liddell Papers, LSU; Caffery Family Papers, SHC; D. C. Hutchison to St. John R. Liddell, October 9, 1844, Liddell Papers, LSU; Will of Moses Liddell, Liddell Papers, LSU; Adams County, Mississippi, Marriage Book, V, 127; Francis D. Richardson Memoirs, SHC.
2. Kenneth W. Rapp to N. C. Hughes, Jr., April 23, 1980; St. John R. Liddell to Lewis Cass, September 17, 1832, October 4, 1832, March 13, 1833, in USMA Archives; Moses Liddell to St. John R. Liddell, October 23, 1832, in USMA Archives; F. E. Plummer to Levi Woodbury, October 3, 1832, USMA Archives; Moses Liddell to St. John R. Liddell, August 22, September 10, 1832, December 4, 1833 in Liddell Papers, LSU; C. Elliott to St. John R. Liddell, September 19, 1832, in Liddell Papers, LSU; F. E. Plummer to St. John R. Liddell, March 27, 1833, in Liddell Papers, LSU; Nancy Liddell to St. John R. Liddell, January 29, 1834, Caffery Papers, SHC.

he was discharged from the Corps of Cadets. Officially, he was dropped "for deficiency in studies," although Military Academy Order #5 states,

> Cadet John Liddell of Mississippi, a member of the U. S. Military Academy, having been reported to this Department for conduct highly subversive of good order and discipline, and for gross violation of many of the Regulations of the Institution, is by order of the Secretary of War hereby discharged from the service of the United States. He will therefore cease to be a member of the Military Academy, from the promulgation of this Order at West Point.[3]

His letters indicate an encounter or trouble of some sort with cadets Cooke and Perry. There were arrests and court-martials and rumors of a duel in which Perry was wounded.[4] Liddell's classmate wrote, "you will receive in a few days a letter signed by the whole corps save seven or eight *Damned* Yankees commending your conduct."[5]

It seems that Liddell went home slowly, by way of Washington, D. C., and Cincinnati, where he had a not unusual financial shortage. Maybe he tried to join the navy. In any event, his West Point friend, R. A. Arnold, wrote him,

> . . . I have always thought that you would do better at home than in the Navy. You have advantages John that everyone cannot boast of *and* my advice to you is to go home, marry a pretty Mississippi Girl and settle yourself down to Farming. Should you be in want of a overseer just let your humble friend know it as he is anxious of obtaining some good situation.[6]

By October, 1835, Liddell was back in Woodville, and Moses

---

3. MA Order #5, February 16, 1835, Engineer Department, Washington, D. C.
4. James H. Perry was admitted July 1, 1833 and resigned December 3, 1835, for deficiency in studies. West Point records indicate, however, that Perry and Liddell "were not on friendly terms." Kenneth W. Rapp to N. C. Hughes, Jr., August 4, 1982.
5. Joseph M. O'Donnell to N. C. Hughes, Jr., July 1, 1959; R. A. Arnold to St. John R. Liddell, February 19, March 2, March 21, 1835, in Liddell Papers, LSU; Moses Liddell to St. John R. Liddell, March 26, 1835, in Liddell Papers, LSU; Grady McWhiney, *Braxton Bragg and Confederate Defeat* (New York, 1969). p. 10.
6. R. A. Arnold to St. John R. Liddell, March 2, 1835 in Liddell Papers, LSU.

set about to find him some good land in Louisiana. Actually the idea seems to have come from Moses' friend (and future son-in-law), Francis D. Richardson. As early as 1832 he urged Moses to buy John a sugar plantation in the Bayou Gula area.[7]

Moses let John look and learn. Letters from this period indicate that John helped plant cotton in Vidalia, Louisiana. He visited many of the budding upriver plantations and journeyed all across northeast Louisiana and southeast Arkansas. He would put this knowledge to good use in the campaign of 1864.

John ran up bills; he quarreled; but he observed. His shopping for land ended in 1837 when he found a tract on the Black River just below Trinity.[8] Moses bought it for him. John was thrilled.

He settled on Black River in 1837 and by 1838 was planting cotton. John's lack of direction vanished as he committed his energies and enthusiasm to his plantation.[9] Brother-in-law John H. Randolph visited him there in July, 1839, as Emily Jane reported to her sister Bethia:

> Mr. Randolph has just returned from a visit to John, on Black River. He was very much pleased with the land, etc., and is anxious to settle there. Can't you persuade Mr. Richardson to settle there too, so that we may all be together. John is delighted with his place. He has just put up a new house which he calls Fancy Castle. John Maynard keeps house, and performs the honors of the table with much grace.[10]

Fancy Castle became Llanda in 1841. All it needed was "Molly."

7. John's younger sister Emily did settle near there in 1841. She had married (1837) a young cotton planter, John Hampton Randolph (1813-1883). They soon turned from cotton to sugar planting. By the outbreak of the war the Randolphs had about 7,000 acres composed of four plantations: Fairvue, Forest Home, Bayou Goula, and Nottaway. Nottaway (1859) became one of the South's ante-bellum show places.
8. He found a tract two miles south of Troy Plantation or Troyville (present-day Jonesville). Black River begins here where the Little, the Ouachita, and the Tensas Rivers merge. Liddell wanted a large tract in this rich historic neck of land. This "watery crossroads of the Catahoula Swamp" is the site of the Troyville Mounds. These great and mysterious Indian mounds had been known for centuries to the Indian, the Spaniard, the Frenchman, and the Louisianan.
9. Francis D. Richardson to Moses Liddell, December 24, 1832, in Liddell Papers, LSU; correspondence between St. John R. Liddell and Moses Liddell, September, 1836—March, 1840, Liddell Papers, LSU.
10. Jane L. Randolph to Bethia L. Richardson, July 22, 1839, Caffery Papers, SHC.

14

John had met Mary Metcalfe Roper about 1839 in Natchez. The daughter of Judge William Roper of Maysville, Kentucky, Mary had come downriver to visit her beloved uncle, Dr. Volney Metcalfe. St. John and Mary were married at Volney Metcalfe's Montrose on September 2, 1841. This marriage extended a wide network of related families from Natchez across eastern Louisiana to New Orleans (Ker, Hollingsworth, Caffery, Baker, Joor, and many others).[11]

The families remained close. Letters, blending easily family, business, social, and political concerns, continued back and forth among them for two generations. The Randolphs and the Richardsons supported St. John Liddell throughout, and showed great pride in his Confederate achievements. Frank Liddell Richardson adored his uncle and became his most effective apologist.

Francis Richardson, a mature, patient, reflective planter, kept in close contact. This classmate and friend of Edgar Allen Poe became a legislator in Louisiana, and a conspicuously successful businessman. Bayside, which Richardson built in 1850 in Iberia Parish, was an outstanding example of deep south plantation architecture.

Ten children were born to St. John and Mary Liddell at Llanda or in Natchez between 1842 and 1859: Bethia Frances, Moses John ("Judge"), William R. (Willie), Volney Metcalfe, Louis J., Louisa R., Sarah (Loulie), James Metcalfe, Mary, and Jessie C. In addition, nine-year-old Carolina Emily Nancy Griffin came to live with them in 1844.[12] John and Mary Liddell adopted this orphaned niece and she remained with them until her marriage to Marcellin Gillis in 1854. The Liddells were devoted to Carolina and this closeness extended past the Civil War.[13]

11. Adams County, Mississippi, Marriage Book, VI, 498; St. John R. Liddell to Mary M. Roper, July 31, 1841; St. John R. Liddell to Dr. Volney Metcalfe, September 9, 1841, Amelia T. Hollingsworth to Mary M. Roper Liddell, November 13, 1849, in Liddell Papers, LSU; 1860 Catahoula Parish, Louisiana, Census; Jane Liddell Randolph to Bethia Liddell Richardson, September 12, 1841, Caffery Papers, LSU; Goodspeed, *Province and the State*, p. 251; 1850 Adams County, Mississippi, Census; 1850 Catahoula Parish, Louisiana, Census.
12. Jane Liddell Randolph thought Carolina "perfectly wild" for a young girl. Jane's sister Nancy (everyone's favorite) had led a lonely life from the time of William Griffin's death the year after they were married (1835) until her own death in 1844.
13. The correspondence between Gillis and Liddell is heavy and continuous, since the former was Liddell's cotton factor in New Orleans. A great many of their letters have been preserved in the Gillis Papers, SHC, and the Liddell Papers, LSU.

By October, 1841, the young Liddells were at work on Black River, carving Llanda out of the swamp. It was hard, often discouraging work. They built their dock, outbuildings, and two rows of slave quarters on the west bank of the river. Llanda, on higher ground, sat back from the water.

Liddell kept a journal describing the activity of each day. Many of the entries are in Mary's hand, however, and as the years went by she took a greater role in the operation of Llanda.

> Sunday just after supper—9 o'clock. About this time every evening I write in this book the occurrences of the day. I having now pursued the custom for 3 years or more, find it like a second nature to me. Feeling as if something was wrong (with me) if neglected, so that with the addition of making an invaluable book of references *(to myself)* in future, I never fail to attend to my evening's work. Frequently in my absence my wife writes in it for me. My father first suggested this plan to me, and what appeared irksome at first, has now become a gratification.[14]

Moses Liddell sold Elmsley in 1846 and moved to Louisiana. He made his residence at Bayside with Bethia and Francis Richardson, and continued to own land in Catahoula and St. Mary Parishes, Louisiana; in Texas; and in Arkansas. His property in Catahoula alone inventoried at $160,000 at his death.[15]

Moses and John corresponded frequently. Moses' letters are long, full of instructions about plantation management, and full of encouragement. John still owed him a great deal of money and continued to borrow more.

> I really had no idea that you would have touched a dollar of the proceeds without letting me know it. . . . I trust that you will refrain from purchasing or going in

14. April 2, 1843, entry in Plantation Diary of St. John R. Liddell, Liddell Papers, LSU.
15. A letter from Moses' son-in-law, William Griffin, is revealing:
   "Should he [Moses Liddell] come, make yourself known to him, render him as comfortable as possible, and behave yourself as well as you can. He is a plain, self-taught, self-made, old gentleman, and of a character as unimpeachable and as highly respectable as that of any man living or dead. He is, however, and has been for several years, very intemperate, in consequence of his second marriage." W. S. Griffin to brother Samuel Griffin, July 13, 1834, in Gillis Papers, SHC.

debt for anything except what you really want and cannot conveniently do without.[16]

Moses' letters to John leave little doubt that, though he admonished him and used a stern tone from time to time, he indulged his only son. The death of Bethia and a disastrous second marriage seem to have made Moses dependent emotionally upon his children.

Nancy wrote John in the spring of 1834:

> You cannot believe what affection he bears for you. He said, "There is not a night I lie down but what John is uppermost in my mind." He would say no more, and tears burst from his eyes. . . . "I love him too deeply— my whole life and soul and feelings are centered in that boy." Such were the words he uttered, while his lips quivered, and tears were coursing each other down his cheeks.[17]

As time passed, St. John Liddell prospered. He continued buying adjacent land. Some he would cultivate; some he would use for pasture. By the end of 1855 his four tracts on Black River totalled over 1500 acres. On Llanda lived 150 Liddell slaves (15 from his mother's estate; 125 purchased from Moses), 65 horses, and 80 cattle.

In the early 1840s Liddell had 60 acres planted, alternating rows of cotton and corn. By 1844 increased planting doubled the 83 bales (1444 pounds each) he produced in 1840. A few entries from his plantation daybook show the variety of his activities:

Jan. killing hogs, clearing ground, rolling logs, piling brush, burning brush, making shingles, women cut cane, salting meat, sewing oats, branding cattle, plant Irish potatoes

Mch. plant sweet potatoes, 9 ploughs running, plant corn, plant cotton, plant garden crops (onions, parsley, red pepper, tomatoes, cabbage, beans, pumpkins, melons)

April scraping and cutting out cotton, 11 ploughs running

May building negro cabin [five technical drawings of a circular saw—how large a piece of timber will it cut? Liddell asked himself]

16. Moses Liddell to St. John R. Liddell, January 16, 1843, Liddell Papers, LSU.
17. Nancy Liddell to St. John R. Liddell, March 18, 1834, in Caffery Papers, LSU.

Aug.  doctor for sick slave, cut cane, hoe cotton, moulding brick, —60,000, killed wild cat, deer

Sept.  pick cotton, gather corn

Oct.  pick cotton, discharged hired workers, Jones—drunkeness and talking with negroes, Martin quit

Dec.  10 holidays

These daybooks, journals, and diaries of Liddell's contain everything from recipes for gumbo to a cure for a foundered horse.

Plantation work fascinated Liddell, as did levee construction. He loved any type of gadget. As evidenced by hundreds of drawings and notations in his diaries, Liddell had a mechanical bent and a talent for sketching. He drew farm animals, and made designs for plows, water pumps, buildings, and all sorts of devices. He invented the "Liddell Attachment," which is thought to have been some sort of plowing implement.[18] He also invented the huge "Liddell Gin," "having one hundred and twenty saws, with the main pulley in the center, and calculated to gin fifteen bales of cotton a day."[19]

To manage a plantation such as Llanda, Liddell required a successful overseer, but an overseer needed too many good qualities, technical as well as personal. Liddell never found (after 1842) the right man. At Moses' request he tried J. Andrew Liddell, but he too proved unreliable.

At its best, Llanda remained a bit primitive and never rivaled the plantations of the Richardsons and the Randolphs. Located between the Black and Little rivers, it was subject to crippling overflows. Without a protective levee system, the threat of high water made life there anxious.

Disease was a constant concern as well, and death was no stranger to Liddell's diary. Nearby Trinity watched its population drop to 200 in 1850. Cholera and dangerous damaging high water ran them off. Twenty-three people died in Trinity within six weeks during the fall of 1850.[20]

18. Correspondence, invoices, broadsides, advertisements, clippings, bankbooks, memorandum books, notebooks, plantation diaries, time books, and lumber books, 1839-1869, in Liddell Papers, LSU.
19. New Orleans *Evening Delta*, October 4, 1857.
20. Sue C. Avery, Alice B. McL. Winegeart, and Alma McC. Womack, *Jonesville Through the Mirror of Time*, 3 vols. (Jonesville, La., 1978), III, 10. (Hereinafter cited as *Jonesville*).

Cholera, whooping cough, inflamation of the stomach, worms, alcoholism, all contributed to making a slave owner's life a nightmare. Slave health was crucial. Liddell even fretted when he found some enterprising river captains had put his slaves in with immigrants coming upriver. He kept books for his slaves as they bought and sold and borrowed among themselves. He nursed them, he whipped them, he mourned them. In 1851 he received bad burns and scars as he nearly lost his life in a futile attempt "to save a little Negro from the flames."[21]

These slaves, the hired hands he employed, and Llanda itself dominate his letters and conversations. He did have other interests, however, and enjoyed a special sort of city life in New Orleans and Natchez.

Liddell went up and down Black River and the Mississippi frequently. A trip to New Orleans was an ordinary event in his life. He continued to venture north and west into "the Pine country." He eventually owned 2700 acres on Boeuff River (Morehouse Parish) which he used principally to produce lumber. He also owned 1280 acres on Bayou Sabine in Bienville Parish, 484 acres on Brush Bayou, Concordia Parish, and 20 acres in Memphis.[22]

Liddell busied himself with the Louisiana Colonization Society in the late 1840s. He became vice-president, believing the effort would benefit his children and his neighbors as "protection from the fanaticism of the abolitionists."

His papers contain numerous drawings of levees. He participated in water control projects and petitioned local and state bodies, requesting action and offering alternative plans and designs. He encouraged lobbying on behalf of the "swamp," and saw that the right persons were present at carefully staged political dinners. He called himself a Whig in the 1850s, although his political stands and activities were not significant.[23]

About 1850 Liddell, through the influence of Mary M. Liddell and her sister, Louisa Roper, became a Presbyterian. His letters henceforth reflect an iron religious determination and a tone of fatalism that may have been dominant in the tiny Trinity Presby-

21. John H. Randolph to Moses Liddell, April 21, 1851, in Liddell Papers, LSU.
22. Plantation Notebook, October 19, 1859, in Liddell Papers, LSU.
23. St. John R. Liddell to R. L. Stanton, August 21, 1848; St. John R. Liddell to Moses Liddell, May 7, 1851, miscellaneous correspondence, 1847-1860, in Liddell Papers, LSU.

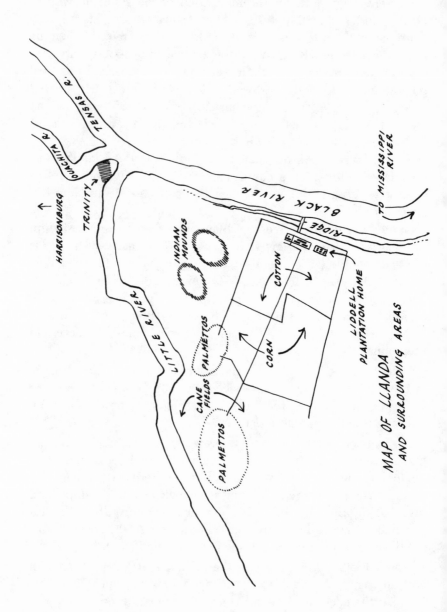

MAP OF LLANDA
AND SURROUNDING AREAS

terian Church. Liddell gave the land in 1858 on which this church, one of the oldest in the Red River Presbytery, was built.[24]

In 1847 Liddell's life changed suddenly and irreversibly. Like some Faulknerian hero, his became a blighted existence, nervously and absurdly fastened to a man and woman dedicated to his destruction. The twenty-three year struggle between St. John Liddell and Charles and Laura Jones is known in Louisiana as the Jones-Liddell Feud or the Black River War. The consequences of the feud between these two families in this dark land dominated by the mysterious Indian mounds widened over the years. Eventually at least fourteen men would die violently, not only in Catahoula Parish on the land between the rivers, but in New Orleans itself.

Charles Jones, a young man the same age as Liddell himself, arrived on Black River about the same time (1837-1840). He acquired, through a land grant patent, Elmly Plantation in 1841, the same year St. John brought Mary M. Liddell to Llanda. It is believed Jones emigrated from Ireland, coming to Catahoula by way of Kentucky.[25]

By 1848 Charles and Laura Jones had built Elmly on the banks of Black River. The early plantation house, though modest itself, was set at the end of a drive, 100 yards long, flanked by magnificent double rows of sycamores. Charles Jones also owned Troy Plantation, the site of present day Jonesville, Louisiana. The 1860 census shows him prosperous, with real property valued at $300,-000 (Liddell, $240,000). This Catholic planter in a largely non-Catholic area of Louisiana, had a reputation connecting him to trouble in Monroe, Louisiana, and in Kentucky. Even the relationship between the Joneses themselves was stormy. In March 1849 Laura won a judgement against Charles and had their property separated.[26]

24. St. John R. Liddell to Bethia L. Richardson, March 26, 1850; Mary M. Liddell to Bethia L. Richardson, March 26, 1850, in Caffery Papers, SHC; *Jonesville*, I, 28.
25. The Census of 1860, however, lists Jones' birthplace as Kentucky and Laura Stewart Jones' as Ohio. One source believes that Jones, while living in Kentucky, may have been involved with the Roper family.
26. At one time the relationship between the Joneses and Liddells appears to have been friendly. For instance, the owners of Blue Cane Plantation, twenty miles south, recalled coming up regularly from their houses in New Orleans and entertaining there and being entertained at Elmly and Llanda by their friends and neighbors, the Joneses and Liddells. Correspondence, 1847-1860, Liddell Papers, LSU. 1850, 1860 Catahoula Parish, La., Census; Judgment #2061, Fifth District Court of New Orleans, Laura S. Jones v Charles Jones, March 10, 1849.

The origin of the feud is obscure. The evidence is contradictory and patinaed with time. One version anchors all to an argument over a flock of Jones' geese. Francis D. Richardson, who ought to have known, stated the men ". . . first met socially at a gentlemen's dining, during which a toast was given by the other reflecting upon female virtue. Major Liddell, who was sitting near an open window, threw out his glass of wine. Here the arrow entered. . . ."[27]

Whatever happened took place by October 1847, for in May, 1848, Liddell wrote, "this man has been in pursuit of my life since October last. . . ." Matters worsened. During 1848 Liddell definitely felt threatened. He observed Jones acting "in the most suspicious manner." Jones through his actions "indicated impudence or hostility."[28]

In April 1848, Jones attacked and wounded a friend of Moses and St. John Liddell with a knife. This assault caused bitter resentment by both father and son. Judge J. G. Taliaferro, perhaps the most influential citizen of that area of Catahoula Parish, tried to mediate the dispute, but Liddell questioned Taliaferro's involvement with Jones. Meanwhile friends and acquaintances provided more tinder. Liddell's good friend Felix Robb reported to Liddell that Jones intended to kill him.[29]

The match for the fire was Eliza J. Nichols, wife of Phillip R. Nichols. The Nichols had arrived as neighbors in early 1845. Volney Metcalfe knew them in Natchez and complimented both highly. Liddell and his wife exchanged visits with the Nichols and got along famously. Mrs. Nichols probably began to serve as Carolina Griffin's tutor, relieving the Liddell's concern for the education of their ten-year-old ward. The Nichols also owned land adjoining Jones. According to one source, Jones coveted this remaining part of his section, so he determined to drive them out of the Black River area by slandering Mrs. Nichols.[30]

In any event, Eliza Nichols, on the morning of April 26, 1848, appeared at the end of the avenue at Elmly to speak with Charles

27. Francis D. Richardson, "St. John R. Liddell." Liddell Papers, LSU; Lanza, "Jones-Liddell Feud."
28. That same October R. H. Curry warned Jones that he and Liddell would have difficulties whenever they met. St. John R. Liddell Diary, Letterbook #15, Liddell Papers, LSU.
29. *Ibid.*
30. Volney Metcalfe to St. John R. Liddell, January 28, 1845; St. John R. Liddell to Volney Metcalfe, January 13, 1845, Liddell Papers, LSU.

Jones. She was accompanied by St. John Liddell. An argument ensued and Eliza Nichols shot Jones in the face. He fled and was shot again as he ran back to the house.

Liddell reported in a letter to C. G. Forshay, "I arrived there only in time to see her shoot him repeatedly and to take her away in safety, for treachery and rascality was apparent all around. That *man's wife* is a bad woman. There is no telling what she will do—already there are reports that she offered a reward to the negroes to assassinate Mrs. N. . . ." In his diary Liddell wrote that Mrs. Nichols shot Jones when he unbuttoned his coat. He regretted that he "did not finish Jones off." "If I had not been there Mrs. Nichols would have been lost."[31]

> Jones seems to persist in it—"that I am his murderer—that I shot him the fatal shot." &— He [(Jones)] certainly is satisfied that he [(is)] not *dead*.—He certainly forgets too that he met me on the Bayou below his place to kill me, & that I was entirely ignorant of his designs upon me—& that there were too many persons along with me. He forgets that this was disclosed to me by Curry's letter to him—exhibited by Judge Taliaferro.—He forgets too his attack upon a member of my family.—He forgets that he has spoken of the manner in which he could easily kill me, viz. when he found me unarmed that he would insult me—that I would rush upon him & he would slay me justifiably.—This was contemplated when he met me with arms on the Bayou. What would he have done with my sister to stop her testimony? as she happened to be along — Mr. & Mrs. Nichols' presence prevented the catastrophe. I only wish now that I had . . . finished the affair for Mr. N.; but I thought that the revenge of his injured honor belonged to *her exclusively* & aided her so far as was compatible with her safety.— Jones forgets that he & his wife have left here with violent threats. Forgets that he has used treachery all along.[32]

Liddell was in danger, even though Charles Jones remained at

31. Lanza, "Jones-Liddell Feud"; Crawford, "Jones-Liddell Feud"; *Jonesville*, I, 28; St. John R. Liddell Diary; St. John R. Liddell to I. L. Mathewson, May 14, 1848; St. John R. Liddell to C. G. Forshay, May 19, 1848, in Liddell Papers, LSU.
32. St. John R. Liddell Diary, Liddell Papers, LSU.

Elmly recuperating from his wounds. Jones' nephew, Sam Smith, threatened to kill those who shot his uncle. Smith also vowed that he would "pick off" Liddell's Mississippi friends "if they did not look out." Jones' friends in Catahoula also began to make hostile remarks about Liddell.[33]

To everyone's relief, Charles and Laura Jones defused the situation by leaving Black River when Jones' wounds had healed. They went to New Orleans, and from there perhaps to Cincinnati. Liddell did not know what they were up to, but friends informed him that Jones intended to return and kill him.[34]

In April 1852, Charles and Laura Jones came back to Elmly. "His return was like a firebrand to the community," reported the Vidalia *Concordia Intelligence.*

Jones brought with him Richard Pryor, "noted blackleg without means or character." Pryor and Sam Smith were seen before an election standing behind some trees near the roadside at a place convenient for intercepting Liddell on his return from the election. "The impression became general that assassination had been contemplated."[35]

An employee of Henry Huntington, a friend of Jones, alarmed Liddell by discharging his pistol in front of Llanda. Liddell disarmed him. Huntington called Liddell a coward and invited him to a duel on the Texas line. Liddell declined, suspicious of being waylaid en route.[36]

Liddell began buying weapons from Kentucky. He remained close to home with three or four friends there for protection, ". . . seriously alarmed as to his personal safety." "I shall stand upon my *named rights* and shall assuredly defend myself, and destroy whomsoever I suspect has designs on me."[37]

One member of the Jones faction was Samuel Glenn, a 33-year-old planter on Little River. He and Pryor "had made some threats

33. St. John R. Liddell to D. V. Metcalfe, May 18, 1848, in Liddell Papers, LSU.
34. The Nichols also left. By November, 1851, Phillip and Eliza Nichols were back in Natchez. Carolina Griffin was also there, either visiting or being tutored, Lanza, "Jones-Liddell Feud"; Crawford, "Jones-Liddell Feud"; St. John R. Liddell to Carolina Griffin, May 17, November 25, 1851, in Gillis Papers, SHC.
35. Vidalia, La., *Concordia Intelligencer,* July 24, 1852.
36. Articles of Combat: Henry Huntington to St. John R. Liddell, May 28, 1852, Liddell Papers, LSU; Lanza, "Jones-Liddell Feud"; Crawford, "Jones-Liddell Feud."
37. Bills of Sale, April-June, 1852, Liddell Papers, LSU; St. John R. Liddell to I. L. Mathewson, May 14, 1848, in Liddell Papers, LSU.

of violence." Liddell learned on June 26, 1852, that the two had gone into Jonesville.

A few hours later Samuel Glenn and Moses Wiggins, a 41-year-old neighbor of Liddell's and a Jones sympathizer, were ambushed on the Trinity Road. Glenn's body was found in the carriage; Wiggins ran wounded until he dropped dead in front of Llanda. ". . . Maj. Liddell professes to have killed both, but regrets that he took Wiggins for another person." Liddell was arrested for murder.[38]

Liddell's friends justified his conduct on the grounds that the numerous threats made against him by his adversaries led him to believe that he was to be waylaid and assassinated. Lewis Ker put it more plainly; we "consider you fully justified in all you have done and all regret there were not a few more travelers in *that* buggy."[39]

"Terrible excitement" reigned in Catahoula as the relatives of the slain men assembled. Under unusually heavy guard, the prisoner Liddell was moved from the jail in Catahoula to that in Concordia. When the trial came, however, Liddell was tried in Catahoula's Eleventh Judicial District. Conducting the defense was the able William F. Martin of Natchez, together with Owen Mayo and Edward Sparrow of Louisiana. It took courage for these men to defend Liddell in the face of "threats of death to any lawyer who should appear for the defense." After two Grand Juries, two "Not True" bills, one regular jury, and a "not guilty verdict," Liddell was finally acquitted in April, 1854.[40]

The high feelings did not die, however. In 1856 Liddell speaks of "my enemies." He was convinced Jones and his friends would have turned Catahoula into a criminals' den if it had not been for his stand against them.[41]

By 1857 calmer heads prevailed and a document was drawn between Liddell and Charles and Laura Jones, "agreeing that Liddell and the Joneses would pass one another as strangers and without recognition." If either party had a grievance they would

38. Vidalia, La., *Concordia Intelligencer*, July 24, 1852; Washington, *National Intelligencer*, July 21, 1852; Lanza, "Jones-Liddell Feud."

39. Lewis Ker to St. John R. Liddell, August 13, 1852, Liddell Papers, LSU; Vidalia, La., *Concordia Intelligencer*, July 10, 1852.

40. Records of the Eleventh Judicial District, Catahoula Parish Courthouse, Harrisonburg, La.

41. St. John R. Liddell to Marcellin Gillis, July 7, 1856, in Gillis Papers, SHC.

alert the other before any action was taken. It is significant that Liddell did not sign the document.[42]

Trouble would come. Everyone knew it. In the meantime, war clouds diverted attention.

A preview occurred in 1860. Moses ("Judge") Liddell had enrolled at the Louisiana State Seminary of Learning and Military Academy at Alexandria, Louisiana. Who should be in charge of the young L.S.U. but Major William Tecumseh Sherman. Judge suddenly left (technically he has deserted, according to Sherman) the State Seminary because he thought he would be compelled to tell on another cadet.

Sherman tried very hard to be diplomatic and fair, but Judge and his father were furious. The fact that Judge was president of the school's "Midnight Marauders" did not make them less vehement. Liddell appealed to the Board of Supervisors but they backed Sherman. Liddell thought Sherman "had made a mountain out of a molehill about an absurd secret society." Sherman deserves censure. "His course has been neither consistent, dignified, nor free from prejudice—three essential qualifications for the control of young men."[43]

Sherman would leave soon for other battles; so would Judge, and so would St. John R. Liddell.

42. Sworn Statement signed by William Beard, Felix Robb, Charles Jones, and Laura Jones, November 8, 1857, Liddell Papers, LSU.
43. Judge appealed to W. B. Taliaferro to intervene. The latter investigated and declined, infuriating the young Liddell. "On fear of getting into difficulty you cannot comply with your promise." You ". . . prefer the friendship of W. T. Sherman to that of truth and justice." C. G. Forshay to St. John R. Liddell, April 17, 1860; W. T. Sherman to St. John R. Liddell, June 26, 1860; St. John R. Liddell to W. T. Sherman, June 5, 1860, July 18, 1860; St. John R. Liddell to Gen. R. M. Graham, August 14, 1860; W. B. Taliaferro to Moses J. Liddell, September 10, 1860; Moses J. Liddell to W. B. Taliaferro, Sept., 1860, Liddell Papers, LSU.

## TO MY SONS

M. J. Liddell, Volney M. Liddell, and Louis J. Liddell

To My Sons, M. J. Liddell, Volney M. Liddell, and Louis J. Liddell,
  I give this record with the hope that the truth will impress you with the instability of all human calculations. In this so-called enlightened age, war as the natural state of man, notwithstanding the teachings of philanthropists, will, some time or other, come upon you. It becomes your duty to provide for such a terrible contingency. I only hope, my dear boys, that like your Grandfather, your life may pass in peace. Whilst he escaped trouble, your Great Grandfather suffered terrible distress in the Revolutionary War of 1776. Do not, therefore, indulge the delusions of a life of long peace and quiet. Do your best, no matter what your station. Be cheerful and seek contentment, but do not forget to be prepared for everything.
  It is natural that changes of man's affairs should occur in cycles of half centuries. Nothing is fixed or certain with humanity. As the seasons change, so may man. We children of men are but atoms on Earth in the hands of the great Unknown.
  Should you ever be induced to publish this record, give yourselves ( I enjoin it) no concern at the animadversions that possibly might arise from public knowledge of the important truths ( to some persons) I have written.

Your Father
St. John R. Liddell
Brig. Gen., C. S. A.

Llanda
October 14, 1866

# AUTHOR'S INTRODUCTION

It is my purpose to write only my impressions, with the facts coming under my own observation during this war. I do so regardless of the motives and acts of those connected with me or of the common enemy. I know well that no two persons see the same thing in the same light. Nevertheless, the truth can only be obtained from the collated writings of all who impart their own observations. I pretend to no more than a simple narration of facts, to the best of my knowledge and recollection.

I know that it is natural for the chief actors in this war to be believed, when truthful men in lower stations will not be credited. In the greater part of this record, I am compelled to write in the first person, though repulsive to my own sense of modesty. I have either to do this or give up the subject. I consider that I owe my record to my children and if ever published by them, which can only be after my death, I hope all allusions to myself will be overlooked, since criticism cannot reach me in the grave. I have written for no present usefulness or profit or even benefit to my Children.°

---

° The editor has spared the reader by removing all but the two final paragraphs of Liddell's eighteen-page introduction. Despite the animadversions that might arise from such editorial harshness, I feel these pages on the cutting floor can be reduced to:

Radical Republicans drove an exasperated South into war.

The South struggled magnificently against staggering and ever-increasing odds. A virtually defenseless nation led by a man of limited vision conducted fatally inactive defensive warfare.

Hannibal and Napoleon are the two greatest generals in history.

# CHAPTER I

# IN SEARCH OF A COMMAND

Impressed with the necessity for prompt preparation on the part of the South, I corresponded with Colonel Braxton Bragg of Louisiana and by appointment met him at Baton Rouge in January, 1860. He was at that time State Commissioner of Swamp Lands. I had not seen him for 26 years, when we were at the same school and in the same class.[1]

I expressed to him my fears that the threatening political troubles would cause collision between the North and the South. I suggested prompt preparation for defense on the part of our State. He readily admitted this to be the probable result of the existing state of sectional animosities but believed the danger to be yet distant. On his part, he only wished my cooperation and assistance as a citizen of the State in organizing and fostering the State Military School at Alexandria on the Red River. This would help prepare young soldiers for the emergency.

I apprehended that no time would be afforded for much benefit to be derived from such a school before war would occur. Something more was needed now. He was of different opinion. He thought any action premature, and to my mind rather made light of the subject. I, on the contrary, had become more strongly impressed with apprehensions than ever as discussion cleared away the mists. I felt free to confess that I would prefer being a subject of the British limited Monarchy than to live under a government such as ours. It was soon to come under the control

1. United States Military Academy, Class of 1837. Liddell's letters of 1849 contain references to Bragg's marriage that year to Elisha Brooks Ellis, a young lady from Louisiana known to and perhaps related to the Liddell-Metcalfe family group.

of Black Republicanism which would not hesitate to disregard or pervert all constitutional rights to their own uses.

I could have no confidence in the stability of things or affairs when a popular majority whose "will," guided by passion or hatred, could execute their higher-law construction of the written constitution of the Union. There could be no worse tyranny under the sun. The greater number of tyrants the most insufferable the tyranny.

Bragg was a strong Democrat and believed in the integrity of republics. He overlooked the fact, an insurmountable one with popular governments, that the masses are ever liable to become fanatical or exacting or venal when controlled by corrupt representative leaders, oftentimes cloaked with religion.

I did not see Bragg again till July, 1861. Meanwhile, some of my premature fears had been verified. The Southern States were seceding from the Union, and great excitement prevailed. War was talked of, and names of active leaders were mentioned on both sides. Amongst them was that of W. T. Sherman, who had been in charge of the State Military School at Alexandria. He had been placed there through the influence of Bragg himself.

Notwithstanding Bragg's partiality, I had no confidence in Sherman, in as much as he had perverted the truth in a correspondence I had with him a short time before.[2] In a subsequent personal interview, I had discovered that it was his nature to do so to attain his objects. I was also satisfied that he was against the South at heart. Bragg said that he had not heard him spoken of unfavorably by any other person. I answered that Bragg himself would find him out before being done with Sherman.

We changed the subject to the probable strategy of both sides in case of Civil War. I alluded to the military policy of the North to get possession of the Mississippi River and divide our territory and cripple our resources. Bragg thought the idea impractical. When I spoke of the facilities of railroad transportation for military purposes for invasion, he rejected its practicability, also saying that such communications are too open to severance. His opinions seemed fixed but were by no means convincing. He lived to learn better by sad experience, the hardest of teachers. At that time, in my ignorance of such things, I trusted sincerely that he was right.

2. Liddell refers to the episode of his son "Judge," mentioned in the prewar chapter.

We disagreed so continually that I feared he was inclined to perverseness, which always will bias good judgment. Some of my views were reasonable. At all events, I felt annoyed that he would not even entertain them at a time when he could have done good from his important standing in the country and well-established military reputation. Apart from the pride of Southern character, every interest I had was at stake, all of which must sink or float with the cause.

A short time after this conversation, it became known that Major Sherman had given up the Alexandria School and gone North. Upon the next time meeting with Bragg, I referred to the facts and wished to know his opinion. Bragg said with a shrug, "That Sherman was just like all the rest of the Yankees, unreliable." Nothing more was said, nor can I call to mind an occasion in which Sherman's name was ever again mentioned between us. I have heard from a young officer of Bragg's staff, and his relative, that Sherman made professions to the former that did not tally with his subsequent course.

I think in July, 1861, Bragg was appointed Brigadier General by Louisiana. Upon the establishment of the Confederate Government at Montgomery, he was transferred with his command to that service. He desired me to take a commission under him, but I declined until necessity for my service should arise. Then I would answer his call promptly. He was ordered to Pensacola and promoted in the fall.

I had never held office of any kind, or sought it. When affairs became so threatening as to require the raising of troops, some few of my friends endeavored to secure for me the command of one of the newly organized regiments in the state. They did so without my knowledge, and, it turned out, without success, as my name carried no political weight. Perhaps it was fortunate for me. I found that the politicians in seeking the new field for distinction were having their own way in the organization of regiments.

I retired at once from competition, pleased to think that they who had used the most influence in bringing on the war were bravely determined to see it out personally. How many stuck, I am unable to say. As the danger of war thickened, I fear all did not adhere unswervingly to their professions of constance. Nevertheless, the majority did, and deserve therefore all the praise due brave and patriotic men.

31

A collision in April, 1861, became more and more imminent. I was not content with passive inactivity and therefore went to Virginia.[3] On my way, I met with Brigadier General Hardee at Memphis, who was going to take command in Northern Arkansas.

We renewed old associations of 1835.[4] We agreed that I would serve as a volunteer on his staff. Bragg had never made any call on me. I was to join Hardee at Pocahontas, Arkansas, after my return from Virginia.

About the 12th of June, I was at Manassas when I saw Beauregard,[5] whom I had known since 1835, now in command of the Army. I found him exceedingly reticent of his designs, giving me very little information. He, however, showed me his maps which put things before me so plainly that I could draw my own inferences of all probable movements, excepting, of course, the time for action and the strength of forces.

I went to Centerville where I found my eldest son, a lad of some 16 years and now Junior 2nd Lieutenant of a company of Guerrillas in Major Wheat's battalion.[6] All were at this particular juncture on duty in front and kept moving on outpost services. Very hard on young tyros.

After waiting several days and nothing occurring, I went to Richmond and was introduced by a lady friend to the President. I had not seen President Davis since my boyhood. I was too young to remember him after the lapse of some 37 years. Our families had lived in the same county in Mississippi and were well-known to each other. I recognized his resemblance to his sister, Mrs. Stamps, a most estimable lady who still remained near the old place of the family.[7]

3. Liddell skips over his activities of the spring. He left his plantation in the hands of an overseer and proceeded to collect weapons and munitions at Jonesville. These were mostly arms seized by Governor Moore's troops at the Federal Arsenal in Baton Rouge.

   He anxiously formed a company of cavalry at Trinity, but could not get its acceptance into the Confederate Service. When he left in search of a command, Liddell gave Mary power of attorney to transact all business and to run Llanda.

4. Hardee belonged to the Class of 1838.

5. Also a member of the Class of 1838.

6. Rob Wheat's Louisiana "Tigers" (1st Louisiana Special Battalion) had been "... recruited along the levees and among the alleys of New Orleans." A tough, hard lot, they became synonymous with dependable fighting. Rob Wheat, a lawyer and adventurer, carried the reputation of being a desperate leader, "reckless as brave." Judge Liddell had joined what was to become one of the most famous outfits in the Confederate Army on June 8, 1861.

7. Lucinda Davis Stamps and her husband William lived in Adams County, Mississippi close to Jefferson Davis' mother's Rosemont.

The first battle of Bull Run had just been telegraphed. Speaking of the next movement of the enemy, Mr. Davis said in reply to an observation from me, "Any attempts to turn our left by passing across our front would be very hazardous to him." He seemed very anxious but confident of the result.

The next day I returned to Manassas, taking with me my second son, 14 years old, who had come from Louisiana with me on this visit.[8] On getting near the lines on the cars, I found them closed, with orders directing all persons not connected with the army to turn back. I succeeded, however, in joining a friend, Captain Keary, now in command of the camp at the junction. I remained with him during the night.

The following morning early, the fight opened with distant cannonading. It gradually moved towards our left front and up the North side of the Bull Run. The movement of troops was plainly indicated by clouds of dust. About 10:00 a.m. the engagement with our left wing was unmistakable. Troops were hurried from right to left with all possible dispatch in support of the small force already there.

I shall not attempt to describe this tumultuous affair. It has already been done sufficiently often by both sides. The enemy had passed our front in column as if in review to endeavor to gain our left and rear, thus clearly pursuing the very movement condemned by Mr. Davis. But what advantage was taken of it was no manner perceptible to me. Men had been pushed forward to meet his flank movement; and there the battle began and ended, the enemy taking the same road in retreat, with his flanks fully exposed and awaiting, as it were, our attack.

It was a matter of wonder to me why our right wing and center were not pushed forward with all possible vigor upon the flank of the disordered mass of the enemy. Then they should have been directed to take up the line of march at once with the fugitives for Washington. The panic was so great that Washington's occupation by our troops can hardly be questioned had the attempt been made.

No good genius whispered to our Hannibal. Peace would have certainly followed, for ours would have become the de facto government, in actual possession of the Capital and all its accessories. The North, disorganized with confusion would have con-

8. Willie R. Liddell.

sented to separation without further bloodshed. I regretted the victory. Better to have lost it and taken the consequences at once than not to have availed ourselves of its advantages to the fullest.

I met no one who seemed to look farther than the glory of the day. The intoxication of success seemed to content men to give no thought for the future. This great opportunity lost forever, our troops remained inactive to give time, as it were, for the enemy to get fully ready. All of the spring we waited for something favorable to turn up. What an unpardonable suicidal policy. They who would be successful must make events, not wait for them.

# CHAPTER II

## BOWLING GREEN

From Manassas in June, 1861, to Donelson in February, 1862, a period of seven months, inaction prevailed on both sides. The Confederate loan in Europe was under negotiation. Now it was apparent that affairs there, if handled properly, would lead to fortune. Any amount of the loan would have been taken up at that period of our struggle when hope of our success was brightest to those who looked on favorably from abroad.

Here was the time and chance. Where was the boasted wisdom of Southern Statesmen? But Mr. Davis, with his singular short-sighted ideas of public economy and the future government liabilities, declined taking more than 15 millions of money. In truth, all that he could possibly get would hardly have been sufficient for our uses. Besides, it was so much the more interest in the success of the Confederacy. Interest rules the passions and hopes of men at last. The active sympathy caused thereby would have turned the scales with the outside world, so much to be desired by the Confederates in their great struggle for separate nationality. This money, if not expended, would not be lost. The interest would be nothing compared to the gains acquired by success.

The whole debt could have been liquidated in five years. Even were it otherwise, why not have enlisted every possible appliance for the benefit of the cause. This loan could have been made the basis of Confederate money and given value to government issues.

Mr. Davis' pinching economy was in positive contrast with the lavish expenditures of Mr. Lincoln. The stakes in the game were incalculable. The costs of success were not counted by the

North, although her people are the closest calculators upon the earth. To win with them was to gain everything, to fail was to lose all. It was hard to conceive of Mr. Davis, educated with the foresight of the soldier and statesman, overmatched by Mr. Lincoln, the plain, uneducated, common-sense exponent of Northern Policy. Whilst the one fails from parsimony, over caution, and unpardonable hesitation, the other succeeds in the end by boldly staking all upon the great issues.

Mr. Davis evidently overlooked the magnitude of the situation. Lacking in self-confidence, he was at the same time too self-opinionated to listen to the advice of the sensible men of the times. How true it is that the world is constantly deceived in human character and ability when placed in untried positions of great trust. The able leader of a great people in war should hesitate at nothing short of the cardinal principles of humanity and honor. Such is the requisite for success, whether in the cabinet or in the field.

In August, 1861, I joined General Hardee at Greenville in the lower part of Missouri.[1] The expedition contemplated in the direction of St. Louis had been abandoned. Hardee was now ordered by General Polk to Columbus, Kentucky, on the East bank of the Mississippi River and thence soon afterwards to Bowling Green. There General A. S. Johnston, now in command of the whole department, established his headquarters. From Bowling Green, a portion of Hardee's command was pushed up to Cave City on the Louisville and Nashville Railroad. Up to this time, all of Hardee's troops were from Arkansas, but he was now promoted Major General of Division. His division embraced men from other states.

I assisted him in drilling and disciplining the troops. There was a great deal of sickness among the young men of the Army. I do not know how many died, but I am sure not less than three thousand from various causes. The waste of life for lack of proper care was frightful. This too at a time when the services of every man were required in support of the cause. I think at one time

---

1. On September 15, 1861, Hardee appointed Liddell as his aide-de-camp with the rank of colonel. Liddell was to serve at his "own expense."

   Judge, meanwhile had left Wheat's Battalion and joined the 1st Virginia Cavalry. Charles Jones, to the astonishment of Marcellin Gillis, had just been elected Lt. Col. of the 17th Louisiana. Within it, the 17th contained two companies from Catahoula Parish.

there could have been hardly less than 16,000 sick and absent out of a total of less than 40,000.

At Bowling Green I became acquainted with Brigadier General S. B. Buckner.[2] Being the best drill officer in the service, he had organized and disciplined the best division of troops in the Army of Tennessee.[3] I learned to estimate this man highly for his many good qualities, affable, high-toned, and able, though not brilliant. He lacked only constancy of purpose to have made a more prominent figure in the war. I thought him to be impatient with superiors and yet lacking in energy when left to himself. Hardee said to me that he was not as good an administrator of his command as General S. A. M. Wood. Buckner was somewhat captious.

I also met here Major Gilmer, C. S. Engineer. Often he wanted me to accompany him in locating defensive works near Bowling Green. As it so turned out, they were never used. Brigadier General J. B. Floyd of Virginia and Bowen of Missouri were here at this period. Also here were Colonel Terry of the Texas Rangers, Brigadier General Hindman, Colonel J. C Brown[4] of Tennessee, and Colonel P. R. Cleburne of Arkansas, names more or less known.

We were inactive the whole winter. Meanwhile the Federals were busily engaged in building gunboats on the Ohio River and accumulating supplies. They concentrated troops at Louisville and on the L. & N. Railroad as far down as Munfordville on the Green River. They were preparing for some decided movement with combined strength, army and navy, Southward. They were

2. Simon Bolivar Buckner (1823-1914). Before the war he was generally thought to be the ablest Kentucky military figure. Buckner worked hard for Kentucky neutrality. He declined high commissions in both armies. When neutrality ended, he and his "state guards" entered the Confederate army. Fort Donelson clouded his reputation, but he remained popular with high-ranking military and political officials.

   After the war he regained his political power in Kentucky (Governor in 1887) and eventually became a national political figure.

3. This is a curious observation on Liddell's part, since his friend Hardee was generally regarded by both armies as "the best drill officer in the service."

4. John Calvin Brown (1827-1889). Lawyer, influential politician, Brown, as a Whig, had a strong following in his native Tennessee before and after the War. Governor of Tennessee, president of several companies, he wielded great influence.

   Just after his wedding to a niece of Mrs. James K. Polk in 1864, a telegram beckoned him back to the Army of Tennessee. A gifted leader, he rose from private to division commander. His Tennesseans were devoted to him.

permitted to get all things ready for their expedition without the slightest molestation, as General Johnston had not sufficient force to assume the offensive.

Johnston's army was scattered from Columbus on the Mississippi to Cumberland Gap. General Polk commanded at Columbus, Hardee at Bowling Green, and General Crittenden at Mill Spring. General Lloyd Tilghman was at Fort Henry and Donelson. Of this whole Army, I suppose that fully one-third were absent or sick. General Johnston was well aware of the designs of the enemy. Unable to thwart them, he sensibly felt his numerical weakness.

At this period, General Joseph E. Johnston in Virginia opposed General McClellan, who was far from being ready to march on Richmond; General Albert S. Johnston in Kentucky opposed Generals Buell and Grant and others, nearly ready to move; and General Price and Van Dorn in Missouri opposed General Frémont and others (General Steele, I think, was among the number).

Except the battle of Belmont above and opposite diagonally from Columbus where the Federal forces under General Grant had been beaten by General Polk, nothing had occurred to disturb seriously the quiet of the fall and winter. At Munfordville, however, Colonel Terry, commanding the Texas Rangers, had been killed in one of General Hindman's fights on the Green River. The time was coming when events must take some shape and remove suspense.[5]

Inclined by nature to method and order, I often commented upon the consequences of the negligence and confusion prevailing in all departments of our Army. On several occasions, I expressed to officers that we would be forced to give up Kentucky and Tennessee. Our policies and means were wholly inadequate for holding them. These reflections were not assented to and by no means believed in. Hence, some thoughtless persons regarded me as a Croaker. They learned different opinions in a few months.

I would have been glad to return to my business in Louisiana if any assurance could have been given me that our cause would prosper. As matters stood, I deemed it the unreserved duty of every true Southerner to lend his faithful assistance wherever

5. During the last week in December, 1862, Hardee sent Liddell to the camp of Terry's Texas Rangers to inspect them. Liddell returned a detailed report on the state of readiness of this regiment, and stressed that "it needs a chief. . . ."

useful. I saw plainly that these sentiments were not general. I saw also the thirst for office and the love of money. The watchful eye of Government was more than ever needed to inspire content with the honest soldier, who could not otherwise fail to become demoralized when he began to feel the sad effects of neglect in his scanty pay. Office and rank gave money and were sought for in most instances with avidity.

I know of a man from my own locality who from poverty at the beginning of the war acquired a half-million through facilities for speculation in the department he served. This man was said to have been repeatedly reported for his conduct, but to no purpose. He had been wounded slightly at Shiloh, which it seems was enough to justify his license to steal and communicate through his wife with the enemy—wounded in our cause and yet a traitor to it. His name is R. H. Cuney, Major, C. S. A., who need not distress himself about publicity since he can find company. I only mention his case by way of illustration. It cannot injure his established character.[6]

On the 9th of January, 1862, General Hardee informed me that General Johnston wished me to go to Richmond on business for him and that I must see him at once to get instructions. I did so and held a long private interview with him on the subject of my mission.

Johnston seemed fully alive to the uncertain condition of affairs. He spoke very deliberately and clearly of everything connected with his situation in holding his present line of the Green River and of the strength and designs of the enemy under Generals Buell and Grant. He regretted very much the inadequacy of his own force and desired me to impress the President with the necessity of sending him reinforcements and arms. Johnston thought both might be spared to him temporarily from Virginia, as no immediate movement was contemplated in that quarter since McClellan was not ready.

In the course of our conversation, I was careful to elicit from

6. Major R. H. Cuney served as Chief of Subsistence, Department of Mississippi and East Louisiana, from 1862 until 1865. He was relieved of his duties in December, 1862, but evidently was reappointed. Service on the staff of General Daniel Ruggles helped him secure this position.

It should interest the reader to know that in the will of Charles Jones, September 21, 1866, he admonishes Laura and his children "to be governed by the advice of Richard H. Cuney in the settlement of my affairs." Jones also served on the staff of Daniel Ruggles.

Johnston a clear understanding of his position north of the Cumberland. He ended the interview saying pleasantly that he left it to me to lay the whole matter open to the President as my judgment prompted. He then wrote a letter to Mr. Davis which would state the object of my visit.[7]

My impression of General Johnston was that he possessed a clear head, without brilliancy. He was comprehensive in his views, with an imperturbable equanimity of manner. Fully seeing the danger surrounding him, he went at his work with calm determination and unflinching tenacity. He hoped to win if possible at the start or to maneuver for better opportunity. I must, however, confess that I was not impressed with the profundity of his combinations. It was his good common-sense views that struck me and won respect. I know no one whose good sense I valued so much.

Colonel W. W. Mackall was chief of staff for Johnston. He was an old Army officer, an old friend and classmate of mine. Our meeting renewed old associations. It justified freedom of intercourse and gave me opportunities for valuable information otherwise unattainable.[8] He also gave me a letter to his relative in Richmond. I carried with me maps and a synopsis of effective strength, 23,000 nearly, and total force of General Johnston's command, 39,000 nearly.

7. A. S. Johnston to Jefferson Davis, January 9, 1862, in Service Record of St. John R. Liddell, National Archives.
8. William Whann Mackall (1817-1891), Relatively obscure, Mackall merited the respect and friendship of the Confederate high command. He excelled as chief of staff under Albert Sidney Johnston, Bragg, and Johnston. Mackall, Bragg, and Liddell were all members of the Class of 1837. In the old army he saw action everywhere: Seminole War, Canadian border, Maine frontier, and the Mexican War. He seemed the perfect adjutant general and held that post many times. In the Confederacy, he remained a staff officer, intensely loyal to his commanders.

   Not all shared in praising him: Taylor Beatty wrote in July 1864: "The removal (actually Mackall resigned because of Johnston's removal) of Mackall is a good move, I think. He has always been opposed to fighting—always predicted disaster. He has been aptly termed the "owl of the army." Taylor Beatty Diary, July 2, 1864.

# CHAPTER III

# A VISIT TO THE PRESIDENT

Leaving Bowling Green early the next morning, I traveled by rail without stopping, over the Cumberland and Blue Ridge Mountain chains. The ground was covered with snow. The bridges near Marion, in Virginia, had been washed away by previous rains. I had to take an open wagon with straw cover over me for protection from the water to get to a distant station. But notwithstanding the cold and these delays, I arrived at Richmond late in the evening of January 14, four days out. I repaired through the snow at once to the President's house.

I was soon admitted and shown into a room by a little negro boy. I found the place very comfortable after so much exposure on the railroad. In a short time, Mr. Davis came in. I handed to him my letter from General Johnston. Whilst he was engaged in reading it, my attention was drawn to his features. They seemed to be disturbed and careworn. A lighted lamp was suspended over the center table between us. As he read the letter, I could not avoid seeing the effect it had. His features seemed to contract as if by pain or perhaps anger.

To my surprise he suddenly exclaimed with abrupt emphasis, "My God! Why did General Johnston send you to me for arms and reinforcements when he must know that I have neither? He has plenty of men in Tennessee, and they must have arms of some kind. Shotguns, rifles, even pikes could be used. We commenced this war without preparation, and we must do the best we can with what we have at hand."

His manner seemed excited and irritated. Whether natural with him or for effect, I knew too little of him to say. I ventured to remark that General Johnston could hardly be expected to know anything more than his own necessities.

Mr. Davis said, "But where am I to get arms and men?" I answered that General Johnston had expressed to me his belief that there must be an excess of arms taken at Manassas. Troops might be spared to him temporarily from the seacoast defenses and other points not yet threatened.

At this Mr. Davis quickly fired angrily, "My God! Why repeat? The people of Virginia were already dissatisfied at my sending General Floyd's brigade to General Johnston. The other states are equally unwilling to spare men. What am I to do?"

I remarked with deference that troops might be spared for the occasion from Charleston, Savannah, Pensacola, and even New Orleans. Mr. Davis petulantly interrupted, saying, "Do you think these places of so little importance that I should strip them of the troops necessary for their defense?" I answered that these places were of importance, but not so much as the heart of the Confederacy. A desperate blow would soon be aimed there. If warded off in time, it might be the means of saving these places. All available means of saving these places and men from every quarter should be sent to Johnston's support. He had but a small army and would soon be attacked on all sides and compelled to fall back before superior numbers to the Memphis and Charleston Railroad on the line of the Tennessee River. Unless he maintained his ground, the connection with the rest would be cut, ending finally by the enemy taking possession of the Mississippi River and destroying our communications with Texas and Arkansas.

"My God!" again exclaimed Mr. Davis very emphatically. "Why repeat?" I now felt nettled at this constant charge of repetition and instantly said, "I am not repeating, Sir. I am trying to make known to you the facts and the dangers threatening us in Kentucky and Tennessee and, if possible, to set forth the remedy."

He now rather considerately said, "I mean only that I have heard similar remarks from others." In that case our opinion only happened to coincide, and I continued, "I came here to represent General Johnston at his special desire, to make known to you his condition and wants. I had no personal considerations of my own to promote apart from the deep interest I felt in the success of the Confederate cause."

This seemed to satisfy him with my motives at heart. He became silent and thoughtful. I then handed to him the synopsis of General Johnston's effective strength. Upon looking at it, he merely remarked that many or most of the absent and sick would go to the field when active operations commenced. I sought the opportunity to say, however, that whatever troops could be sent to Tennessee or Kentucky might be returned to their places at a future time when needed. Meanwhile, everything depended upon General Johnston's holding fast to his designs.

As to the objections made by the States relating to the transfer of their troops beyond their separative limits, I thought he ought to disregard them altogether. The people of the Confederacy had placed him at the head of their cause and would look to him alone to provide for the common defense. Whenever he thought the greatest beneficial results were to be obtained, then it was for him to use his authority to put forth the full strength of the Armies. For by united efforts only could success be assured.

In my opinion, everything available for offensive action should be concentrated into the two armies of Virginia and Kentucky to enable each to take the initiative. We should do this instead of waiting, as we were doing, for the enemy, secure and unmolested himself, to watch for the opportunity to unite his forces for attack. In short, "we must make him feel the weight of war on his own soil."

Mr. Davis quickly assented to the views zealously urged by me and said that he had such objects in contemplation but that we were not prepared for the attempt at this time. Meanwhile, all we could do now was to make the best possible use of the means in our hands. That better time never came. I now saw that Mr. Davis was not altogether satisfied with his own views. Yet he distrusted the views of others and seemed disinclined to believe the representations I made of General Johnston's critical condition. I had heard that he, General Johnston, was an especial favorite of Mr. Davis and was naturally surprised when I saw no point was stretched to afford him prompt aid.

Disappointed at this fixed determination, I arose to leave. I expressed nevertheless my regret and concern at the mistake made by the General in selecting me to go on this fruitless mission. I wished that a man of well-known ability had been sent in my stead who could have made the condition of things unmistakably clear. Then the object would have been gained for Johnston, but now I felt serious apprehensions for the future.

As I started to go, Mr. Davis got up from his chair and, coming towards me with extended hand, said, "No sir, I do not regret your coming. It is right that I should know all the facts though I might not afford the desired relief. When do you leave for Bowling Green?"

"I shall rest tomorrow and leave the next day. I am tired of traveling in crowded cars in cold weather."

He then invited me to dine with him the next day at 6:00 p.m. Surprised at this sudden civility, since up to this time his manner had not been at all cordial, my first impulse was to decline. But I reflected that my own feelings were not worth a moment's consideration when so much was at stake. Perhaps tomorrow might bring changes in his mind. Accordingly I accepted the invitation.

Much more was said than I have written. I confine myself to the most important points. I might have prolonged the conversation, but Mr. Davis seemed impatient and yet not uninterested. It was disagreeably perplexing to him. I therefore desisted and hastened to leave, cherishing the hope that there was still a chance left on the morrow.

It struck me forcibly that he did not grasp the magnitude of affairs with the view to combined operations throughout the Confederacy. Nor did he seem inclined to listen dispassionately to the views or weigh the suggestions of those who were candid enough to express opinions at variance with his own. It is doubtless true that the active execution of indifferent plans is better than indecision and non-execution of good ones, yet such important matters should be discussed freely and fairly before determined upon. Keeping his own counsel, Mr. Davis could well have afforded to listen and ponder the promptings of patriotic and sensible men. No one man can be expected to know all things, any more than he can be expected to do all things. Even after the mind has been definitely made up, common sense suggestions from ordinary men may modify or improve the wisest determination. Decision, without good judgment and wisdom to sustain it, amounts to obstinacy and cannot avail much after all.

In the report of my interviews with Mr. Davis, I give the substance and full import of the language used. Of course, after the lapse of four exciting years, much has to be trusted to memory. I feel assured, however, my memory has not failed me, and certainly not as to my impressions, which are stamped for life upon my brain. I must say, however, that at that time I had no idea of writing upon the subject. Therefore I did not take notes.

I spent the following day in visiting a number of friends in the city. In our discussions on the all-absorbing topic of the war, I unreservedly expressed my doubts of the government policy and of the ability of the War Department to carry us through. I found the impression gaining ground slowly that the means of the South were being misapplied or wasted through the acts of incompetent or ignorant officials. Nevertheless, we flattered ourselves with hopes that our fears were groundless and our doubts, caused by anxiety, were surely imaginary.

At the appointed hour, I was again admitted to the President's house and found him again alone with his family. It was much later than my usual dinnertime, but my anxieties dissipated my desire for food. We had quite a long social conversation. He seemed quite another man and was delighted to speak of his schoolboy days, of our teachers, of the old Citizens, of the Country in which he lived. In short, he spoke of every local occurrence that had transpired in our earlier days, ignoring altogether the subject most important to my mind. At several intervals I attempted to introduce it, but he often avoided it as if out of place and once so pointedly that it seemed to give him pain. Hence, it became proper on my part to cease all further allusion.

He brought up the fine scholarship of the Rev. J. R. Shaw, of New England, our old teacher in 1825.[1] He commended him in the highest terms, mentioned having met with him in New Orleans after his own political advancement to the U. S. Congress, and of the gratification it seemed to give the Doctor. He then related anecdotes of old Citizens well-known to both of us. He spoke of a certain Captain Jack Stewart, a Scotch loyalist and retired British officer, whom I well recalled to have seen about the year 1824 dressed in the red uniform coat in which he greatly prided to the last.

Mr. Davis said that in riding to and from the Academy, which was some distance from his home, he was often accidentally

1. Although Davis was seven years older than Liddell, both attended Wilkinson Academy in Woodville, Mississippi. The principal was John R. Shaw. This Bostonian, according to Davis' biographer, Hudson Strode, remained the model teacher in Davis' eyes. Moses Liddell paid Shaw for teaching St. John in 1824, but Shaw seems to have made no impact on the younger boy.

brought in company with the stout old Captain Jack who was always sociable and would enquire about his progress in Latin, where he was, what book and line. Upon being informed, the old man would take it up from memory and repeat the whole. This was no uncommon thing with him, and Mr. Davis thought that he was the most thorough Latin scholar he had ever met.

He took so much interest in these reminiscences that it must have given him relief from his cares in public perplexities. I must confess, my thoughts ran all the time in an entirely different channel. I could not separate my thoughts from the present troubles that convulsed our Country. I could listen only with forced attention to the end.

When I started to leave after dinner, Mr. Davis said, "Tell my friend, General Johnston, that I can do nothing for him. He must rely upon his own resources; but I expect to get 38,000 stand of arms shortly from Europe from which I can furnish him." I quickly said, "All, No, only his share."

He continued to talk as we approached the door of the ante-room. On my asking for dispatches, he directed me to call on Secretary J. P. Benjamin, who would give them to me. Getting into the anteroom, I requested him not to trouble himself. I knew how to get along now.

"No. No," he said, "it gives me no trouble." Then taking my overcoat from the hook, he kindly assisted me in putting it on. On shaking hands with me, he used the words, "May God bless you," as though he especially meant me well. I felt him to be sincere and reciprocated my honest hope for his health and that we might meet again in better times.

I found it very cold on the streets in Richmond and hastened to the war office to get the dispatches that I might be ready for the cars at daylight. On applying to Mr. Benjamin, he told me that he had given the dispatches to Earl Van Dorn, who had left that morning for Bowling Green.

The next morning I found the air very cold and the crowded cars very disagreeable. I was quite unwell when the train reached Chattanooga about 9:00 p.m. the third day. I pushed on, however, and arrived at Bowling Green the next evening, January 20, 1862.

# CHAPTER IV

# RETREAT

I repaired forthwith on foot through rain and mud to the General's Headquarters and made known to him the results of my mission. I detailed all the particulars and ended by expressing my sincere regrets that he had not selected a more politic man for the business whose ability might have influenced the President to grant all that was desired. General Johnston answered with candor, "No sir, I am glad that I sent you. You have told the plain facts. I will be justified now in whatever I may do. I am satisfied."

I then asked him if he had secured the dispatches from General Van Dorn. "No." I then told him what Mr. Benjamin had said to me. He sent at once to enquire of General Van Dorn, who had preceded me by one day, and received for answers, no dispatches had been given him by Mr. Benjamin. All persons present were surprised Mr. Benjamin had told a deliberate falsehood, for what object I never could perceive.

I have never had any faith in him since. His conduct generally has not been of benefit to the Confederate cause. He might well be pardoned by the Union Government for his wretched mismanagement, resulting in actual benefit to the side he was against. Why therefore should this man fly the country to England after the war had ceased? What harm can the Union Government intend? He could not by his counsels and deceptions have served the Union purposes better. It was not necessary for David to forgive Hushai.[1]

My trips across the mountains had cost me a bronchial affection

1. David's servant and his spy. Furthermore, no stranger to Charles Jones' Elmly was wealthy sugar planter Benjamin.

47

with painful cough. To be relieved I sought and obtained permission from Hardee to go South for 30 days.

The disaster at Mill Springs and the death of Zollicoffer[2] had occurred on the 19th, and I began to feel more anxiously impressed with our critical condition. I therefore asked the consent of General Johnston to use the information I possessed to get assistance from the Governors of Mississippi and Louisiana, since the President said that the States were unwilling to send men beyond their own borders. Perhaps now they would see their own danger and would unite for the common good. But General Johnston, after a few moments of reflection in which time he took, as usual by way of stimulus, a large chew of tobacco, declined granting the permission. "It would be useless," he said.

Generals Floyd and Buckner had now gone to Fort Donelson with their commands. Heavy rains had been and were still occurring. The Tennessee and Cumberland Rivers were very high and rising.

I hastened on and arrived in New Orleans about the 26th of January and did not delay long before going to see General Lovell[3] in command there. I informed him of the probability of an immediate movement of Buell and Grant against Johnston. If he could possibly spare men from his command, he should do so quickly, sending them at once in Kentucky. After I had posted him on our affairs, then he said that he would do so. He himself, however, must be the judge of the necessity of his troops being sent there. He didn't wish to be cheated again out of any portion of his command. General Polk had requested some reinforcements from him which he had sent, with the understanding that they were to be kept no longer than absolutely necessary. But Polk afterwards, not wishing to return them and without reference to time, had obtained the consent of the War Depart-

---

2. Felix Kirk Zollicoffer (1812-1862). Editor of four or five newspapers before the war. Member of Congress from Tennessee, state Printer and Comptroller. Fought as a young man in the Seminole War. This early brigadier general and department commander held the right of Johnston's extended front. George H. Thomas tore him and his army apart at Mill Springs and thereby heightened the pressure on Albert Sidney Johnston.

3. Mansfield Lovell (1822-1884). Lovell, a professional soldier, jumped from Deputy Commissioner of Streets in New York City to Confederate Major General. Davis entrusted him with New Orleans. Considered able by Lee, Johnston, and Hood, he could not be ordered to active field command after early 1862 by the War Department, since he bore the debilitating reputation of the general who lost New Orleans.

ment to keep them. Lovell emphasized, "he would not be cheated out of his troops again."

I asked him how would it sound to him for General Johnston, at the distance he was from him, to insist upon being the judge of General Lovell's necessities in New Orleans before he would aid him?

"Well," he said, "I will send a staff officer to enquire into the facts, and afterwards send the troops if I find they are needed."

This was right enough, as I had no authority to demand troops, only to place the facts before Lovell for timely co-operation.

The question of judging the necessities of General Johnston was, however, foolish. Ordinary good sense in a commander on the ground of operations surely ought to know more than the man at a distance. General Johnston had good sense, and he made no professions of superiority, which certainly was something to his credit in these times of military pretension and arrogance of official station. No one inspired more respect for integrity of character. How then could General Lovell apprehend being cheated by such a man?

I was at my home only a few days when all kinds of reports reached me of the attack and fall of Fort Henry on the 6th of February, and of the opening of active operations in Kentucky. I could not remain quiet under such circumstances and hastened to New Orleans to take the train back to the Army.

I arrived there the day before the fall of Fort Donelson. This fact and that of the capture of the garrison and Buckner's command was telegraphed on the 17th of February (I think).

It was clearly seen now that the enemy was trying to get in Johnston's rear and force him to withdraw from Buell's front. Johnston was altogether too weak to hold his ground, having lost at Mill Springs, Fort Henry and Fort Donelson about one-third of his command. Thus were my fears one by one realized. The miserably spread-out policy of the Confederate Government was reaping a deplorable harvest of disasters. Nothing was ever done in time. Change for the better could hardly be hoped for. I saw that misapplication would render useless all the means possessed by the South, even were they twice as much.

I felt so much depressed with the dark prospect that distressing dreams disturbed my rest. My dear Father, buried five years before, appeared to me for the first time. His strangely pleased expression surprised and troubled me. I ungenerously had reproached him for the inheritance of "Slavery" he had left me and had desired me to retain. My own judgment inclined me to get rid of such interest, to avoid the terrible uprooting day of the whole system. Now I was assured the time had come. My reproaches changed his pleasure to distress, which awakened me.

It was but a dream. Yet I have never been able to divest myself of the impression that, whilst my poor honest old Father was satisfied with the honesty of my motives, he could not but feel for my distress at the sinking fortune that awaited the South. Her cause had been confided to the smartest of her sons. Jefferson Davis was well-known to my father 40 years before. Yet his wisdom could not save it. Certainly, it looked as though the fates had so willed it.

The Confederate Government knew well the military policy of the enemy, knew his superiority in numbers, in resources, both at land and water. Then why allow him also to use all the strategy? This superiority surely he should not have been allowed to claim.

Why neglect concentration at the proper time, when effective blows might have been struck? Why spread out and lose piece-meal, until concentration eventually give no strength to avail much?

Again when the enemy was most depressed, why not push advantages gained, however slight, to allow him no time for recovery from his losses, only to return with increased strength? Buell should never have been allowed to unite with Grant at Shiloh. I could never comprehend the fatal apathy that seemed to exist in the conduct of the Confederate affairs.

Though these things were apparent to me at the time, I had resolved to do my share of the work faithfully to the end. I trusted that the wisdom of "the powers that be" saw the way clearly, though it was not perceptible to my darkened vision.

Johnston's army was bound to fall back, too weak after the Donelson affair even to resist Buell's column. Reinforcements must come forward now or never. I went to see Governor Moore[4]

4. Thomas Overton Moore (1804-1876). Powerful, popular, secession Governor of Louisiana, Moore convinced mulitudes in his state to oppose with arms that "Black Republican President." He organized Louisiana military units early and established military points throughout the state, particularly on Red River. A distinguished political career ( U. S. House and Senate) came to an end in 1864 when he fled to Cuba. His state government operating in Opelousas and

of Louisiana, then in the City (New Orleans). I eagerly urged the necessity of sending a telegram to the President suggesting that the numerous steamboats at the wharves of New Orleans could be used in transporting Price and Van Dorn's commands from Arkansas to General Johnston in Tennessee. This would be sufficient to bring it to the notice of Mr. Davis, who might then take immediate action. Otherwise the chance may escape his attention.

I urged that time and celerity of action were with us. Delay might be fatal, even to New Orleans and Louisiana. The possession of the Mississippi would follow failure on our part. It was all to no purpose. The Governor hesitated and finally declined doing anything, saying that he had nothing to do with the military.

I then called aside E. W. Moise,[5] State Attorney General, who was said to possess the brains and conscience of the Governor. I entreated him to use his influence with the Governor and get the telegram sent, which would cost nothing. But this man, far more prompt and decided, said quickly and jerkingly, "The Governor has been repeatedly snubbed by the President and will not subject himself to any further indignities from that quarter."

I was so shocked at the vindictive absurdity of the excuse. Disaster was threatening the very existence of the State and City in which these two men ruled. I could only say, "Well, I would take a thousand snubbings to save the cause."

"Well," Moise said, with a determined shake of his head as he turned away, "the governor will not, and it is useless to talk further about it."

What folly! Those two big men, whom I well knew personally and by character, have meekly borne far greater indignities from other men of less note than the President. It is astonishing Moise's tender care and regard for the snubbed feelings of Governor Moore. How was the Confederacy to succeed when the very men whom the deluded people had put in "office for the general good and public safety" were ignoring their dangers. Instead of looking after the vital interests, they were engaged in keeping up absurd and nice points of etiquette?

Shreveport had become virtually an underground organization. His splendid sugar plantation in Rapides Parish had been confiscated.

He returned to Louisiana after the war, but lived out his life quietly trying to restore what had been done.

5. Edward Warren Moise, onetime doctor and lawyer, became a Supreme Court Justice of Louisiana.

There was strong indisposition on the part of some State Governors to assist and co-operate with the Government. Each wanted independent authority and desired no superior. They seemed to pull away from Mr. Davis and to thwart his objects. Surely, if they did disapprove his conduct of affairs, it did not justify neglect of faithful co-operation with him. Can anyone wonder then that Mr. Davis should have had a hard time, with so many persistent drawbacks from those very ones who had invoked the war?

They felt so sure of Southern Independence that they foolishly overlooked the contingency of ruin by failure of the Government. They regarded its iron struggles with fatal indifference. An insignificant telegram! I myself would have sent it if I had possessed the influence and character to give it weight. Coming from the Governor of Louisiana, it is fair to conclude that the President would have given it his immediate attention. The troops of Price and Van Dorn would have arrived in ample time to share in the battle of Shiloh. Had such occurred, what might have resulted from the efforts of the 18,000 to 20,000 men, veterans of Elkhorn and Oak Hills, in that day's fight? Great events sometimes hinge upon small things.

Although by no means recovered from my railroad exposures, I hastened to rejoin the army. About February 20, 1862, I found it near Murfreesboro, whither it had retreated before Buell from Bowling Green. Nashville had already been seized by the enemy. Before getting to Murfreesboro, I met troops well-known to me from Hardee's command, moving southward to Decatur on the Tennessee River.

The drift of affairs was too plain now to be mistaken. Everything was moving to concentrate for a battle below the Tennessee. Troops were now coming forward that ought to have been sent a few months sooner. Confusion prevailed everywhere. From the disasters of Henry and Donelson we had lost some six thousand men of Buckner's division. This does not include those lost under Tilghman at the first-named place, supposed to be about one-third more. These losses of men and arms could not be made up and were seriously felt.

The matter of the surrender of Henry and Donelson was pretty freely discussed. In regard to the latter, it was not clearly decided upon whom the blame should rest, whether Floyd, Pillow, or Buckner. Each had his friends and enemies. From what I could learn, General Buckner was the first to make the propositions of surrender. He asserted that his men were demoralized and indisposed to fight any longer.

Under the circumstances, General Floyd, who was the ranking officer, refused to surrender. He determined to withdraw his own brigade. At the same time, he turned over the command to General Pillow, next in rank. Pillow immediately passed it to General Buckner and sought occasion to withdraw with what part of his command he could take away with him.

Buckner, now fully in command, sent his proposition to General Grant, who accepted it, though Grant purposed to attack the place the next day. I don't remember much of what General Buckner afterwards said on the subject. Grant's proposition, at all events, was not assented to by General Buckner. He closed the matter himself by capitulating with the surrender of his entire force. The death of General Johnston at Shiloh, nearly two months afterwards, prevented, somehow, an investigation of this affair. It remains to this day unsettled and subject still to disputation.

It was plain enough to me that Floyd's and Pillow's brigades, which had declined to surrender, were themselves too weak numerically to prolong the fight. Buckner insisted on surrender. Since his force, nearly two-thirds of the whole, declined further struggle, no other alternative was left to the two former officers but to withdraw, if they could, from a hopeless contest. Buckner was the only military man of the three by profession and educacation. It was natural and proper for the others, surrounded with so many strange perplexities, to look to him for advice and the solution of all difficulties, But, to surrender, in their opinion, was not the solution. They could not agree with him that this course was the best. He gave no other advice. In this uncertainty, they preferred to withdraw from responsibilities and leave him to take the steps he had advised.

The possibility of withdrawing our forces safely from Donelson to escape surrender I don't think was ever sufficiently considered by the commanding officer. It is the part of a wise commander to secure his means of retreat, except in isolated positions contemplated to be held to the last extremity for the purpose of delaying hostile movements. I saw several officers and men who had escaped from the fort even after the surrender. They were united in the opinion that withdrawal of the garrison could have been effected. Of this, I do not pretend to know. I never visitied the place and knew nothing of its localities or topography. General B. R. Johnson and his adjutant general Ellis escaped after the surrender. So did Colonel N. B. Forrest, with others of his regiment.

At all events, I deem it my duty to do justice to General Floyd's memory. I conversed with him several times at Bowling Green and had met with him at General Johnston's Headquarters more than once. From preconceived political prejudice, I had gradually learned to respect him. I feel now bound to admit his foresight. His comprehensive views of the military policy of the Confederate Government inspired me with respect. I feel this way, notwithstanding all the abuse that had been heaped upon him by his enemies. Floyd was no time-server.

Although no soldier by profession, I thought Floyd would have been better, like Carnot,[6] supervising and directing the general conduct of the war. Why he was overlooked by Mr. Davis I could not understand. I knew of no trouble between them.

From what was observed by me, General Johnston had the highest regard for him. Such a man, I firmly believe, would have made the South a good President in her iron struggle. This man, unlike his surviving confederates, died, as he had lived, free. I have been told, however, that Floyd died heartbroken at the ruinous course pursued by the Government he had helped to initiate.[7]

At Murfreesboro, I joined again my friend Hardee. He seemed sadly depressed at the state of affairs. He doubted the ability of General Johnston to conduct such extended operations. He considered him then as having been overrated for military leadership, an opinion more than once expressed to me by Colonel Mackall, Chief of Staff. The recent disasters were all attributed, during the excitement, to Johnston's want of ability. The public clamor against him at this period rose to its highest pitch.

I knew enough of Johnston's private views and the efforts he had quietly made to avert disasters, not to abandon myself to such want of confidence. I must confess, though, that my faith for the moment was somewhat shaken. Why could he not have

6. Lazare Carnot (1753-1823). Young French military engineer who harnessed the resources of his nation to defeat the Royalists, 1794.

7. Not many have treated Floyd as kindly as Liddell. Usually Floyd and Pillow, even more than Buckner, are roundly abused by contemporary observers and by historians.

anticipated retreat and transported his large supplies of provisions at Bowling Green, Clarksville, Nashville, and other places by timely removal by railroad further southward? His not doing so caused immense loss of subsistence to our armies. Again, why not order the timely evacuation of Donelson? Or go there himself with his whole force as soon as he discovered the weight of the opposing force. Why divide his strength, thereby sacrificing himself virtually in detail. The loss of men and arms surrendered at Donelson were more irreparable than the evacuation of all his positions. How were they to be replaced?

By preserving and uniting all his forces, he could have opposed and perhaps overthrown one column at a time. The enemy had divided, as if offering gratuitously the chance; Buell on the Nashville and Louisville Railroad and Grant on the Cumberland and Tennessee Rivers. Their distance apart was too great for timely support. Buell's overthrow would have brought Grant back to the Ohio River.

Still, as so much was looked for and expected at the hands of General Johnston, he, to meet it zealously, overtasked his physical resources in men and means in trying to hold too much ground. He depended upon his friend Mr. Davis too greatly to sustain him with reinforcements when the pinch came. A generous military critic will pass over this severe lesson taught the General on self-reliance, since it was to a great extent unavoidable from the circumstances not entirely in his control. The place and responsibilities were new and trying, but he was fast learning and would have undoubtedly succeeded had God spared him.

In the retreat through Murfreesboro, General Johnston had with him only Hardee's and Crittenden's Divisions. I did not see that latter General to know him. He had the reputation at that time of being an incurable drunkard. From this cause, with good reason, he stood very low in the estimation of the Army. After the Mill Springs disaster, he fell back and effected a junction with the balance of the army near Murfreesboro.

I am bound to say that this was even better than the Henry and Donelson affairs. I have never yet been able to see the gain effected by the sacrifice of troops, however few, even in isolated places, or seacoast fortifications, abstruse military writers to the contrary notwithstanding.

# CHAPTER V

# RICHMOND, AGAIN

Several days after my arrival at Murfreesboro, when I happened to be in conversation with Colonel Mackall at Army Headquarters, General Johnston saw me. Approaching with a friendly salutation, he pulled by the lapel of my coat gently to one side, saying, "Colonel, I wish you to go for me to Richmond again."

The very thought of such a trip was unpleasant to me.[1] I forthwith begged him to excuse me. I had not yet recovered fully from the effects of the last. Furthermore, I did not wish to see Mr. Davis until better times at least had come. I knew that I should not be welcome, etc. He persisted, however, saying, "I know you to be patriotic and deeply interested in the cause. Besides, I have no one else at hand with whom to entrust the business. I depend on you. Come to my room adjoining this tonight, where I will give you instructions and papers."

There being plainly no alternative, I reluctantly consented and returned to his quarters at the appointed time. We had another lengthy conversation upon the state of affairs. Amongst other things, General Johnston told me that he utterly disregarded the public clamor against him for evacuating Kentucky and Nashville. When the facts became fully known, his course would be fully approved and justified. Beauregard had approved the step, or the necessity for such. Johnston said his mind was not in the least disturbed by foolish newspaper publications, which often misled public opinion and might change at any moment. When the true history of the war was finally written, his course would

1. Liddell said the same thing in a letter to Mary on February 28. He added that he was disgusted with Johnston's bungling the retreat through Tennessee.

57

be fully vindicated. Notwithstanding this apparent indifference to what had been said of him, I thought he was touched or he would not have laid so much stress upon it in his remark. His manner was calm, very plain, and earnest.

I asked him familiarly where he contemplated giving battle. He said, "South, or below the Tennessee somewhere."

"But," I said, "will you not fight before leaving this place?"

"No, unless I am pressed. Then assuredly. I shall concentrate everything I can below the Tennessee for a decisive blow."

He told me that my papers were chiefly in reference to the matter of the surrender of Donelson.[2] He was not sufficiently satisfied in his own mind to come to any definite conclusion. The reports he now sent from the commanders might serve to throw some light upon the subject satisfactory to the President.

I left him very glad indeed to see him struggling cheerfully against all adversities, whether from foe or friend. It was an evidence of solidity of mind and will rarely be met with amongst men.

This information he gave me of his designs reaffirmed my views made known to Mr. Davis in January as the natural consequence, should General Johnston be unable to hold his line in Kentucky. The General had not mentioned this to me then or ever alluded to any probable retrograde movement. His object was solely to maintain the line which he was then holding, or, to use his own expression, "the line of the Green River." Lack of natural advantages, though, required a heavy and concentrated force. It was a wide field surely, requiring enlarged views to embrace the whole strategy.

The Federal strategy was correct: to strike for the Memphis and Charleston Railroad where it nearly touches the Tennessee River, allowing the close approach of gunboats and transports. Thus they would gain Kentucky and middle of West Tennessee by the same turning movement. To do this, however, they directed a column from Louisville by the railroad upon Nashville, which later was under Buell's immediate command. The only error was the separation of the columns. This left the choice to General Johnston to concentrate everything upon Buell, destroying his force. By a forward movement, he could then compel the with-

2. Johnston also sent by Liddell "a dispatch containing my purpose for the defense of the Valley of the Mississippi and for cooperation or uniting with General Beauregard, who has been urging me to come on."

drawal of the other column under Grant. Why, on the contrary, he preferred to fall back and meet the advanced column at Shiloh, thus giving time to the other to come up and converge from Nashville to the place of attack and combine with the first, I am unable to understand in so thorough a tactician. To divide an enemy, to overthrow him, evidenced the highest skill in all great tacticians. When the enemy divides himself, there must be strong reasons for his course, which were unfathomable to my common-sense views.

At all events, I was satisfied that Johnston's clear head was grasping the state of things rapidly. His death at Shiloh was untimely indeed and, to my mind, equivalent to the loss of a great battle. I appreciated the good opinion he had seemingly formed for me. Had he lived, I might have been useful to him, for he was clearly reasonable and approachable. He listened to, and yet was not confused by, the various opinions of his subordinates.

Another tedious and disagreeable trip ended in my reaching Richmond about the 7th of March. On seeing Mr. Davis, who was not again in a very pleasant humor, I was surprised that he limited his remarks altogether to finding fault with General Floyd and Pillow. He thought they were to blame for all disasters that had occurred at Donelson and for which he said they were now suspended from command. I thought, from the tenor of his remarks, that he was fooling me. Therefore, I was careful to say nothing. The little knowledge I had gained on the subject from hearsay had led me to a different view, however.[3]

I soon left him but saw, with concern and regret, that he would allow himself to give way to fits of vindictive prejudices. This prevented his making just allowances for honest service or ability. Outward circumstances could cause the unlucky to fall under the ban of this lamentable weakness in one so high in position. Strange too that he stopped all further pursuit of the object of his displeasure at this point. On the other hand, with singular tenacity, he upheld those who had met his favor, no matter how poorly rated by public opinion. What was the secret by which such attachments or such prejudices were formed, I never knew. He was approachable or not, as it happened. It is just to conclude

3. On March 11, 1862, Benjamin wrote General Johnston, "The reports of Brigadier Generals Floyd and Pillow are unsatisfactory, and the President directs that both these generals be relieved from command. . . ."

that all this contrariety of temper may have been caused by his long years of ill health.

Surely he was a good man and at heart meant well to everyone. It was not the nature even of his family stock to be otherwise, at least that part of it known to me. So far as the fortunes of the Confederacy were concerned, it was very unfortunate that he could not quickly penetrate the character of men, to attach them to him, and make use of each one in his proper sphere for the common good.

On this visit to Richmond, I saw Edward Sparrow,[4] senator from Louisiana, who amongst other things, told me, as coming from Mr. Benjamin, that the President frequently deluded his cabinet. He would direct their attention to other objects of discussion than his real designs. Such want of confidence implied distrust of their integrity. This should have been met with immediate withdrawal from official position.

But Mr. Benjamin was not the man for such spirited action. He was a genuine timeserver and, I have reason to believe, was absolutely displeased with all people who presumed to visit his President without his patronage. In his own official state, Benjamin was an unapproachable Solomon.

I had been in Richmond but a few days when the news came of the destruction of the *Cumberland* and other U. S. ships of war by the *Merrimac* and by her contest with the *Monitor*. The indestructible construction of these two vessels has been the cause of great changes in naval affairs.

I am of the opinion that the little *Manassas* at New Orleans originated the idea, since so remarkably improved on. The events of the *Merrimac* created the greatest excitement and hopes in Richmond at the time, but the injury received by her gallant commander seemed to have deprived this vessel of all future usefulness. Commodore Buchanan figured again upon the *Tennessee*, a vessel of like construction, in Mobile Bay, single-handed against a whole fleet but was compelled to surrender to the great odds.

At the Spotswood Hotel, I met with an old friend, Colonel

---

4. Edward Sparrow (1810-1882). Planter and Louisiana politician, Sparrow became important in the Confederate Congress as Chairman of the Committee on Military Affairs.

W. L. Brandon,[5] commanding the 16th Mississippi Regiment. He was a Southern palladin, who under the weight of some 65 years cheerfully took his chances in the field with the most hardy. In the battles around Richmond subsequently, he unfortunately lost a leg and still lives to bear, as bravely as he fought, the misfortunes of the "fallen cause." I honor his indomitable manhood.

Our conversation at the time was, of course, chiefly taken up with the condition of the South to carry on the war. I felt free to confess to his friendly discretion my firm belief that the suicidal defensive policy of the President, ignoring concentration for quick effect, which together with the reckless waste of our limited resources for subsistence, was fast leading things from bad to worse. If not soon remedied by judicious and decided changes, the *sooner we made terms the better.*

The Colonel was very much disturbed, not to say shocked, at my conclusion. He exclaimed, "Oh my God! no, we must fight it through." I told him I would do my part in the contest.

But he could not reconcile himself to my views. He proposed to visit the President together, for he knew him well, was a personal friend, and had no doubt of getting his ear. I knew Mr. Davis was unalterably fixed in his determination; but at all events, we could simply pay him our respects.

Unluckily for us, President Davis had gone out with General Lee on some military inspection. We had nothing left us, but to faithfully and honorably discharge our duties in support of the Government. No matter how much we differed in regard to its policy, we should not create or support the most factious opposition to its determinations.

No one breathed a doubt of Mr. Davis' purity of nature. The fear was that he was too persistent in error, when his mind was made up. I must say that each interview I had with him confirmed these impressions of his character. My time being up, I could remain no longer in Richmond. I have never again visited it to this day. This was about the 10th of March, 1862.

The East Tennessee railroad bridges had been destroyed by the Tories and deserters of that section only very recently. These

---

5. William Lindsay Brandon (1802-1890). A prominent planter in Moses Liddell's Adams County, Mississippi, Brandon was admired by two generations of Liddells. His plantation, Arcole, his familiarity with medicine, and strong leadership qualities impressed Liddell.

interruptions of travel compelled me to return by Petersburg and Atlanta to Chattanooga.

I began to feel sick before leaving Richmond. To improve on the cars was not possible, in my case at least. By the time I reached Huntsville, Alabama, where I luckily found Hardee, the nature of my increasing malady indicated typhoid fever. It became so fully developed at Tuscumbia as to prostrate me completely. My anxiety doubtless aggravated the disease. It was intolerable to think of being left behind, utterly helpless and exposed to certain capture in the event of any forces leaving the place.

General Hardee, finding from the report of his surgeon, Dr. Lawrence, that my condition was very precarious and critical, sent a telegraphic dispatch immediately to my wife in Louisiana. Meanwhile, he considerately and kindly nursed me himself, sleeping by my side and momentarily caring for my wants, so long as his duties allowed his stay at Tuscumbia. He provided a house for me, anticipated my wants, and exhibited the greatest anxiety and regret at the prospect of losing me. When the moment came for him to leave me, he shook my hand feelingly, as if for the last time. How much do I not owe him? But what would not be my gratification to see him again long after the close of our struggle before the end of life. After my recovery, our associations were long renewed. Although our relations were from circumstances sometimes misunderstood, they were never changed. I know Hardee to be a good man and, as Bragg said to me, "a true soldier," reliable truly as friend or foe.

Hardee placed me under the care of Mrs. J. B. Barton in Tuscumbia. To this lady I am indebted for the preservation of my life. She forced my mouth open, parched with typhoid fever, and poured the necessary acids and food for subsistence down my throat. I have seen this old lady in New Orleans since the war. Notwithstanding all her troubles, from robberies from the Federal soldiers, I am pleased to know that she had enough left for competence and even independence. She was a southern woman in all her sentiments and all her relations.

The telegram of General Hardee brought my wife and young son Willie, a lad of 15 years, to my bedside. Luckily, I had passed the crisis of the fever and was slowly recovering.[6] The boy pe-

6. Mary Liddell had been having her problems, too. She was accumulating debts, and had to rid herself of kinsman J. Andrew Liddell as overseer. "I can get along much, very much, better than you think. I cannot live with Andrew. He has several times been very *violent* and disrespectful."

titioned his mother for permission to join the army at Corinth and share in the engagements. It was given with hesitation and reluctance.[7]

It was a risk to one so young going alone into an army unknown to anyone who might care for him if wounded. All we could do was to ask a friend going there to look after him. But the lad, soon after getting there in the midst of confusion, boldly struck out for himself. He felt and worked his own way, sharing with the troops the dangers of the battle of Shiloh throughout.

From my sick room at a distance of some 55 miles, I could distinctly hear the sound of musketry and cannonading at Shiloh for two days. News came that we had driven the enemy to the banks of the Tennessee River, then of General Johnston's untimely end, then of Buell's coming up with fresh forces to Grant's relief, then that our troops had gradually withdrawn, exhausted, from further contest.

All this was exciting enough for a sick man, but the effect was not injurious. I steadily improved under the kind care of Dr. J. Koon of Tuscumbia and gained, in a few days, strength enough to walk a short distance to the station and make arrangements to leave for Corinth. It was time, for we narrowly escaped capture on an open train at Bear Creek Bridge. It was burned by the enemy only a few minutes after we had passed. The smoke of the burning bridge was visible to us looking back. I have nearly forgotten to state that Colonel Helm,[8] a relative of President Lincoln, helped me to escape from Tuscumbia. He commanded our cavalry at that place and ordered the trains to move in time.

We stopped at Brownsville and camped with Colonel J. S. Scott, Cmdg. 1st Louisiana Cavalry, for a day or so and afterwards.[9] With the use of his ambulance, we managed to get to Corinth, though a road was blocked for miles with trains.

At Corinth affairs were in great confusion from the result of the

7. Frank L. Richardson wrote his father on April 10, "I saw Willie Liddell. He was in the Wirt Adams cavalry. He told me that Uncle John was very sick at Tuscumbia and expected to die with typhoid. And we agreed to go down and see him, but we were told by Col. Perkins, another one of General Hardee's staff, that he had just received a dispatch from Uncle John and that he was better and would be here soon." Frank L. Richardson Papers.
8. Benjamin Hardin Helm (1831-1863). Helm married Emily Todd, half sister of Mary Todd Lincoln. A Kentucky politician sought by both sides, he joined the Confederates and ultimately assumed command of the Orphan Brigade. He died at Chickamauga leading Kentuckians.
9. Scott would be Liddell's close confidant and trusted cotton factor after the war.

recent battle. Crowds of wounded and sick men were at the railroad depot awaiting removal. In many instances they were accompanied by their distressed wives or female relatives. They had sought and found their loved ones in mangled helplessness or on the bare earth in ruined health from exposure. The scene was pitiable to the feeling heart. Yet the constant sight hardened the soldier to eventual heedlessness of all human calamities.

It was a great relief to our parental anxiety to find our boy Willie alive and doing well. He was making his way bravely through the crowds and picking up friends by his manly frankness everywhere. It was as if he enjoyed the wild excitement of war, regardless of the accompanying horrors. He had always been a gentle and affectionate child. It was incredible to us, his parents, this complete and sudden change in his character. It leads to the reflection that the natural instinct of man is violence. Civilized cultivation only suppresses it until the opportunity is offered for the display.

This boy's new suit of homemade clothes was perforated in many places by bullets. His person had escaped all injury. He could not account to his mother for the injury done to them and unavailingly complained that the material was bad. Poor fellow, he lived long enough to learn the cause in subsequent bloody affairs.

I went with my wife and Willie as far as Memphis, where they left me for New Orleans.[10] They arrived in that city only two days before the surrender, April 25th, 1862. They had to fly, in time at least to escape the persecutions of General Butler, known afterwards as the "beast" from his cruelties to defenseless citizens.[11]

At Memphis, I saw Generals Van Dorn and Price, whose troops had arrived there from Arkansas to join Johnston's army, some

10. In a letter to Mary written just after she and Willie departed, Liddell expressed concern about the high water. "You must therefore stir up the people around you to look after their levees in time." He cautioned her about protecting the slave quarters, and ended his letter in high frustration, ". . . the *gross mistakes* of men in office. I think I could have done far better than most of the officials of Jeff Davis, but if *they* will *only secure me my rights.*" Liddell to wife, April 21, 1862, in Liddell Papers, LSU.

11. On August 13, 1862, Marcellin Gillis was arrested by Butler and placed on Ship Island "without communication." He remained there in the fall. When released, Gillis decided to become more active in the Confederate cause, and joined as a private in Capt. C. E. Fenner's Battery stationed near Mobile. This 38 year old Frenchman had "dark eyes, fair complexion, and dark brown hair."

Meanwhile, Major Liddell's operation of Llanda had resulted in a $2,000 indebtedness to Gillis. Correspondence between Carolina and Marcellin Gillis, March 30, 1862 - October 3, 1863, Gillis Papers, SHC.

four weeks too late. The timely arrival by a few hours of Buell's forces saved Grant's army. Might not the timely arrival of Van Dorn's and Price's forces have saved Beauregard, who had succeeded to the command of the Confederate Army after Johnston's death?

To Buell is justly due the Federal success at the battle of Shiloh. It was the first great turning point in the war on the Federal side. It is a matter of surprise that no favor has ever been shown that man for his success on this important occasion. He seems to have been completely neglected and even set aside, whilst less worthy men, by the favor of chance or the accident of overwhelming numbers, have reaped the harvest of his glory and plans.

At Memphis, I took special trouble to see General Van Dorn and in honest eagerness proposed to him that he should get for himself from Beauregard the command of all our cavalry forces, about 9,000 strong and fresh. He could make an overwhelming movement with them through middle Tennessee into Kentucky upon the communications of the enemy. The effect would be of incalculable advantage to us in holding Corinth. As his fitness for that particular kind of service was generally acknowledged, I had no doubt whatever that success and glory awaited him. This is exactly what ought to have been done before the battle of Shiloh, which would have prevented Buell's coming up.

Upon my representation to Van Dorn of this opening for his enterprise, he drew himself up, to my great surprise, with stiff dignity. With studied politeness, he coolly bowed to me, without deigning to reply. Pretending not to notice this disturbance of his dignity, I continued very earnestly to extol the project and to advance my reasons; but not a word was elicited from him. His profound bows at my presumption in addressing him became interesting. His frigid manner increased almost to intensity. There was now no mistaking the fact that he considered my suggestions to be presumptuous and unworthy of his notice. It only remained for me to beat a polite retreat, returning respectfully his bows until entirely beyond the pale of his lofty presence.

I could now breathe freely and laugh at the absurdity of the snubbing I had met with. I have often observed in my intercourse with men that there were but few, however insignificant, from whom some good might not be extracted. In this instance, I found myself not too old at 46 to receive a lesson from a young man, the good effect of which was to make me in the future more cautious and polite in approaching self-sufficient officials.

This man and his acts will come up again in the course of my record. I would not now put this incident down, but that such little matters frequently serve to elucidate the character of public men. Besides, I cannot tell the whole truth and leave out a part.

On returning to Corinth next day, I mentioned this occurrence to Hardee who seemed to enjoy it very much. He laughingly remarked, "It was asking too much of Van Dorn to give up a Corps of Infantry for a cavalry command."

I replied, "Perhaps so; but I was only looking to the good of the cause. I really think the movement suggested to him ought to have been made, and Van Dorn couldn't see it. If I am not badly mistaken, he has not the ability for dashing enterprise that he has been credited with. He certainly should not command a corps. Time will disclose the truthfulness of my opinions."

Hardee could not agree with me and spoke, I thought, rather pointedly on the subject. This caused any further allusion to cease until nearly a year afterwards.

# CHAPTER VI

# CORINTH

During my stay at Corinth, my strength gradually returned from the constant exercise in riding that my duties required.[1] Our lines were very extended. Hardee occupied the right, Bragg the center, and Polk the left, whilst Van Dorn and Price's divisions were held in reserve. It was an open position without any natural advantages.

On one occasion I accompanied Generals Bragg and Hardee in a short reconnaissance beyond Farmington across the Seven-Mile Creek. In commenting upon the management of the late battle, I heard the former speak very regretfully that our successes had not been pushed at all hazards without a moment's delay. It was the critical period with the enemy. We might have prevented Buell's force from crossing the river. It seems that Beauregard, after Johnston's untimely death, unfortunately ordered the withdrawal of the troops, thus losing all the fruits of Johnston's previous success. Johnston had said that we should "water our horses in the Tennessee River." So bent, so determined was he upon success. He had made his calculations and staked all upon the result. For such men, these moments are afforded once in life.

The general impression was that failure to continue the attack was fatal. I fear this blame will fall upon a good man, but lacking in indomitable energy and purpose for a commander of an Army. I mean General Beauregard. He is a man with French impulses, but devoid of English resolution and tenacity. I regard

1. "Uncle John Liddell and Willie are at General Hardee's Headquarters about two hundred yards from here and I see them every day and very often dine with Gen. Hardee, that is with Uncle John, who messes with him." F. L. Richardson to F. D. Richardson, May 8, 1862, in Frank L. Richardson Papers.

and respect him sincerely. I truly regret putting this in my record, for I have never met with anything but the greatest kindness and consideration from him. But I am not writing to protect my friends in making a faithful record.

Whilst making observations on Hardee's front, my attention was attracted to the high ridge beginning at Farmington, three miles east of Corinth. It extended southward, gradually circling round our right and rear, and presenting positions at several points sufficiently near to command Corinth. I took sketches of those most exposed, showing the easy approach and advantages presented to the enemy by their occupation. It led to the conclusion that to hold the place we must first hold the Farmington Ridge. This side must be the one from which the enemy's approach would be made. Up to this time, the enemy had not moved forward from Shiloh Church more than some ten miles or more distant.

All this I made known to Hardee, who doubted. To make sure, he went out with me the next day. I pointed out to him in addition, by occular demonstration, the fact that the present location of the lines of work had caused the only good water for practical uses to be thrown outside. The little clear stream at the base of this ridge was supplied by five springs. All advantages were, as it seemed, given voluntarily to the enemy. The water in Corinth itself and within the works was so wretched as to be the supposed cause of the great numbers of sick in the hospitals and camps.

Hardee, now becoming cognizant of such thoughtless oversights, seemed to be annoyed and distressed at not knowing the state of things before. "I will inform Beauregard and see if some remedy can be found. I wish that you had been here before the works were constructed."

"That would have been to no purpose," I said, "for I would not have been listened to."

"No, but I would have required it. Besides, you knew Gilmer (Chief Engineer who had been some time since assigned to duty in Virginia or the Carolinas), who was friendly to you.[2]

The next day, at Hardee's desire, I went with him to Beauregard's Headquarters, where there was to be a council of officers.

2. Jeremy Francis Gilmer (1818-1883). Well connected, this major general had advanced rapidly in rank and responsibilities. He supervised the construction of the defenses in the areas which the War Department deemed most important.

On the way, he told me that an official military map of the battle of Shiloh had been made by topographical engineers. The first line of battle was represented to be under the joint command of himself and General Gladden,[3] whereas he himself was in sole command. The injustice was clear and annoyed him. I insisted upon his referring the matter to the General Commanding for correction. His character and position would be a subject of history and truth was all he wanted. He still hesitated from a sense of modesty, but finally gave into my reasoning and the mistake was promptly admitted and rectified. He said to me afterwards that he owed it to me for simply doing justice to himself.

I had not waited long before I was sent for. On entering the room, I found Generals Beauregard, Bragg, Polk, Price, Van Dorn, and others. Most of them I knew, the three first since 1835. I was kindly received by Beauregard, who asked me to explain any views I had relative to the positions around Corinth. I did so in a short time, using my sketch for the purpose. I ended by telling him that I believed the attack upon the place would come from the direction of Farmington, repeating in substance all that I had said to Hardee on the subject.

Beauregard seemed to be much interested and asked to keep the sketch until copies could be made, and complained at the same time of the inefficiency of his topographical engineers in not furnishing him with prompt information. Generals Bragg and Polk each asked me for copies, but Beauregard said he would attend to that. I don't know but my frigid friend Van Dorn got one and doubtless must have felt increased annoyance at my presumption.

About this time, April 27th, intelligence had been received of the fall of New Orleans. The effect was disheartening to everyone. A growing impression of doubt as to our final success seemed to enter the mind of every reflecting man. It was perceptible that nothing short of superhuman efforts could save us the Mississippi River. There was but one way that I could see. Carry the war back to Kentucky and contend for the line of the Ohio River.

3. Adley Hogan Gladden (1810-1862). This South Carolinian earned a military reputation in the Mexican War. In the volatile days of 1861, he became Lieutenant Colonel of the 1st South Carolina, then moved and became colonel of the 1st Louisiana Regulars. Along with Johnston, Gladden became a conspicuous casualty of Shiloh. At Shiloh he led a brigade.

On May 1, 1862, the enemy pushed up a force, as I had surmised, and crossed Seven-Mile Creek to seize the Farmington Ridge. I had ridden to the village with instructions to the colonel commanding the brigade holding this position. He reported the enemy's immediate advance, and the disordered condition of his regiments. He requested me to take control of one of these for the occasion. Its field officer was inefficient and the men, in consequence, greatly demoralized.

I complied and attempted at once to move it forward to extend the right of his line. This brought the regiment in open view of a battery of the enemy, just coming into position on a ridge and unseen by me. Instantly from a thicket of underbrush about 450 yards distant across an open field between us, six guns opened upon the regiment, not yet in place, with shell, grape and canister, and with heavy and rapid discharges. I saw at once that the men had not gotten over the effects of the Battle of Shiloh. I encouraged them, by riding along their front, to move up. But they hesitated and halted. The bursting shells over and amongst them caused them to drop down in sections and companies, a few brave men excepted. Notwithstanding the efforts of their officers, they would neither move forward nor arise from the ground. They were clearly unreliable and, for the time, had lost all spirit and usefulness.

I had nothing left me but to direct their withdrawal to the base of a hill in their rear where they might safely await further orders. Their fears construed these instructions to mean precipitate retreat. Accordingly, away they went headlong, pell-mell—past the line upon which a company or so of more determination had established themselves. The rest disregarded all orders or attempts to stop them. To use a common expression of derision in the Army, "They were stung with a bung and slightly demoralized." Since I could do nothing with them, I directed their only field officer present to get his men together again if possible. He could then rejoin the brigade and get orders from the commanding officer what to do next.

I have seen these very men in subsequent prolonged engagements behave in the most gallant manner: not flinching even after losing one-third of their number in open fight against all odds. It proved to me that the bravest often have their moments of panic when the nerves are unstrung by unexpected circumstances. I have seen men totally indifferent to the fire of musketry in their very faces shrink from exploding shells. In other instances, I have seen the opposite. For this reason, I abstain from giving names on this occasion and merely confine myself to the incidents.

I rode hastily back to the place where the line had been established and discovered that the enemy's fire had suddenly ceased. I could find none of our men. It seemed that the whole brigade had in like manner, discreditably and precipitately, retreated through the woods and thick brushwood. The battery which had done good service, finding itself unsupported with infantry, had also withdrawn. The enemy was left in quiet possession of the open ridge. Seemingly but a brigade only in strength, it was satisfied with having secured the position, and made no further attempt to move up.

Farmington was just to our right. I rode among some scattered trees, between the enemy and the village, to reconnoiter. When satisfied as to their strength and apparent object, I made my way back (overtaking many stragglers by the way) to Corinth and reported to Hardee. I found him with Beauregard at General Price's Headquarters.

The heavy cannonading, heard so distinctly at Corinth, had created considerable excitement. Troops were moving to positions. But my report quieted apprehension of any advance *in force*. Beauregard remarked to me that he would have that force of the enemy in a day or so. Hardee was exceedingly indignant at the conduct of the brigade which belonged to his command, but I don't know what he did by way of punishment to the officers and men. The enemy followed up this success. They came into Farmington on the following day and made a reconnaissance in force on the ridge, almost in sight of the lines.

General Bragg was now directed to attack him, which he did successfully on the 5th of May (I think), driving everything back across Seven-Mile Creek. I thought now that we would occupy the regained ground, but it was not done. The enemy returned in a few days in larger force under Major General Pope, reestablished himself, threw up earthworks, and pushed his operations on the ridge, as I had already foreseen.[4]

To give up this ridge was to give up Corinth. I therefore

4. On May 21 Hardee gave Liddell his first command: a demi brigade composed of the 17th Tennessee and the 48th Tennessee Cavalry. These units, together with any other posted on the Danville and Farmington roads, constituted Liddell's temporary command. Special Orders #49, May 21, 1862, Third Corps, in Liddell Papers, LSU.

represented to Hardee that Corinth would now be shelled from the spur nearest to our lines. To stop the enemy's progress we had to hold the ridge ourselves. Wherefore, at Hardee's instigation, some earthworks were thrown up and occupied by Van Dorn at a high point, just on the south side of the cut of the Memphis and Charleston Railroad.

This had the effect to check all further flanking operations on our right, south of the railroad. Beauregard now laid plans to attack General Pope's Corps in Farmington. In the execution of his designs, however, Van Dorn, who was to conduct the flanking column, allowed himself somehow to be led astray by his guides. This frustrated the whole arrangement, greatly to the dissatisfaction of Beauregard. In this affair, Beauregard gave me, unsolicited, the command of a detached brigade,[5] which, upon the signal of Van Dorn's fire, was to march up the Farmington Ridge in cooperation.

On the evening of the 27th May, the enemy threw three shells into Corinth from the spur alluded to. The next day, our forces evacuated Corinth.

We had immense numbers of sick and wounded, between 14,000 and 16,000, which reduced our effective strength to about 26,000. The place was very unhealthy. The bad water added to the bad food, bad care, bad clothing, and bad protection in camps led thousands of young men to premature graves. The sad conviction enters the mind that their services were unnecessarily lost to the cause. Such a waste of valuable life was unpardonable and betokened ill success to the South, who could not supply the vacancies.

These facts were patent to the merest private. Many, becoming disheartened at the gloomy prospect even after fighting faithfully for the season, deserted to their homes never to return, notwithstanding the many offers of pardon by the President. These people chose to exercise their own judgment. When they considered the constant want of success brought about through unskillful leaders, their confidence in ultimate success was at an end. They thought their lives would be thrown away unnecessarily. The greater number were shaky by nature and had never possessed the true Southern Spirit.

Whenever I now see the brave Confederate private soldier

5. See preceding footnote.

who manfully stuck to his flag and cause to the end I cannot avoid the reflection that he deserved more respect and consideration than the general officers that led him in the ruined cause. His should be the honor and reward. For *his* was the endurance and *his* the suffering in true faith, hopeless of distinction to the last.

The day preceding the evacuation, I was dining with Hardee when instructions came to him from the commanding general to burn the Mobile and Ohio Railroad Bridge over the Tuscumbia River at a fixed hour the next day. This was on the line of retreat selected for Hardee's Divisions. The Adjutant General, Captain Roy,[6] read the order to the General aloud. I remarked that I wished he would instruct the officer in charge of the burning to hold on until the last train had passed. Hardee told his adjutant to add that to the order and "gratify the Colonel." Then turning to me, said with raillery, "Anything more that you desire?"

"Yes, General, tell him to make *sure* that the *last* train has passed."

"Roy, add that also." He was evidently amused at *my* expense. All the rest of the staff enjoyed the General's raillery. Pushing me still again, he asked, "Have you any other *wish?*"

"None, General, but to direct the officer to be *certain* of the fact that the *last* train has passed the bridge before he burns it." The laugh by this time was outright against me, but the result will show how fortunate was this persistent caution, considered so provoking to ridicule at the time.

A brigade under General B. R. Johnson[7] was stationed at the dirt road bridge a short distance below the railroad just alluded to. Johnson was to retard the crossing of the enemy should he pursue us. A small redoubt had been thrown up and a battery placed in position to rake the approach.

The next morning early all the troops had passed the bridge and were moving Southward towards Boonville Station, incessant

6. Thomas Benton Roy, Hardee's faithful adjutant and friend, married Sallie Hardee and lived close to the General in Selma, Alabama, after the war.

7. Bushrod Rust Johnson (1817-1880). This Ohio born schoolteacher attended West Point (Class of 1840). He participated in the Florida and Mexican Wars, but from 1847 until 1861 teaching was his profession. He fought steadily as a brigade commander under Bragg. Under Lee at Petersburg in 1864 he rose to command of a division that bore "much of the sternest, bitterest day-by-day fighting in the hideous, red trenches of Petersburg." Sayler's Creek cost him his division and failure continued to stalk him throughout his postwar teaching career.

heavy cannonading was heard ten miles ahead. Upon getting there, it was found to have been caused by the burning of an ammunition train. A force of Federal Cavalry the night before had succeeded in gaining our rear at the Boonville Station and seized the train. They kindly moved the sick from it to a safe distance before setting it on fire. Afterwards, they managed to escape scot free, amid the confusion created by the explosion of the heavy ammunition. The track was uninjured, however. It caused little delay beyond that of removing the wrecks.

Hardee's route to Baldwin Station crossed the railroad to the left or east of this place. I wished to make myself acquainted with the country and roads on the west of the railroad, so I took that side. After riding about ten miles, I came up with Beauregard and staff who had halted for dinner at a house on the roadside.

I stopped and discussed with him the danger of the capture of Johnson's Brigade left to guard the Tuscumbia Bridge. He said too that it was unavoidable, since it was better to sacrifice a brigade than endanger the retreat of the army. I asked how long he intended that it should remain at the bridge. He answered that it would be ordered to evacuate tomorrow. I then represented to him that the object he had in view could be accomplished without sacrificing the brigade. He could direct General Johnson to hold his ground until 9 p.m. at all hazards. Then Johnson could silently withdraw under cover of *darkness*, taking the road west of Brownsville. To avoid touching there, a special guide would be needed. Beauregard unhesitantly issued the orders in accordance with my suggestions.

General Johnson was heavily pressed during the day. He had repulsed the attacks with severe loss to the enemy though so far with but little to himself. He held on bravely to the appointed time after dark when he got off unperceived. Meanwhile the enemy concentrated his forces and during the night had crossed the river above and below him to enclose his brigade. The next morning, to their surprise no doubt, no force was there. The game was gone, having detained the pursuers over two days. There had been a general impression with the brigade that they were to be sacrificed. They were greatly relieved by this unlooked-for escape.

We had not been long at Baldwin Station when Hardee expressed indignant astonishment at the intelligence that we had lost some fourteen *loaded trains* on the Memphis and Charleston Railroad by the *premature* burning of Tuscumbia River Bridge. This bridge was on General Polk's line of retreat from Corinth. The officer in charge of the business, Col. Thos. Claiborne, had too strictly obeyed his orders. After destroying the bridge, the trains that came up had to be destroyed to prevent their falling into enemy hands.

I quietly asked Hardee if we had suffered any loss in this way on *our* line, by the Memphis and Charleston Railroad.

He replied, "None that I know of."

"Then you see, General, why I was so particular in Corinth to make *sure* that the last train had passed."

"Yes, yes. I see it now and wish sincerely that they had used the same precaution on the other road."

Our forces, a short time after this, reached Tupelo Station where they halted to reorganize. The enemy followed us only a few miles south of the Tuscumbia River. Now having gained possession of the Memphis and Charleston Railroad, he opened communications with the Mississippi River at Memphis, which with Corinth had fallen into his hands. Thus in five short and eventful months in our country's history, from the time of my interview in January with the President in Richmond, had all the disasters occurred that had been apprehended by me and made the subject of unpleasant conversation between us.

Only Vicksburg and Port Hudson prevented the possession of the Mississippi River by the Federal forces. What a short gap to make the intersection of Confederate territory complete. I had not expected the fall of New Orleans so soon, nor did I think the attack upon that city would come from the direction of the Gulf. On the contrary, everything being favorable, it should have come with the possession of the river from above. I had overlooked naval operations and knew nothing of the nature of the defenses *below* the city.

My opinions had been formed from men and officers who seemed in every way confident of the strength of the defenses to repel any attack by naval or land forces from the direction of the Gulf. It is certainly regretted that the engineering skill of Beauregard had not been used early to hold New Orleans. Its loss cost us the use of the Mississippi and greatly encouraged the enemy.

There can be no doubt whatever that *skillful handling* of our means, although limited, would have produced splendid results. For the first and second years of the war, the progress of the enemy was very slow and very discouraging to him. But now and then from *our own folly*, he would gain a point. When a great one like New Orleans fell, it served to animate his energies afresh. Mr. Davis hugged the delusion *too long* that the batteries of Fort Jackson and St. Phillip were irresistible to the passage of gunboats. I have heard he absolutely scorned the representations made to him of the possibility of the loss of the city from such causes. One of the wretched mistakes of Mr. Davis was the disregard and contempt he had for *private* enterprise. His military education had inspired him with what is vulgarly called "old fogyism." Nothing good could be seen except in the *beaten path* of the *past*. In private enterprise consists the *spirit of the times*. The man in high position and in trying times who fails to employ such means for success cannot be the man for the occasion.[8]

I have so often seen this the case in this great war that I have been beside myself with anger at the ruin before me. There was no help for it. *God* deprived us of Sidney Johnston, who was the only man known to me capable of seeing these things. And then, as if to make sure of our ruin, took from us our last hope—Stonewall Jackson, the other Johnston. Can it be possible that the fate of the South was fixed by immutable decree of the Almighty in the outset? Then why sacrifice so many thousands of innocent lives? Why such utter ruin to the land of that people, themselves innocent of the cause of national wrong? My reason tells me that Providence leaves man with the privilege and chance of being the architect of his own fortune. If he fails his object, he has no one to blame but himself and his own follies.

Such is the history of the *"fated"* Confederacy.

---

8. On a loose piece of paper tucked in the middle of his manuscript, Liddell wrote, "Nobody ever *doubted* for a moment Mr. Davis' motives—but everybody *knew* and regretted his partiality for relatives and favorites—whilst they deplored the intensity of his dislike, not to say hatred, of those who differed from him in opinion. Thus it was, that incompetent men were placed high in the most responsible positions and *held them*, in spite of public clamor, to the eventual ruin of the Confederate cause."

# CHAPTER VII

# BRIGADE COMMAND

Up to this time, June, 1862, I had been giving my services free as a volunteer with Hardee. The expense was inconsiderable compared to the interest at stake, but my funds were nearly exhausted. It became, therefore, necessary for me to replenish for my own subsistence. I could withdraw from this army, to try it again in that army nearest my home. There I could occasionally obtain supplies, if not money, to keep me going. I made known my status and designs to Hardee. I told him that by going nearer to home, I could look after the necessities of my family. No longer would I support myself here and, at the same time, do my part in the war. But this did not meet his views. He protested my leaving the army and began forthwith to cast about to prevent it in some way. He even offered to secure me a commission as Captain in the Confederate regular service on his own staff. He would assist me with pay from his own funds.

Although my own education, in great measure, had been military, I had never been on actual service. Hence, I was indifferent to official position and only sought to do my individual part in the war. We were about the same age, and having myself no military reputation, I felt myself too old to be governed by ambitious notoriety for distinction. All I could do was simply my *duty* in support of the cause.

Whilst this offer of Hardee's evincing esteem and friendship was being considered by me, it seems that five Colonels of as many regiments of Arkansas troops had, unknown to me, made application with the approval of Bragg, Hardee, and Beauregard, to the War Department for my appointment to the command of their brigade. When the matter was made known to me, it was altogether unexpected. To be their unsolicited choice greatly flattered me. I often wondered whence was derived the confidence these officers reposed in me that should have led them to my selection. Nevertheless, I was averse to taking such command inasmuch as I was not from their state. This position I considered to be justly due one of their own people.

Hardee, who was desirous of having me on his staff, proposed Colonel John Pegram to these officers in my stead, which I approved.[1] At my desire, the matter was left to Beauregard, Commanding General. Beauregard said that he could not spare Pegram from his place as Chief Engineer, but that if I could get a commission of any kind in the service he would put me in Pegram's place as Chief Engineer. I told him in reply, "no matter," that I would serve in *any capacity* for the good of the cause.

Meanwhile, the brigade colonels were not satisfied. They preferred my appointment to any other. In accordance with their wishes, I was put in command by order on 10th June, 1862, to remain until the War Department could decide upon the confirmation of my appointment. The officers who had selected me were Colonels D. C. Govan, 2nd Arkansas; J. H. Kelly, 8th Arkansas; L. Featherston, 5th Arkansas; Samuel Smith, 6th Arkansas; and D. A. Gillespie, 7th Arkansas. They were persons of high character in their own state, but only known to me by recent association in the Army.[2]

I feel bound to state that from first to last, not only with these but with all other officers of this brigade, I had always the most amiable relations. I have ever found them, without exception, courteous and brave men, high toned and honorable throughout, amid all trials and hardships. But these facts will show for themselves as my record progresses. Of the original five colonels, only General D. C. Govan survived the war.

General Bragg's Army of Tennessee was organized in the months

1. John Pegram (1832-1865). This highly respected officer belonged to the old army establishment and taught under Hardee at West Point. Opening his Confederate service inauspiciously with a surrender of his cavalry command to Rosecrans in 1861, he became Beauregard's and Bragg's chief engineer in 1862. Chief of Staff for Kirby Smith, he moved on to become a good cavalry leader in the Kentucky Campaign. Murfreesboro and Chickamauga brought him more recognition. In 1863 he took command of a brigade in Early's Division and transferred to Lee's Army where he became a distinguished division commander. He was killed at Hatcher's Run.
2. Liddell's promotion to Brigadier General came on July 12, 1862. Register of Appointments, Confederate Army.

of June and July, 1862. Toward the end of July, we were ordered to Chattanooga, preparatory for the Kentucky campaign of 1862.[3]

I moved my brigade on the Mobile and Ohio Railroad to Mobile, thence both by river and rail to Montgomery on the Alabama, thence by rail to Chickamauga Station near Chattanooga. We had *lost* the road from Chattanooga to Memphis, hence this roundabout way.

At Chickamauga, I received about 10th August, 1862, official notice of the confirmation of my appointment as General of Brigade, to date from July 12. The effective strength of my brigade was about 2,000. I had taken great interest in their drill and discipline. The evident improvement had inspired an *Esprite de Corps* that could not fail to excite the pride and raise the confidence of all in its future usefulness. It pleased me to drill them; and evolutions of the line had become as familiar and easy of rapid execution by practice as regimental drills. Instead of being a hardship, I was often solicited by both officers and privates to practice the maneuvers.

My staff were young men, sensible, brave and energetic: Captain G. A. Williams of Missouri, Adjutant General; Captain J. L. Bostick of Nashville, Aide-de-Camp; and Lieutenant J. A. Dulin of Arkansas, Brigade Inspector. They constituted my military family. Of these, at the end of the war, Williams and Dulin survive, though often wounded. Poor Bostick, the very soul of honor, fell in harness—dying as he had lived, a free man. Changes of command in the progress of the war separated us towards the last, but the time of their association with me constitute the most pleasant part of my service.

---

3. While we were at Tupelo, we heard of the battles around Richmond, Virginia, resulting in the discomfiture of General McClellan and forcing him to raise the seige of that city.

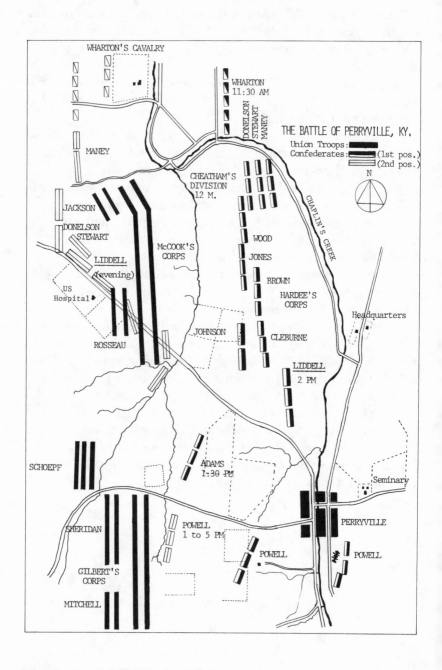

THE BATTLE OF PERRYVILLE, KY.

Union Troops:
Confederates: (1st pos.)
             (2nd pos.)

N

WHARTON'S CAVALRY

WHARTON
11:30 AM

DONELSON
STEWART
MANEY

MANEY

CHEATHAM'S
DIVISION
12 M.

JACKSON

DONELSON
STEWART

LIDDELL
(evening)

McCOOK'S
CORPS

WOOD

JONES

BROWN

HARDEE'S
CORPS

US
Hospital

CLEBURNE

JOHNSON

ROSSEAU

LIDDELL
2 PM

CHAPLIN'S CREEK

Headquarters

ADAMS
1:30 PM

SCHOEPF

Seminary

POWELL
1 to 5 PM

SHERIDAN

POWELL

PERRYVILLE

POWELL

GILBERT'S
CORPS

MITCHELL

# CHAPTER VIII

# KENTUCKY CAMPAIGN

While Bragg was organizing at Tupelo, General Buell on the Federal side had made an effort to seize Chattanooga. Forrest's cavalry frustrated his plans by cutting the railroads and interrupting his communications at Nashville. This was a part of the object I had in view when proposing to Van Dorn to command of all the cavalry after the Battle of Shiloh. At that time I believed firmly it would have helped to hold Corinth.

If General Buell had received the aid he furnished Grant at Shiloh or Pittsburg Landing, it is not at all unlikely that he would have taken Chattanooga. At all events, his *objectives* indicated the true strategy for the Federals, which was subsequently carried out by them.

Bragg's movement in Kentucky completely turned Buell's position in Tennessee. It compelled Buell to withdraw and attempt to intercept Bragg in Kentucky. This was the *first* instance of turning strategy by parallel movement exhibited since the war began. It was readily seen and followed by others: first by Rosecrans, who at Tullahoma tried it on Bragg himself; then by Grant on Lee in Virginia; and, at nearly the same time, by Sherman on Johnston first, and last on Hood in Georgia. General Lee was the only one who made application of the countermovement. The defense of Richmond, however, restricted his chances and necessarily kept him from the full scope of his purposes.

General Buckner, having been exchanged and promoted by the President very recently, arrived at Chattanooga and was assigned to the command of a division comprising Wood's, B. R. Johnson's, Cleburne's, and Liddell's brigades. General Patton Anderson was assigned to the command of a division comprising his own brigade, D. W. Adam's Louisiana brigade,[1] and some other brigades. These two divisions comprised Hardee's Corps.

General Cheatham's Division of Tennessee troops and General Withers' Division of Alabama troops comprised the Corps of General L. Polk. I do not remember the names of all the brigade commanders.

The corps of General E. Kirby Smith was at Knoxville and moved before us into Kentucky, turning Cumberland Gap. It was evacuated by the Federals upon his gaining Crab Orchard in their rear. The garrison managed to effect their escape in a northern direction through Eastern Kentucky. Shortly afterwards, Kirby Smith won the Battle of Richmond, chiefly through the good management of General Cleburne, who with his brigade, had been detached from Buckner's Division at Chattanooga and sent to Smith in time to go with his advance into Kentucky.

Antagonistic armies at this time were Lee against Pope in Virginia, Bragg against Buell in Kentucky, Van Dorn and Price against Rosecrans at Corinth in Mississippi, and Grant near Holly Springs in the same state endeavoring to approach Jackson by the railroad. The date of these positions may not correspond precisely, but the events were nearly contemporaneous. We started from Chattanooga about the 7th of September, 1862, and marched across Walden's Ridge into Sequatchie Valley. This we followed up to the head (Pikeville). We passed over another spur of the Cumberland Mountains to Sparta. On we went, to the Cumberland River, which we crossed not far above Carthage, near an island. We proceeded through Glascow, Kentucky, to Cave City on the Louisville and Nashville Railroad. We pushed on to Munfordville on Green River where we invested and captured Wilder's Brigade, garrisoning the works near that town.[2] Before we got up, General Chalmers rashly attempted to carry the works by storm, which resulted in his severe repulse with heavy loss.

1. Daniel Weisiger Adams (1821-1872). Son of a Federal judge, Adams shot and killed a public critic of his father in 1843. A lawyer of Mississippi and Louisiana, Adams entered the Confederate service early and with a high rank, thanks in part to his friendship with Governor Moore. As colonel of the 1st Louisiana, he gained recognition at Shiloh (wounded), Perryville (wounded), and Chickamauga (wounded). He ended his civil war career as a cavalry officer in north Alabama. D. Hill said of him, "It was difficult for me to decide which the most to admire, his courage in the field or his unparalleled cheerfulness under suffering."
2. Liddell and his men would have an unpleasant return visit from Wilder the following fall at Chickamauga.

Information was soon received of the approach of Buell from Nashville to relieve Munfordville. Bragg ordered Hardee's Corps to move back and meet him at once. But Buell, for some cause, seemed disinclined to come to an engagement. Our supplies for twenty days had become already reduced to less than two, very scanty at that. It was out of the question to wait upon Buell or to follow him back toward Bowling Green. It was very compulsory, therefore, upon us to go forward for *subsistence*.

Bragg accordingly resumed his line of march to Nolin on through Hodgenville to Bardstown, where we halted and found an abundance of good supplies. In the meantime, Buell had inclined his route further to the west of the railroad in order to pass us and to reach Louisville before us. He also expected heavy reinforcements there.

I have frequently heard it said that Bragg *ought* to have fought Buell at Munfordville. But the truth is that he could not wait without starving. There was nothing in that section in the way of provisions at that time, and Buell, knowing Bragg's necessities, could defer fighting as long as he pleased. Apart from these facts, no useless delay should have occurred in uniting Bragg with Kirby Smith's Corps for effective and decided objects. Doubtless Bragg knew Buell's intentions. In this little game of tactics, Bragg decided upon the best course held out to him. I believe he was right.

Up to this time, everything had progressed as well as could have been expected. It only remained for the General commanding to carry out his plans unswervingly, and with self-possession and good judgment. He could feel the positive assurance of being well-seconded in any and all things by the troops under him.

So far, our march had been delightful. The season was propitious, dry weather with pleasant days and cool, bracing nights. The constant movement and change of scene in a high country, sometimes mountainous, had improved the health of the troops. Their spirits were buoyed with the brightest hopes of success. They had the fullest reliance upon the skill of their general. His previous military reputation had justified every fair promise for the future.

The people of Kentucky seemed to be gratified at our coming, at least so far as my own observation went. In most places they were not slow to afford us every friendly facility in their power. Yet after all, it was plain to the close observer that there was something which indicated distrust of finality. It caused them to hesitate in taking open active steps that might in any degree compromise the safety of their persons and families or the security of their property in the event of ultimate failure on the part of the South.

I could not blame them. It was natural for any people to dread the horrors of war at their own doors. It was natural to wish that their own community and state should escape from being made the battleground for large contending forces, animated with the hatred inspired by civil war. However much they may wish success in their hearts to the side of their sympathies and interest, it was at last only human nature to desire that the threatened calamities should be turned aside from their own hearthstones. It is true that it was selfish to avoid the risk common to all the states by inaction and by submission to the strongest side. Yet, Kentucky was luxurious from prosperity and lacked the energy and bold determination of her Virginia founders.

She *might* have done better by the South. She had, after all, suffered comparatively nothing. Many, *very many*, joined the Federal side, whilst but a few thousand, true representatives of the old stock, bravely hazarded all hopes of self in the cause and adhered to the fortunes of their Southern brothers in arms to the last. These *must* constitute the best people of Kentucky, and it will be so considered eventually, when time shall have swept away the mists of faction and hatred.

In our march through Kentucky, private property was respected everywhere. I never saw, nor did I ever hear of, any authentic instance of plunder or injury of citizens by the troops of Bragg's Army. Orders were very stringent against the minutest violations of person or property. If any wrong was done, I feel assured it must have been at the hands of wretched deserters or pretended adherents to our side. Kentucky's hesitation as a "border" state— so different from gallant old Virginia—her lame halting between parsimony, love of ease, and her duty to her Southern sister states, did not justify this kind consideration at Bragg's hands. She should have shared the fate of the balance.

I heard Bragg feelingly deplore the inaction of the state and the indifference of the people from whom he had been led to expect great efforts. Kentucky, of all the Southern states, had less to complain of and more to be ashamed of. May she enjoy the blessings she *sought*. Kentucky showed herself indifferent to

84

this stain in her history by losing her state rights, which her greatest men so carefully guarded in the Kentucky resolutions of 1798.

Bragg halted one part of his army at Bardstown for some seven days. He proceeded to Frankfort. There, unwisely, he traveled out of his line of legitimate military operations to inaugurate Governor Richard Hawes. This premature and absurd formality was interrupted by alarming reports of the rapid approach of Buell's forces. Now was the time for Bragg to concentrate for a great blow. Truly all sensible men believed that such was his fixed purpose. Unfortunately, civil and military policy are seldom combined in any one man. The want of either quality, when attempted, disturbs the free action of the other.

About the 2nd of October our division was ordered to take up the line of march for Springfield. Passing through that place, I stopped at a house to receive some orders from General Polk in command of our wing. He placed in my charge three Federal cavalry officers (a major, a captain, and a lieutenant) who had been captured by the Texas Cavalry in Bardstown not long after we had left. For some cause of retaliation, he directed me to dismount them and turn their horses over to the quartermaster. The saddles (McClellan "trees") were to be specially reserved for him and his staff.

Although very positive in manner, I could not help observing General Polk to be in the highest spirits. Hardee was with him and seemed to share his elation.

I proceeded at once to execute the orders, to the disgust of the three mounted prisoners. Two of them I found to be Kentucky union men. Like all traitors, they used very abusive language against the South. They were captured in their own town (Bardstown) when they attempted to enter at the head of their squadron for *effect* with their friends, particularly female friends. Their sad disappointment must have increased their natural rancor against us. The third officer was a northern man whose courteous manner contrasted in every way with these Kentucky Unionists.

I bore the talk of the Unionists with patient forbearance and continued to treat them as kindly as my means permitted. I shared my rations with them in the day and my blankets at night, as it had now become quite cold after sunset. When these men, shortly afterwards, were separated from my care, they must have felt some sense of self-reproach. They sent their thanks by messenger for my considerate attention.

Before getting to Perryville, we found the roads very dusty and the water very scarce. Passing through Perryville, we halted for water and rest on the Chaplin Fork of Salt River on the Harrodsburg Road, only a mile or less from the town. Buell's column was now fast coming upon our heels. It was high time for us to turn upon him.

We were separated from Kirby Smith's wing, which was somewhere near Frankfort and constituted more than half of our effective strength. It was the general belief that Bragg would *refuse* battle until he had effected a junction. No one, not in on the secret, knew precisely where Kirby Smith's command was. Common opinion was reduced to every confidence that it was within striking distance, at least, or sufficiently near to turn any doubtful scale. I, like all the rest, knew nothing beyond rumor. The sound of artillery on the Springfield Road behind us indicated the coming of the enemy. If Bragg was going to fight at all, it was expected that he would be prepared for it by having everything *on hand* for telling effect. Hence there was no uneasiness.

On the evening of the 6th October, I prepared to camp after having passed a short distance on the Harrodsburg Road from Perryville. Hardee rode near me with his staff and called me to go with him. He wanted to look at the ground north of the town, with a view of fixing upon a line of battle. He wanted prominent points sketched, and asked me to bring paper and pencils.

As we rode along together, Hardee remarked that we *must* fight, since he could not march with the enemy so close at his heels. The enemy must be driven back or checked to save the supplies we had at Danville. Hardee asked what was my opinion of the position to give battle. I unhesitatingly answered, saying that we could hardly have a better one. The road that the enemy was coming on for some ten or twelve miles back was exceedingly dusty and dry. Since we possessed the road, this inconvenience would be seriously felt by the enemy. In the fatigue of battle, if we only succeeded in holding our ground for two days, the result must be favorable to us. Hardee readily concurred. He told me further that General Polk had been communicating with Bragg at Harrodsburg or Frankfort to get his consent and to arrange things for general engagement there.

After examining different positions between the Springfield and

Mackville Roads, we returned to Perryville. We rode through to a house in a commanding position for a battery. The place we found was owned by a Widow Padlock, who had a large family of females. The gallant General was now quite at home with the ladies, bandying compliments, particularly with the widow. Widow Padlock, not one to be beaten, expressed her sincere sympathy for the General that one so advanced in years should be engaged in the dangers and troubles of war.

"Why, Madam," exclaimed the General, horrified and touched to the quick, "how old do you take me to be?"

"Well, Sir, I am seventy-two and I think you are about a year younger."

"How! What! Why, Madam, I am not as old as that man," pointing to the writer. But the lady shook her head in utter disbelief. The General, now quite concerned, fell seriously to work trying to convince her of her error. In the eagerness of his arguments, Hardee appealed now and then to me for confirmation of his assertions. I was busily engaged in making out my sketch of the localities of the expected battleground.

I saw clearly that he was making no progress in convincing the lady. I therefore, proposed to beat a retreat. We could not afford to waste any more time upon the subject *now*. I did say freely in his support that we were nearly of the same age. But the lady shook her head, not at all satisfied. We, however, got off, Hardee partially satisfied with the last word.

Amid the exciting events that followed, I had forgotten this disputatious affair; but Hardee recalled it to my mind a month afterwards. Rather feelingly, he said, "The absurdity! That this old lady should insist upon my being seventy-one years old."

I saw now that it was not so much of a joke with him after all and tried to comfort him with the usual unsatisfactory consolations. The old lady had discovered his anxiety on the subject and only persisted in it to quiz him. This pleasantry came up subsequently at Shelbyville, Tennessee.

Later in the evening, Hardee sent me an order to move back on the Springfield Road about a mile and take position in a strip of woods between the Springfield and Mackville roads. This ground had attracted our attention in the previous reconnaissance. When Wheeler's Cavalry was forced back, I must endeavor to retard the advance of the enemy as much as possible, or until the line of battle could be decided upon and occupied. Accordingly, I was soon in the designated place.

Wheeler's Cavalry held their ground gallantly until the next evening (7th October) when the pressure became too great. They were compelled to fall back and retire to our flanks, leaving the future contest to the infantry. It was late in the evening when the cavalry withdrew from my front, and the enemy moved up to the vacated position. I had made all my dispositions with the expectation of a daylight attack. Through the night, all was quiet except an occasional shot between the advanced pickets. This proved to me that my own men were on the alert, which rendered a night surprise improbable. Resting at the root of a tree, though sleepless, my thoughts reverted continually to the probable events of tomorrow. The moments were full of anxiety.[3]

Daylight on October 8, 1862, came and yet no movement. Sunrise was hailed by a shot, another, and another along the picket line, increasing rapidly in frequency until the firing became general. Soon, the batteries of the enemy opened, drawing fire from mine at every opportunity. I was sent for in haste to look after a section of my battery on my right. A charge upon it was apprehended. I superintended and directed its fire with good effect upon the head of a column of cavalry, debouching from a point of woodland in the valley below us, causing it to retire in apparent confusion. An order interrupted me to report immediately to General Buckner, who had just arrived on the field from Frankfort. He had been assisting Bragg in inaugurating Hawes Governor of the State.

All things in my front seemed to be going right, so I rode hurriedly to find General Buckner. He was not far from my left flank and close to the Springfield Road. Saluting him, I asked at once if he knew the ground or had seen the rough sketch I had furnished Hardee. On receiving a negative reply, I endeavored to explain. I found it impossible to do so with any satisfaction without a diagram, so I quickly set to work drawing one from a piece of paper I had (sitting on horse all the while) and for which he patiently waited on me to finish.

We were in good view and under direct fire from a battery

3. Leonidas Polk described Liddell's position as, "General Liddell's Brigade of General Buckner's division was thrown forward in observation about one mile in front of Perryville, between the Springfield and Mackville roads." *O.R.* I, 16 (1), 1110.

hardly five hundred yards distant. It fired grape and shell incessantly. It was trying, but we had to stand it. After giving Buckner the diagram and making such explanations as were satisfactory to him, I proposed riding close to the enemy's position that I might show him an important point.

He quickly agreed, and we rode together towards this battery playing upon us. Luckily, we descended a slope, which enabled us to pass *under* the line of fire aimed at us. Upon getting to the base, we turned to the right, passing between the opposing lines unharmed. I said now to General Buckner that if a general engagement at this place was determined on, we must hold the height. I pointed it out to him on the far side of the valley of Doctor's Fork just below us. It became known afterwards as the "Burnt Barn" position and, in my opinion, was the key to the whole field. His quick perception grasped the advantages offered by its occupation. He said that he would go forthwith to General Polk, who was not commanding the forces, and get him to hold the position in the event of its being decided to fight, and immediately rode.

The firing was now increasing before me. About 10:00 a.m., the enemy pressed back my skirmish line, which, however, I quickly reinforced and forced him back in return. A line of battle closely followed the skirmish line of the enemy and again forced my line steadily back. It was soon plain enough that I could not maintain my skirmish line against the division before me. I drew it in and got ready to receive the attack in line with the three remaining regiments. My skirmishers obstinately contested the ground. Notwithstanding the fire from the line of battle, they slowed the enemy's approach.

Soon both sides were in opposite woodlands. My men in the skirmish line had been forced across the narrow interval of open valley between. While the enemy was apparently hesitating to take this open space, orders reached me from General Polk that we were ready.[4] I must give up the position and take post in reserve, withdrawing without confusion from the front. In the face of the pending attack, before I could accomplish this order, I suffered a loss of seventy-two killed and wounded. The 5th and 7th Arkansas regiments, in skirmish deployment under Colonels L. Featherston and D. A. Gillespie, were principally engaged in this affair.

4. In his official report, Liddell says that Buckner ordered him back. Liddell crossed Chaplin Fork about 11:00 a.m. *O.R.* I, 16 (1), 1158.

They had bravely held back, since the previous evening, a division of the enemy. My men were favored by the woodland cover that concealed and probably magnified their numbers.

Bragg had arrived, and it seems that there was some hesitation with him as to the propriety of giving battle at Perrysville. But he finally gave in to his advisers and threw the command for the occasion upon General Polk, though intending to overlook the operations personally.

Meanwhile, pending all this unwise delay, the enemy was making use of his opportunity in pushing up and deploying his columns. General Bushrod Johnson's Brigade had been ordered to take the position at the "Burnt Barn" in accordance with my suggestions to General Buckner. Afterwards, Johnson was unaccountably ordered to withdraw, and then again ordered back. So vacillating were the decisions of the council.

Before Johnson could retrace his steps to reoccupy the place, however, the enemy came up and took possession of it. The enemy's thirsty men were joyfully engaged in filling their canteens from the water in the Doctor's Fork close at hand. At 1:00 p.m. he had become too securely posted behind stone fences for Johnson to dislodge him. Johnson tried, nevertheless, but met with severe repulse. Cleburne, who had again joined the division with his brigade of veterans, was now ordered to take Johnson's place and regain the position.

Meanwhile General Cheatham's Division, some distance to the right and low down on Doctor's Fork, had become heavily engaged with the Federal commands of Generals McCook and Rousseau. Cheatham succeeded in slowly driving them back to the Mackville Road which they had crossed for some distance.[5]

From my standpoint on the ridge, I saw General Cleburne's Brigade assault and carry the "Burnt Barn" and then hold the place against the repeated attacks of fresh troops thrown against them. The brigades of Johnson and Wood were now moved into the interval between Cleburne's right and Cheatham's left. All were hotly engaged after 2:00 p.m.

Before this, I had been placed in a commanding position, with

---

5. Benjamin Franklin Cheatham (1820-1886). No other soldier is more closely identified with the struggles of the Army of Tennessee than this popular Tennessean. He performed creditably at every level of command he held. Frank Cheatham's men fought with enthusiasm for this outspoken, unpretentious, convivial farmer. He exemplifies the volunteer Confederate leader.

instructions that, if our forces were beaten, I was to hold my ground at *all hazards*. This would enable the balance of the army to get off safely under the cover of my fire. General Buckner gave me minute instructions and then went forward to the fight with the remainder of his division. Although I was then entirely out of sight of the enemy's line and probably some one and one-half miles distant, his missiles passing over the intervening high ridge fell in my ranks and killed several men.

Changes were rapidly occurring. Notwithstanding all preconcerted arrangements, I soon found myself subject to new directions. Hardee ordered me to the crest of this high ridge, whence, as already stated, I could overlook the entire field of battle. It was plain to me now that we had only three divisions present: General Withers' Division of Polk's Corps was near Mackville and Kirby Smith's Corps was not in supporting distance. Hence the disparity of strength was unmistakable. We had but fifteen thousand men to oppose Buell's whole army.

The battle was going on below us, and the movement of the contending forces in the valley had the appearance of actors in a great amphitheater. The arena was encircled by the high ridge for the use of spectators. Hardly high enough, however, to be indifferent to the danger. It was very imposing—the advance, the repulse, the charge, the retreat, the fire from the numerous batteries, the incessant rattling of musketry—all combined—rendered the spectacle interesting in the extreme. High as we were above the plain of battle, shot and shell fell thick over and amongst us, killing and wounding my men, now quietly, but uneasily, looking on.

Solid cannon balls would ricochet to the top. Some would strike detached rocks below us, would turn at right angles upwards, visible until distance carried them out of sight. I saw a flag of the Union carried forward in the center of a regiment until it came exactly between my line of sight and the rays of the declining sun. Shining through the folds and stripes gave the sun the appearance of a flame of fire. I could not suppress the sudden misgiving that the Union *flame* would yet consume the Confederacy. Our ancestors had given us this right by helping to make this flag for our own protection. Perhaps it would have been better for us to fight for our rights in the Union under the same flag.

The sight was an ill omen to me, but I had no longer time to give way to reflections of this nature. Hardee sent his aide-de-camp Hardin Perkins with orders for me to come down immediately into the plain.[6] Perkins rode with me until the head of my column, marching by the right flank, reached Doctor's Fork. Then he turned suddenly to me, saying with a grim smile, "I had like to have forgotten. The General says go where the *fire is hottest.*" He then quickly left me.

The order evidently gave me the latitude to use my own judgment. No time was to be lost. The sun had just sunk behind the trees. I looked around for the hottest place. It seemed to be everywhere.

I crossed the creek, my command following, when suddenly it struck me to attempt the capture of a heavy battery I had seen from the ridge firing over its own lines from the rear of the Union left wing. I now ordered the men to move rapidly and did not call a halt until I had reached nearly the extreme right of Cheatham's Division. This done, I spoke a few cheering words to the men. I assured them that their vigor and bravery would decide the battle. I felt confident that they would not fail. A cheer and a voluntary fixing of bayonets was the answer.

When we pressed forward in line to the work before us, we met crowds of stragglers flying towards the rear. A young officer in violent language and manner wildly called on his men to halt and return to the fight. Having rallied a company, he requested permission to join my command. Recognizing his gallant try, I granted the permission.

As we neared the front passing through a battery captured by Cheatham, the roar of firearms rendered it difficult to be heard. At this moment, General Cheatham, pipe in mouth, rode up to me, waving very excitedly and loudly, "General, you can save the fight! Go on and save it."

I replied to him, "I shall try, General, but come and show me your line. It is now getting too late to distinguish colors clearly. I might fire by mistake upon your men."

"No—go on and save the fight. You will find the line." Still marching forward, I appealed to him again, but to no purpose.

The full moon was high up, and the twilight of a clear October evening had rapidly merged into a bright moonlight. Suddenly we confronted a dark line hardly more than twenty-five paces off on the crest of the elevation we were ascending. Immediately, with-

6. Col. S. H. Perkins reached Liddell about 5:30 p.m. *O.R.* I, 16 (1), 1159.

out orders, a desultory fire issued from my line. It so happened that at this moment a sudden and, to me then, unaccountable cessation of firing took place on both sides. In this momentary silent interval a distressing cry came from the dark line before us, "You are firing upon friends; for God's sake stop!"

In an instant everything was still. Uncertain who was before me and not having found another line, I was just about to give the order to forward with bayonets fixed when General Leonidas Polk rode up. I don't know whence he came, but he quickly expressed his delight at seeing me in that place. I interrupted him by informing him of my men having fired by mistake into Cheatham's Division. General Polk seemed shocked at the accident and said, "What a pity, I hope not. I don't think so. Let me go and see. Open your ranks."

It was done. The brave old man spurred his horse with a jump through the opening. My suspense was but for a few seconds when he hastily returned, exclaiming, "General, every mother's son of them are Yankees. I saw the colonel commanding the brigade and looked closely at the dark clothing of the men and am sure of not being mistaken."

I waited no longer. The news was circulated loudly, "Yankees!" The trumpet sounded to "fire.' A tremendous flash of musketry for the whole extent of the line for nearly one quarter of a mile in length followed. It continued for some fifteen minutes. I discovered that the return fire had ceased and therefore directed the trumpeter to signal the cessation on our part. The smoke soon cleared up, which enabled General Polk to ride forward with me and see the result.[7]

The Federal force had disappeared everywhere. The ground before my line of battle was literally covered with the dead and dying. I returned to the line and announced the cheering fact that the field was ours. It was answered with repeated cheers and then followed loud cheering *far to our left,* which we supposed to be from Anderson's Division. But it turned out to be the enemy, who had driven in our left wing, as we had done their left.

7. Polk reported the timely arrival of Liddell and noted the high spirits of his men. ". . . It was the enemy, and in obedience to orders that veteran brigade, under its gallant commander, closed the operations of the day in that part of the field with a succession of the most deadly volleys I have witnessed. The enemy's command in their immediate front was well-nigh annihilated." *O.R.* I, 16 (1), 1111.

I now directed my battery to move forward and had the bodies removed from its path for that purpose. General Polk asked my object. I answered that I designed taking the heavy battery, which I knew to have been withdrawn from its first position and was then in the edge of the woods in advance of the skirmish line. General Polk objected, "I want no more night fighting. It will be a waste of ammunition. Await orders just as you are." I ventured to remonstrate that I knew now nothing to be before me but the panic-stricken enemy. Let me go forward and secure the fruits of our success. He was very positive in refusing and then rode off to some other part of the field.

All I could do now was to look after the wounded, removing the Federals to a hospital established by them during the day, which was close at hand on the Mackville Road. I detailed a field officer to attend to this business. As it was repulsive to him, he tried to get off. I refused to excuse him, and a few hours afterwards he thanked me for making him do a charitable act. He stated that the gratitude of the poor wounded and dying men amply repaid him for the labor and made him feel, besides, the inhumanity of ever hesitating again to attend such duty.

The ground was strewn with small arms. Since they were in our way, I ordered details to stack them in large piles. We got tired doing this after two hours work and scarcely seemed to diminish the number. I suppose that there could hardly have been less than 4,000 stand lying around.

The baggage ambulance of General McCook was captured and sent at once to General Bragg. Another one was taken with it.[8] Generals McCook and Rousseau were reported by the prisoners to have made their escape but a few moments before the last firing. An officer brought me a canteen of whiskey from General McCook's ambulance. Its wretched, sickening taste led me to doubt that the property was his, but someone present who knew him well said, "He drinks no other kind." The man was right, for Bragg got all his letters, papers, and clothing.

Prisoners were brought in from all sides by the skirmishers. A colonel commanding a brigade was brought to me on his horse and whilst talking with me was suddenly attacked by a furious officer who had ridden up unperceived on my left and was determined to cut him down. I seized his sword arm, expressed

8. In his report, Liddell thought the second ambulance was that of Rosecrans.

my astonishment at his conduct, and angrily ordered him back to his regiment. The Yankee Colonel was conducted to the rear. I never saw him again, although he published an account of this transaction just before the Battle of Chickamauga. He mixed up my acts with those of General Polk, and said that he now sought satisfaction of the officer who attempted to cut him down. He called him "a fiend in human shape."

It was probably this man in the Yankee line whom General Polk accosted with the sudden exclamation, "What are you firing on friends for? Who are you?" The officer, thrown off guard by the sudden imperative question and the confusion around him, stammered some excuses. Before he could recover his senses, General Polk had discovered the state of affairs and hastily galloped back to my line.

I gave the paper containing the statement to the offending Confederate officer, who told me that he had failed to obey the signal to fire in consequence of the deception practiced on him by this very colonel. This Yankee colonel called out *in his front* not to fire on friends, which assured him that we were killing our own men. When he discovered the facts from the lips of the colonel himself in the conversation with me, just at the close of the battle, he felt disposed to kill the man who had deceived him. I told the officer that it was a common maxim of war to lie to your enemies, but be truthful to your own side. He, therefore, could not blame the colonel for looking to his own safety and success. He said that he was now sorry for it but was ready in case of opportunity to give the colonel all the satisfaction he was seeking. Here the matter ended, and I don't think that they ever met in any of the numerous subsequent engagements.[9]

Among the officers of my brigade who parleyed with the Yankee officers on this occasion was Colonel J. H. Kelly,[10] 8th

9. Probably the Union officer referred to was Col. Michael Gooding, 22nd Indiana. Liddell stated that Gooding's regiment "was said to have caused great havoc in Arkansas, and it seems as if retributive justice had at last been meted out to it by the very men most injured by it." *O.R.* I, 16 (1), 1160.

10. One of Hardee's young West Pointers from Alabama, Kelly was given his start by his former teacher who put him on his staff with rank of captain. By Shiloh he commanded the 9th Arkansas Battalion. During the reorganization of the Army of Tennessee in the summer of 1862 he became Colonel of the 8th Arkansas. He was in all the hard fighting that followed and got a brigade of infantry in late 1863. By 1864 this 24 year old led a division of cavalry competently. His shooting star fell on September 2, 1864, at Franklin, Tennessee. Cleburne said, "I know no better officer of his grade in the service."

Arkansas, who, calling out to know the regiment before him, was answered, "Indiana." Thinking it might be Louisiana, called again and was answered "Indiana." "Do you want us down there." "No," said Kelly, stay where you are," and immediately began the attack. These parleyings happened almost simultaneously along the whole line of both sides. Colonel Kelly captured the Yankee colonel alluded to.

When I sent General McCook's ambulances to Bragg, they were loaded with arms. I requested that both of them be returned to me for my wounded and sick, as I was destitute of such conveniences. This was not done until long afterwards, when not so much needed. It gave rise to a misunderstanding between Bragg and myself, unsettled until the Battle of Murfreesboro. I understood from Hardee that McCook wrote to him to have his baggage restored to him.[11] McCook laughed that his clothing must be too large for any Confederate General except Humphrey Marshall.[12] But Bragg had disposed of the effects, probably to destitute soldiers. I cannot help thinking that courtesy required their restoration.

About 11 p.m. General Buckner sent for me to meet him at the "Burnt Barn." He expressed himself highly pleased with the movements and conduct of my brigade. He was dissatisfied, however, that I was ordered away by Hardee from the position he had placed me in reserve without *advising* him. In consequence, he had lost sight of part of his own command until accidentally discovered after the battle, through the instrumentality of one of his staff. He then intimated to me the intention of Bragg to withdraw. He gave me instructions to be ready to move after midnight or as soon as it was made known to me that all other commands had preceded mine, being then the most advanced. He told me that General Cleburne was wounded at the "Burnt Barn," as was also his next ranking officer, Colonel Polk.[13]

About ten days after this, I saw Cleburne, who was fast recovering. He told me that at the time my command attacked from

11. McCook served as an instructor under Commandant Hardee at West Point. They were warm friends.
12. Marshall was the undisputed heavyweight among the Confederate general officers.
13. Lucius Eugene Polk (1833-1892). Where Cleburne went Polk went. This nephew of Bishop Polk developed into one of the finest combat officers in the Army of Tennessee. Wounded at Shiloh, Richmond, Perryville, and Kennesaw Mountain, Polk returned on crutches to his home in Maury County, Tennessee, in 1864.

the slopes of the ridge, the enemy was closing his lines around him. He and his brigade would certainly have been captured but for the fortunate movement made by me on the enemy's left. My attack disconcerted the enemy's designs and caused a sudden withdrawal from Cleburne's front and flanks. Cleburne, being wounded, would have been unable to escape.

At the proper time, I quietly moved, as ordered, to the Harrodsburg Road east of Perryville. My men seemed deeply concerned and shed tears at leaving the field. They generally believed that Bragg surely would not lose the chance of pushing the advantage gained and bring up all his force. I saw Bragg the next morning. As he rode by me, he said, "Be ready, General, to fight at any moment." Great anxiety seemed to be depicted on his face. His look was so unusual that I feared some unforeseen calamity. I did not ask him, as I thought that I would hear the trouble soon enough. I was often astonished at the readiness with which soldiers acquire indifference to consequences.

We passed through Harrodsburg late in the evening. Then we continued leisurely across the Dick's River to Camp Robinson, where we remained several days in the quiet enjoyment of abundant supplies.

In all this time, I never heard a word of the locality of General Kirby Smith's command. What the matter was I could not discover from anyone.

I think it was 12th October that Buckner sent for his brigade commanders to make preparations to withdraw from Kentucky through Cumberland Gap.

Alas! All our cherished hopes were lost. We had gained two fights, Richmond and Perryville. Why not now concentrate all our strength and contest for the possession of Kentucky? This would give us Tennessee. What was the object now of this expedition? Where the strategy? What do we gain by this absurd retreat in the face of success? The initiative and the prestige of success were with us. To unite *all* for the grand trial of strength was all that was wanted. Elation was with us. We would have won, I verily believe.

Dissatisfied with Bragg for this step, I spoke outright. He never forgave me. The arbitrary detention of my captured ambulances added to my dissatisfaction.

Bragg was an able officer and considered by Mr. Davis as the best of his generals. He had been unfortunate. He had the great fault of being easily led astray or turned aside by petty side issues. Not foreseen in his original program, they completely upset him in trying moments and ruined *all* his well laid plans. In a word, he was no tactician to execute his own strategic combinations.

I well recollect on the retreat to Cumberland Gap, in the presence of Hardee, censuring Bragg severely for throwing away his chances. Hardee said, "You speak very plainly. I am half inclined to arrest you."

I answered, "Very well. Do so. I speak the truth at all events." Hardee was jesting, but at the moment I was nettled and did not perceive his humor. Hardee remarked further that when all the facts were known, General Polk would be credited for saving Bragg's Army in causing its timely retreat from Kentucky.

This remark proved to me what I suspected. Bragg was not well supported by his generals, on whom he had every reason to rely. I afterwards heard that he wished to concentrate his wings to give general battle. Unfortunately, Bragg gave way to the pressure of his council officers. With his own apprehensions, this quickly turned the balance. As commander of the forces, however, he had to bear the blame. Therefore he should have held on to his own original purposes—bearing blame only for his own acts, not for those of others who diverted him from his objects.

Bragg should have fought in Kentucky *for Tennessee*. Instead of fighting at Murfreesboro, Tennessee, subsequently, he could have pushed Buell with far better chances for success in Kentucky. By one victory he could have gained both states. These successes would have forced the withdrawal of Grant from Mississippi to defend the line of the Ohio River. Our chances were better in Kentucky than elsewhere—but alas! Bragg's failure here now deferred the whole thing. This was the last, aye, the *very last* chance to accomplish anything by *strategy*. The plainest man could see the fates were against us. All chances were destined to be recklessly thrown away. Literally, wantonly thrown away.

I firmly believe that many gave up the struggle in utter despair. They withdrew from the contest to save something to themselves from the impending wreck of the South. To them, success in Kentucky and Tennessee would have revived hope and brought *all* back to the Confederate standards. Truly—yes, truly—it was worth a struggle, aye, a death struggle.

If we failed, we could make the best terms we could, for the tenure of Virginia depended upon keeping back the hardy men of the populous Western States. General Lee could not in such case hold his own. The West had been overlooked. No adequate resources of men and means had been sent to Bragg's support. Everything was called for and given to Virginia, overlooking altogether the back door to the capital of the South.

Who is to blame? The Southern people had *voluntarily* placed Mr. Davis in the Presidential Chair to gain their independence if he could—to compromise if he *must*. But Mr. Davis, in the very confidence of foregone success, had made up his mind in the beginning to compromise in no sense whatever short of Southern independence. Ruin *must* come before he would yield. He adhered to his determination at home, abroad, with friends and with foes, and was persistent in his course.

Everything in the Confederacy reached the point of military authority and rule. No one set himself against the government or expressed an opposed opinion. There was danger of arrest by the military; but from Mr. Davis personally, no one had anything to fear. Kindhearted and generous, he would, could, and did constantly forgive the bitterest of his enemies and at the same time, alas!, the enemies of the South. He seemed to think that everyone inimical to the South was *his personal* enemy, but that his official position justified him in overlooking the injury. There was no discrimination, and no good results from misplaced, ill-timed leniency. Nevertheless, let justice be shown Mr. Davis. A good man at heart, he was not the man for the occasion. The South was awfully mistaken in him.

# CHAPTER IX

# BACK TO TENNESSEE

We took up our line of march for Cumberland Gap, passing through Crab Orchard, London, and Barbourville on the route. I saluted General Polk, who was passing my column, and he called me to come and ride with him. We conversed familiarly for some time upon the course pursued by General Bragg and of the mistakes of the campaign. When I thought the subject exhausted, I prepared to return to my command.

General Polk said, "No. Come with me. I command the Army now. General Bragg has gone to Virginia. Besides, I have a point of difficulty between us to settle."

At this I was quite surprised and said, "Well, General, inform me, for I am unaware of any cause of trouble."

He then said, "You reported me on returning to your line at Perryville to have said, 'Give them H—l, General'—emphasizing the expression in the manner usual to those habituated to such expletions."

I was amused at the absurdity of the thing, as well as the good General's theatrical manner. I said, "If you had used the language, General, it would have given me excuse to do the same. Those very words were on the point of my tongue, but my respect for your profession restrained me."

With this answer, which was the precise truth, the old General seemed relieved as well as gratified. He quickly remarked that my "statement of facts was fully satisfactory," and he would be "indifferent to all further talk on the subject." I assured him that I knew no proper foundation for the report, and we afterwards remained the best of friends.

He was truly a good man, lofty in sentiment, gallant and enthusiastic in the cause. He possessed all the requisites of a great soldier, except strategy and tactical combination. His name alone carried great weight in the army, and his lamentable death in the field was felt from one end of the Confederacy to the other. The South had lost one of her bravest and most unyielding paladins.

Somewhere about the last of October, 1862, we passed Cumberland Gap, an impregnable position for a determined garrison. Starvation only could reduce it. The view from both sides of this lofty ridge of the Cumberland Mountains was truly magnificent.

The army, after reaching Knoxville where it remained a short time, was transported by railroad back to Chattanooga, thence to Murfreesboro.[1] Most of the troops had already preceded Buckner's Division. When we reached Estill Springs, we were disembarked from the trains and ordered to Shelbyville on Duck River. Here we stopped for a while to await further developments.[2]

At Shelbyville I visited a friend's house one evening. Meeting with several ladies, the subject of conversation turned upon Hardee's gallantry to the ladies, which I confirmed and, upon the promise of secrecy as to the author, related the General's dispute with the old lady at Perryville. Two days afterwards, I met Hardee at a review of the troops near Shelbyville. He asked me very abruptly why I had told that story on him to the ladies at Mrs. Matthews. I realized that the promise of secrecy had been broken, but pretended not to understand him and avoided any acknowledgment until I could know how the matter got out.

The ladies told me afterwards that the General was very much perplexed at the story having reached their ears before his arrival. He wanted to know the author, of course. This was evaded, notwithstanding all his suggestive questions, until, just as he was leaving, one of them happened to mention that I had been there

1. At Knoxville Liddell and his staff had their photographs taken. George A. Williams, Liddell's adjutant, lost his and secured a copy after the war from Liddell. The editor, however, does not know of a copy that still exists.
2. George A. Williams remembered Liddell, ". . . of striking appearance, dignified; of soft speech, gentle, winning manner, graceful in gesture; he was the type of the cultivated gentleman of his time and kind. He endeared himself to his staff by his considerate treatment; to his soldiers by his careful attention to their wants and comfort in camp, as well as by his gallant bearing in action, where he shone like Rupert in the charge. . . . His patriotism was pure; his motives disinterested; his service distinguished. He was a Louisianian who commanded troops from another State; for this reason he has never received, at the hands of Louisiana, recognition for the honor he reflected upon them." G. A. Williams Speech at presentation of Liddell's portrait, Howards Memorial Hall, New Orleans, Louisiana, 1902.

the evening previous. He quickly exclaimed, "Liddell is the author; denial is useless." I gained my point in fixing the story on him, but I saw clearly that ladies were not to be trusted with secrets.

Mr. Davis visited Murfreesboro early in December. He withdrew from Bragg 12,000 men. He sent them to Mississippi to confront Grant's army, moving down on the New Orleans and Ohio Railroad.

I lost for *my share* all that part of the 12th Arkansas Regiment that had been incorporated in my brigade, in all about 270 effectives. They were destined for the defense of Port Hudson in Louisiana. I parted from them with regret. They took with them the best wishes of their comrades, to whom previous service had endeared them. When the hour of parting came, the line under arms saluted them. It was greatly to be deplored that Mr. Davis did not permit all this force to remain until after the Battle of Murfreesboro.

I for one never could understand why Bragg, a man extremely pertinacious of his rights in all other respects, should have consented to this fatal depletion of his strength in the very face of an impending battle. He knew that this battle must involve the absolute existence of the Confederacy, and that the enemy was *divided,* part in Mississippi, part in Tennessee. Concentration upon *one part* was a matter beyond question. Bragg should have tendered his resignation rather than give away his troops at this critical time. This *great* opportunity was lost to us forever by the wretched blunders of Mr. Davis. It is of no use to cry about it now.

Hardee and I were riding along the principal street of Shelbyville one morning when a field officer of cavalry rode rudely and brusquely between us and saluted Hardee, who seemed to know him. Something in conversation between them caused my name to be used by the General. The officer quietly turned to me and asked if I was any relation of Lieutenant Willie Liddell? Thinking perhaps some trouble was on hand, I answered deliberately, "Yes, he is my son."

"Well, General, I only know you from character, but I do know that boy personally. He is as brave and gallant a soldier as belongs to the Army of Tennessee. By G-d, sir, I have seen him in close places. I know he will go eye to eye with the bravest."

Then abruptly bidding us good morning, he struck spurs to his horse and was soon beyond sight.

I was so much astonished at the abruptness of the man, his singular speech, and the subject, my son, that I rode thoughtfully and silently along without it ever once occurring to ask his name of Hardee. To this day, I don't know who he was. No comment or remark was made by either of us upon the strange incident. Whenever we afterwards met, other subjects occupied my mind to the exclusion of one. Now that all is over I would like so much to know this strange friend of my lamented boy.

From Shelbyville we moved to College Grove, which was the extreme left of our line.[3] Whilst Mr. Davis was at Murfreesboro, a competent officer was desired by him to be placed in command of Mobile and its defenses. General Buckner was selected on Hardee's recommendation. General Cleburne was promoted over his seniors, S. A. M. Wood[4] and B. R. Johnson, to the command now vacant by Buckner's transfer to Mobile. This promotion was effected through Hardee, who was very partial to Cleburne.

I heard him relate with considerable glee a little story told by Mr. Davis on application being made to him for Cleburne's promotion. There seems to have been some hesitation about the matter. Mr. Davis yielded finally to Hardee's wishes and said that when he was a cadet at West Point, there was a famous bugler leading the band named Willis. Willis in time had a pupil (Barnes or some such name) *nearly equal to himself.* Mr. Davis, perceiving it, sought to compliment Willis upon the skill of his pupil. "Yes," said Willis deliberately, "Yes, *Barnes* is a good bugler; Barnes can't be beat; Barnes is the *best* bugler in the U. S. *I* made Barnes." The application was apparent and subject of amusement. Mr. Davis desired to compliment Hardee with making Cleburne. When Hardee told the story to me, he said with a laugh, "Yes, *I* made Cleburne."

3. George A. Williams, Liddell's Adjutant General, remembered this Christmas of 1862. "Christmas day found Buckner's Division at College Grove, west of Murfreesboro. It was here that Liddell, out of his own purse, provided a Christmas dinner for his entire command. He had his commissary scour the surrounding country for sheep, pigs, poultry, and vegetables, and furnished a feast for his men that was unique as far as known."
4. Sterling Alexander Martin Wood (1823-1891). This young Alabama lawyer and editor won a popular election as Colonel of the 7th Alabama in May, 1861. Unlike many political officers, he excelled and saw hard fighting at Shiloh, Perryville, Murfreesboro, and Chickamauga as a brigade commander. Mysteriously, he resigned following Chickamauga and returned home to his law practice.

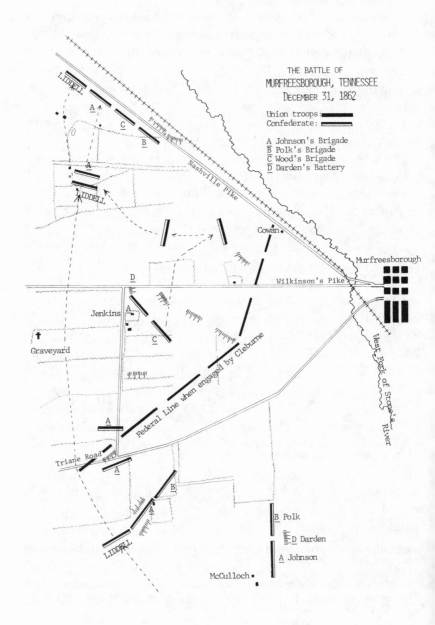

THE BATTLE OF
MURFREESBOROUGH, TENNESSEE
DECEMBER 31, 1862

Union troops:
Confederate:

A Johnson's Brigade
B Polk's Brigade
C Wood's Brigade
D Darden's Battery

LIDDELL

Nashville Pike

Cowan

Murfreesborough

Wilkinson's Pike

Jenkins

Graveyard

Federal Line when engaged by Cleburne

West Fork of Stone's River

Triane Road

LIDDELL

B Polk
D Darden
A Johnson

McCulloch

# CHAPTER X

# THE BATTLE OF MURFREESBORO

On the 26th December, 1862, Cleburne's Division was ordered to Murfreesboro to meet Rosecrans. Rosecrans had replaced Buell and was advancing in force from Nashville upon Bragg's position at Murfreesboro. When we reached this place (north of town and east of Stone's River), my brigade was posted in the second line in rear directly of Brigadier General Hanson's Kentucky brigade, in the first line front on Stone's River and near the Murphy house.[1]

Hanson was a large fat man. But as all (even the blind) could see, he possessed the soul of a hero, true as steel to his purposes, sincere and unsophisticated as a child, the very man whom all honest and good people would flock to for advice, friendship, and protection. This man drew me to him by his *natural* nobility of nature. I helped him like a brother to establish his lines and prepare himself for the conflict, before it might be required of me to come to his relief. Poor *man*, how much I do regret his death. God takes away the *best*—leaving the unworthy behind to weather the storm.

On the evening of the 30th of December, the enemy's skirmish line was in sight from the Stone's River railroad bridge. Polk's Corps was posted in two lines on the left bank or west side of the

1. Roger Weightman Hanson (1827-1863). This popular Kentucky political figure made a reputation as a staunch Unionist and as a violent man. Events carried him along, however, into the Confederate army where "Old Flintlock" became the beloved commander of the Orphan brigade. On January 2, 1863, he became furious at Bragg's plan for a frontal assault on the Union left. Hanson had to be restrained from going to ". . . headquarters and kill Bragg." He knew it would be ". . . simply murder to carry out the order." Nevertheless, under the tormented eyes of division commander Breckinridge, Hanson and the Orphans were cut to pieces doing their duty.

river across an open field, directly in front of Rosecran's advance. Watching the movements, I happened near the bridge with my Adjutant General George Williams, when General Bragg with numerous staff approached. Not desiring to have an interview after all that had passed, I turned to go back to my command when one of his staff, Colonel David Urquhart, rode up hastily to me saying, "The General wishes to see you."

I rode back to the General, expecting an unpleasant meeting. After mutual salutation, he said, "General, I have to regret the .detention of your ambulances. I thought Polk had captured them. I knew nothing of the facts, and some of my staff, without my knowledge, had taken the responsibility of keeping them. I must say that some members of my staff have too often done things in opposition to my wishes. General, you shall not only have your ambulances, but as many more as you need for your command."

I was surprised. My indignation was gone. I had done Bragg an injustice. Unworthy men had used *his* name for authority to do improper things. I now so much regretted my hasty language. No man needed friends more than Bragg. I had misunderstood him. Henceforth, I would do all I could to help him. I felt we were friends again. We had been classmates, and it was right that I should uphold him in every good motive, at least until it was seen beyond peradventure that he was not patriotic, which never could be said of him. Bragg said to me feelingly, "General, I have no children. Hence, I look upon the soldiers of my army as my own—as *my* children."

Thinking the remark only an exhibition of feeling on the eve of a great sanguinary struggle, I turned to leave with a bow of assent and wish to retire, when he called me back. He repeated the assertion and added, "General, I wish you to tell this to your men. I am in earnest." I bowed assent and withdrew to my command. Upon reaching my men, I wrote out as precisely as I could remember the words of the General and ordered their circulation among the regiments of my brigade.

My adjutant sent the circular around immediately. There was some maneuvering in answer to this paternal speech. Men were heard to say, "He has a very large family and sometimes causes his boys to be shot."

About 4:00 p.m., December 30, the enemy opened upon Polk's lines from across Stone's River with numerous heavy batteries of artillery. Polk's guns replied with equal spirit if not strength.

106

Great volumes of smoke rolled over the plain, and soon the incessant rattling of musketry added to the din. The sound seemed to me like the roar of a Southern tornado. There were but few of the bravest men who listened with any assurance that they would escape harm in the coming conflict. Before sunset tomorrow they knew that thousands would fall, but the excitement of troops moving in all directions preparatory to action obliterated all impulses of feeling save that of the fiendish nature of man. I was forcibly reminded of the expression, "war is the natural state of man." So it will ever be to the end, notwithstanding the generous efforts of philanthropists to secure to humanity the blessings of eternal peace and goodwill.

Before dark, I received orders to move at once. Following my guide, I found myself and brigade after midnight across Stone's River (above Murfreesboro) in extension of the extreme left of our position and in the second line under Hardee. Polk held the first line. As soon as the men had debouched, Cleburne sent for me. I found him at a deserted house in conversation with the young General Rains[2] of Nashville, now commanding a brigade under Major General McCown.[3] I soon found Rain to be an able and prompt officer. By reference to my locality the day before, he quickly made known to me my new position which had been taken in the dark. This brave young man was killed the next day at the head of his men. His death was greatly regretted.

Bragg's designs were now apparent. He intended to throw all his available force (except Breckinridge's Division) across Stone's River in conjunction with his left wing. By a sudden, grand swing or right wheel of the whole line—the pivot flank touching Stone's River—he would overlap and turn Rosecrans' right wing. This plan of attack would give Bragg the advantage of the initiative and at the same time force Rosecrans to take the hazard of changing position in the face of vigorous attack. It was an admirable plan. If everything went well, it would be only necessary to persist in this design and bring up reserve to ensure complete success—neglecting his right wing, which was protected by the precipitous bank of the river.

2. James Edwards Rains (1833-1862). Not yet thirty, Rains had made his mark politically in Middle Tennessee. As a lawyer turned soldier, he proved to be a leader and promised to become an effective general.
3. John Porter McCown (1815-1879). A Mexican War hero, this Tennessee major general's rapidly rising star dimmed after Murfreesboro. He never again held an important command.

Unluckily for us, Bragg halted his lines in the midst of success to look after his right under Breckinridge. He then precipitated his right into a useless fight, where the enemy was well prepared to receive attack. If, on the other hand, Bragg had *kept to his original purposes,* if he had re-formed his right and pressed forward his left wing, if he had sent all reserves, including Breckinridge, to the extreme left and secured a foothold in rear of the enemy, Rosecrans would have been completely cut off from all resources and supplies. He would have been hemmed in between the railroad and Stone's River and compelled to suffer inevitable disaster.

In this event, the whole face of affairs in the West would have been changed. Vicksburg and the opening of the Mississippi River would have been relieved from Grant, who would have been compelled to return to Kentucky to oppose Bragg. Both armies, strengthened by all reserves called in, would again try the issue in Kentucky—but with far better chances for the South.

At daylight cn December 31, I was moving with the division, General John A. Wharton's Cavalry on my left.[4] About sunrise, we came up in rear of General McCown's line, which had just engaged and repulsed the enemy. I halted my men and rode forward to see General McCown, who told me that his men were considerably cut up and he wished me to take the advance. I replied that my orders were to support him, but we could compromise by letting me come up on his line. The arrangement was agreed to, and I moved up on his right.[5] I then told my men in few words that we were about "to go in," and that I did not wish them to stop to take charge of prisoners, which would weaken our strength by escorting them to the rear, but that every man must stand to the front, for we needed all. The prisoners would be provided for by cavalry detailed for such purposes. Then without waiting on General McCown's movements, I gave the orders to advance to the attack.

---

4. Liddell's Brigade at Murfreesboro consisted of most of the Arkansas troops in the Army of Tennessee. He commanded the 2nd, 5th, 6th, 7th, and 8th Arkansas Infantry Regiments.

   Liddell's Brigade, plus those of Lucius E. Polk (Cleburne's old brigade), Bushrod Johnson, and S. A. M. Wood made up Cleburne's Division. This division, J. P. McCown's division, and the brigades of Wharton and J. K. Jackson, constituted Hardee's Corps. Breckinridge's Division, nominally under Hardee, was held back by Bragg as Army reserve.

5. In an unusual tribute, McCown devoted a paragraph in his report to the prompt and effective assistance rendered by Liddell.

A fence on the edge of woodlands and partly hid by under-growth was about 150 yards before us. When we got within 75 yards of it, the enemy's line was developed in ambush behind this screen. The fire from it was very trying. My men, seeing the great advantage to the enemy and the certain destruction await-ing them, dropped down, almost as if by common consent, on their faces, and commenced firing with great accuracy and pre-cision through the interval between the rails and brush. I tried to move them forward and ordered the charge sounded repeat-edly—all to no purpose. They had deliberately set themselves to work to kill all they could. I had nothing to do but await the denouement, which I knew could not be long deferred under the heavy fire then going on. I and my aide dismounted. Men were killed and wounded on every side of me, but there was no sign whatever of giving way. A second line of the enemy fired over their first line at us, but we were too close to the first to notice them. This deadly contest continued for nearly an hour.

When the enemy began to waver, I seized the favorable mo-ment to sound the charge. At last it was answered with loud cheers and a rush. My horse bravely carried me forward with excitement in the interval between two Yankee regiments. My death or capture was avoided because of the rapid advance and wild hurrahs of my men.

The enemy's front line now gave way in great confusion. The panic carried to the second line, which also quickly yielded to the pressure. It fell back rapidly to the third that was posted about one-fourth of a mile still in its rear and was covering a large hospital near the Wilkinson Turnpike.

We continued to press on cheerfully and resolutely. Then the third enemy line, under Major General Joshua K. Sill, engaged us at the hospital. Firing from the window caused Colonel Govan to direct his men to fire on all men mounted near the hospital enclosure. The enemy's line of battle at this hospital, stretching far to the left, sustained our attack only a short while before giv-ing way. My artillery fired at the retreating masses just as they crossed the Wilkinson Turnpike. Here, the ammunition being exhausted, I ordered a halt to fill up cartridge boxes.

Someone now told me that my son Willie was killed. I felt deeply distressed. I knew that it was a fact of war, consoling myself with the reflection that he could not have fallen on a more honorable occasion. Just then my Aide-de-Camp Bostick came up (I had lost sight of him for sometime past) and told me that my son Willie had been badly wounded in the first engagement.

Willie had fallen from his horse, and Lieutenant H. Shannon of my battery[6] called Bostick's attention to the fact that Willie was in the way of his battery. He should be moved at once or he would be under the flame of Shannon's guns. Bostick rode to Willie immediately, dismounted, examined his wound, and, with the aid of some Yankee prisoners, placed him on his horse. But the horse's head was cut off at that moment by a cannon ball. Bostick picked him up and removed him slowly to an ambulance that happened to be at hand. When Willie was in good hands, Bostick mounted the first horse at hand and pushed forward to join me.

Generous, whole-souled J. L. Bostick! How much I owe you for this favor. My son and you are both numbered with the dead in this deplorable war, and the only satisfaction I have is that your fate never could have been better. My bugler John Shlosser was shot near me and carried off the field. I escaped so easily that I could not understand why my men were shot, nor did *they* understand why I was not hurt! Poor fellows! They sometimes got around me for safety. But the charm to me did not extend to them and death fell in their midst without respect to persons.

The Federal General Sill was killed near the Wilkinson Turnpike by one of my men, who took his gloves with his name on them. Many prisoners were brought to me. I sent them to the rear and their captors back to the front line. The prisoners seemed troubled and asked what they should do. I told them that no one would molest unarmed men. In marching to the rear they would find the officer in charge of this business. But if they wished to escape and thought the thing practicable, I had no objection, provided they promised never to fight us again. This pleased them. One man seized my hand, saying, "We agree, you are the man for me." The hospital yard was full of them, whither they had gone to escape the fire of the line. Wharton's Cavalry and other commands took them all in charge.

General McCown by this time came up and directed his brigades to oblique to the right to make connection with the line we had severed in these engagements. This change again threw me on the extreme left. McCown's command passed on whilst

6. Shannon commanded the Warren Light Artillery.

my men were renewing their supply of ammunition. We were far in advance of the balance of the line, and the enemy had not yet recovered from the effect of our attacks. We had passed through fields and woodlands and over hills, which intercepted our view of the action to the right of us towards Stone's River.

Soon after McCown's Division left me going towards the right, my men were ready. We moved forward again through the woods in pursuit of the enemy. Colonel John H. Kelly of the left wing sent word to me that cavalry were threatening his flank. I sent orders to him not to delay his forward movement because of threats only. Luckily, they turned out to be our own cavalry, some of the men being dressed in Federal overcoats and pantaloons.

The morning was cold and frosty, but excitement kept us warm. We soon approached an open field with a Federal line of skirmishers in view. When my skirmishers advanced, they retired below the brow of a ridge. When we reached it, we saw the enemy's lines scattered over the valley of Overall Creek and beyond. We saw large trains with bodies of men marching in confused masses on the turnpike in direction of Nashville. As they were beyond the range of musketry, I ordered the battery to shell them. The Texas Cavalry now made its appearance in the valley not far from Overall's Church and charged upon those trains. I aided this operation by sending shells among the masses until they had disappeared entirely from view.[7]

Evidently we were now in rear of the enemy and close enough to be in command of the Nashville pike and railroad. Now was the time to press forward and cut off Rosecran's communications, but I had no more than 1,000 men left and as a subordinate could take no steps to bring forward troops.

Discovering that I had diverged too far to the left and was without support, I moved, following along the turnpike, through the woods towards Murfreesboro. We had passed over half a mile or more when we met men flying towards us and heard heavy firing following them. The fugitives made known to me that Generals Rains' and Ector's brigades had met with some repulse in the cedar thickets and the enemy were now in hot pursuit.

---

7. Hardee made heavy mention of Wharton's Texans in his report. In a "day of brilliant achievement" Wharton swept the Union cavalry aside. "The field was favorable, the charge irresistible, the conflict short." Several hundred wagons, over 1500 prisoners, and several pieces of artillery were captured.

I immediately moved forward to interpose and save our men from capture. Just as we reached the edge of a small field, we confronted a brigade of Federal regulars. The conflict immediately began. For a half hour or longer at the distance of sixty-five or seventy yards, these men fired with the most determined obstinacy into each others bosoms. In the very midst of it, a regimental surgeon, Dr. W. R. Kibler rode alongside of me and saluting me with a smile, said, "General, I am ordered to come and look after you or your staff should any be shot."

I answered, "You are too close up for a surgeon. I fear you will be shot."

"No, I think not—I am not afraid."

Just at the moment, casting my eyes to the enemy's regiment on my right, I saw it waver and begin to double up in confusion. The moment was critical. I spurred my horse forward with a cheer through the interval between two of my regiments and waved my cap to my men to advance with me. Impatient at the tardy movement and nearly halfway between the lines, I drew my revolver and fired repeatedly into the enemy's ranks. At the fourth shot, Dr. Kibler, who had ridden forward, carried away with the excitement of the moment and was cheering lustily by my side, exclaimed, "My God, I am shot."

"Where, Doctor?"

"In the side."

I put up my revolver to help him, but he fell from the horse before I could catch him. Thinking I could do nothing for him now, as the shot must be fatal, I rode away to attend to the attack on my left. The infirmary corps soon came up and took off the doctor. What a quick change! He had come to relieve me but a moment before and now was carried off the field, a victim to his own temerity. The line soon came up, and the enemy fled, leaving a long line of dead and wounded on the ground.

At this place, General B. R. Johnson's brigade joined me again, having been separated since sunrise. We moved forward together towards the cedars on the turnpike and railroad with the enemy in full retreat before us. The general and I congratulated each other upon our success up to this time. I started for the left flank of my brigade to find some commanding position for my battery to enfilade the enemy's position that we were now approaching in the cedar thickets. On passing a second hospital full of Federals, I halted for a moment and was asked protection from apprehended molestation by my troops. I told the chief surgeon to chalk my name on the walls and claim it for me.

These things seemed to take up but a moment of time, but casting my eye towards the line I had just left moving forward, I saw, with distress, the troops hastily falling back. I was astounded and flew to head them off. They were Johnson's men, and I soon met the General, in like haste looking for them.[8] He told me that my brigade had also fallen back. I found them a short distance from us on the edge of the woods where the last fight had occurred. The men did not know why they were there.

It seems men were falling back to the rear from the right towards the left from no perceptible cause, and my senior colonel, Govan, thought it was a general understanding to do so. No enemy was in sight, and none had pursued. Directions were now sent us by Cleburne and Hardee to halt and await further orders.

In the evening Hardee came along. I took the opportunity to call his attention to the fact that we were in command of the railroad and the Nashville Turnpike. By bringing up all reserves and driving Rosecrans towards Murfreesboro, and by attacking him in rear, I had no doubt that success would be with us. From some cause, Hardee would not listen to me, saying that "he was disgusted." I gave it up and visited my wounded son in Murfreesboro during the night.[9]

I have ever afterwards blamed myself for not going to see Bragg in person and persuading him to come and look for himself. It would have resulted in my failure, though, with no thanks for the obtrusive opinion. The truth is, I *ought* to have gone, since no one else would do it, even if I had been arrested for it. If I lost my place, honor was safe, which was far the most valuable to me. Perhaps this little circumstance might have been the means of changing the future of the Confederacy. Such chances once lost are seldom offered again. Truly, truly I ought to have risked *all* for my judgment, but we are all failures at last. It struck me that Bragg did not know whom to trust. He

8. This precipitate, disorderly retreat by Bushrod Johnson's brigade ruined the success of the Confederate attack. To the astonishment and dismay of Johnson and Liddell, the brigade fled at the moment "our men were in sight of the Nashville pike; some have said they were on it. The enemy's right was doubled back upon their centre. Had we held this position the line of communications of the enemy would have been cut." *O.R.*, I, 20 (1), 879-880.
9. Liddell lost more men killed and wounded than any brigade in Hardee's Corps (86 killed, 503 wounded).

113

was not popular with his generals; hence, I feared that zealous cooperation on their part was wanting. If he had caused one or two of us to be shot, I firmly believe the balance would have done better.[10]

On Friday evening, January 2, 1863, Hardee came back to where I was posted on the extreme left and reconnoitered the position. He discovered the advantages presented for attacking the enemy, which I told him I had endeavored to draw his attention to two days before.

While conversing with him on this subject, we heard the firing from Breckinridge's attack. It was far to our right, at least three miles from us. We listened attentively and finally heard the shouting of the Federals at the successful repulse. My hopes, I freely confess, sunk within me. What folly could have caused this miserable disaster, when all was successful hitherto. But, as it could only be a severe repulse, it was not too late for all reserves and reinforcements to come to us and press the enemy from a point least looked for by him.

That night, Cleburne's Division was ordered to withdraw from the left to the right across Stone's River in support of Breckinridge. It commenced to rain very hard when I moved that night. I found myself occupying my original place in rear of the lamented General Hanson's Brigade. I sought shelter from the cold rain in the Murphy house and to my surprise, found Bragg and staff in possession.

I did not hesitate to enter and see the General. I inquired out his instructions and our hopes. His manner, it seemed to me was thoughtful and hesitating. He finally gave me to understand that the troops were exhausted with such continued fighting and that to withdraw from the contest was necessary for their repose. I replied that my men had been doing some of the hardest work and I felt assured that they would carry the thing through with the rest of the army, at all hazards. He then told me that the

10. William Howard Russell saw Bragg as "spare and powerful frame." ". . . face is dark, and marked with deep lines, his mouth large, and squarely set in determined jaws, and his eyes, sagacious, penetrating, and not by any means unkindly, look at you from bettle brows which run straight across and spring into a thick tuft of black hair, which is thickest over the nose. . . ." ". . . He wears such regulation whiskers as were the delight of our generals a few years back. His manner is quick and frank, and his smile is very pleasing and agreeable." Russell, *My Diary North and South*. New York: Harper and Brothers, 1863, pp. 45-46.

enemy were receiving large reinforcements. Surprised, I asked him his authority. He answered, "Wheeler!"

I said, "It can't be so, for I have just come from the extreme left. I could have clearly seen the reinforcements approach, and I have seen none. Where is Rosecrans to get them from?"

Bragg said, "It must be so. Wheeler seems assured of the fact."

I then said, "General, don't regard his reinforcements. Even could I believe such to be the case, everything depends upon your success here. If you will throw your army between Rosecrans and Nashville, you will cut off all reinforcements. They will withdraw at the sight of your forces. Then I would fight Rosecrans to the last. I would rather bury my bones here than give up this field and our previous successes. Great results will follow complete victory. You have Rosecrans in a close place. You have only to push him to extremities."

To this he said, "General, I know that you will fight it out, but others will not."

I exclaimed, "Give the order, General, and every man will obey you."

After some hesitation, he said, "No, it has now become a matter of imperative necessity to withdraw. It must be done at once." I don't recollect his precise words. I give the substance with the words as well as I can recall them at this time.

I saw now clearly that Bragg had decided to retreat. A brigade commander had no weight beyond his ability to hold his ground in the field of active operations.

Even by remaining in place two days longer in threatening attitude, ready to seize upon mistakes, would have given to Bragg more than his utmost expectations. Rosecrans had nearly exhausted his ammunition and supplies. He anxiously awaited something to enable him to get out of his compressed situation between the railroad and Stone's River. We were in command of the approaches in his rear. Bragg listened too much to Wheeler's report of reinforcements. None ever came, unless they were the demoralized troops that were brought back after having been driven off the field.

I thought that this was the chief turning point in the war. If we had to fail, let it be done here where so much was to be gained by success on our part. Such great results were worth a desperate effort. When I went back to my command, some of the men familiarly called out to me, "What's up now, General?" I answered impatiently, "Ask General Bragg." They saw the hidden meaning and said, "Well, boys, retreat again. All our hard fighting thrown away, as usual." "One more struggle and the day is ours." This last being an allusion to words used in a published circular to the troops two days previous by General Bragg, assuring success to our efforts.

It rained very hard and turned very cold that night. Our march was slop, slop through sleet and water till morning. We had not retreated twenty-five miles before the facts of the enemy's situation became known from returning scouts and citizens. I saw Hardee and spoke feelingly on the subject, for I was sadly disappointed.

Hardee told me that Bragg had called a council of war before I saw him (which Bragg did not mention to me at our meeting). There all the officers agreed to retreat. Hardee, himself, had only concurred without advising. I replied that I wished to God I had been permitted to come in. I might have lifted my voice against such an unfortunate step. It now turns that Rosecrans about the same time called a council of war in which his officers also urged retreat. But he determined upon holding on a day or two longer to get off his sick and wounded. Rosecrans awaited some opening that might present itself to draw off with safety. He was rewarded for it by the unlooked for, God-sent withdrawal of Bragg.

This must have caused Rosecrans to have overweening confidence in his future judgment and good fortune. He subsequently committed mistakes too glaring to be overlooked by his Government and was eventually removed.

Had Bragg's officers generously encouraged him on this occasion with zeal and good advice, our affairs would have been different. The best-laid plans must fail for lack of faithful cooperation. We were fighting for the Independence of the South, our own cause, not for Bragg, though he was in position representing that cause.

Bragg's manner made him malignant enemies and indifferent, callous friends. Ambition made men overlook success, little thinking that a day might come when they would have cause to regret every other feeling, save active devotion to the cause in which they voluntarily embarked. Can all such men say with their hands on their hearts, that they were entirely free from personal con-

116

siderations or animosities engendered at the expense of Southern success?

Such men cannot blame Bragg now, and if the truth should ever come to the surface, they will generously confess themselves to blame in great extent for his ill success. I, for my part, honestly confess myself open to censure for not doing all my judgment told me that I might have done even at the expense of my office. But I do blame Bragg for allowing himself to be swayed from his own plans. These outsiders, who could not and did not help, seized the occasion to censure him, after his adoption of their own policy.

Napoleon selected the best men he could find for his purposes. Bragg had to take only such as were given him. If he had the authority given him to select his own officers, would he have done better?

He had such poor judgment of character that I doubt even such probability, for I have known him to overlook men whose actions and zeal entitled them to wiser consideration, and it became the general belief that not service or enterprise entitled men to credit and promotion, but favoritism only.

My losses at the battle of Murfreesboro were 607 killed and wounded, out of an effective total of 1,706, which was over one-third of the whole.[11] Bragg's total loss was over 10,000 killed and wounded. His whole force did not exceed 35,000 effective of all arms. That of Rosecrans was said to be 70,000.

---

11. Cleburne reported: "Brigadier General Liddell led his brigade with a skill, courage, and devotion which, I believe, saved my left flank from being turned by the enemy." O.R. 1, 20 (1), 850. Liddell's own report about the Battle of Murfreesboro may be found in the same volume, pp. 856-860.

# CHAPTER XI

# SPRING IN MIDDLE TENNESSEE

Soon after getting to Estill Springs, I received orders to move back on the railroad and occupy Wartrace Station about twenty-nine miles from Murfreesboro. This place was on a fork of the Duck River and derived its name from the valley being on the old war path or trace of the Creek Indians in the forays on Nashville and Kentucky previous to 1800. A branch of the railroad led to Shelbyville eight miles lower down the Duck River.[1]

The locality was beautiful, and better winter quarters could not have been assigned me. I found clever people living in the neighborhood; and the house of Colonel Andrew Erwin, a relation of Henry Clay and John Bell, was the resort of all good and intelligent people. Its society was improved by the charms and benevolence of Mrs. Erwin, who made everybody welcome.

At his summons, I went to see General Hardee one day at Tullahoma. He wished to show me a letter to General Bragg signed by Generals Withers and Cheatham, the two division commanders of Polk's Corps, written during the battle of Murfreesboro, stating in substance that Bragg's army was demoralized and not to be relied upon. General Polk endorsed that which his

---

1. In two letters to Mary in mid-January, Liddell sums up Murfreesboro this way, "We had a hard battle on the 31st Dec. and we drove him 4½ miles, but he ensconced himself behind the railroad from whence we could not drive him." Frank Richardson had given him information about Mary and the children. Willie suffered a wound in the thigh. ". . . I only had time to ask 'if mortally' and go on to the front. How hard!"

St. John ends these prayerful letters choked with emotion, "Use your own judgment, dear wife, about going to Texas. I cannot advise you." Maybe send away the Negroes for safety. If the enemy takes them, "it will only be to send them to Cuba for sale." Liddell to Mary Liddell, Jan. 12, 14, 1863, in Liddell Papers, SHC.

two division commanders had written. It stated further, in effect, that he was satisfied the army could now withdraw with credit, but that delay might be disastrous.

I give the substance, as I have not the copy with me and it doubtless will be produced by General Bragg or Hardee at some future day. General Hardee allowed me to take this paper with me to copy, and I placed the copy in my aide-de-camp's hands for preservation.

I now understand Bragg's expressions to me at our interviews in the Murphy house. I could not understand how Generals Withers and Cheatham could know so much of the demoralization of Hardee's Corps. They had nothing to do with his men, nor did I see either one of them on that part of the field where we were. Nor could I see them leaving their own so-called demoralized troops to report those of Hardee's Corps. Why not attempt to stay the demoralization amongst themselves? General Polk's endorsement I sincerely regret, for he was a good man, meant well and was a true patriot. Unfortunately, he saw this thing with other eyes.

The Rev. Dr. Quintard visited me one day at Wartrace. An allusion was made that some of our officers were too much under the influence of whiskey during the battle. I remarked that I heard that General Cheatham was on his high horse. "Yes, I am sorry to say, he was on his low horse, too."

"How so, Doctor?"

"Why, he fell, he went under," said the doctor, suiting the action to the word.

I had before this heard Hardee say that he had to report Cheatham to Bragg for being drunk on the field. I don't know how it was, but this flagrant fault in discipline was passed over by Bragg. It caused other troubles and misfortunes to the Confederate service.[2] An example of severity was needed. But when the opportunity offered in high position, Bragg failed to apply the screws. The disaffected generals of Bragg's Army had but small barriers to their expressions of dissatisfaction with him. It was to break out openly against him at a future day.[3]

2. Bishop Quintard was not the only witness. See Christopher Lossen, "Major-General Benjamin Franklin Cheatham and the Battle of Stones River," *Tennessee Historical Quarterly*, Fall, 1982, XLI, 287.

3. Bragg ". . . is very unpopular and is universally pronounced unfit to be the Commanding General. This you know has been my opinion of him before the war, and experience has established my judgment then formed." Liddell to Mary Liddell, February 18, 1862, in Liddell Papers, LSU.

I could have spent a very pleasant winter at Wartrace Station, with the many agreeable associates around me; but as I foresaw the troubles ahead in trying to keep up the cause, I became restless and discontented. I felt that remedy for our sinking condition was fast going by, and I indulged the vain hope that some able men would yet spring up to relieve us. But none came.

Cleburne visited me one day, and in our conversation on the state of affairs he said, "Would you be willing to give up slavery for the independence and recognition of the South?"

"Willingly," I said.

It seems he had been thinking on the subject for sometime and felt around for support amongst other officers. I agreed with him and believed that the South could no longer have sincere fraternal regard for the Northern people. They, by their course, had forced a war upon the South to preserve her true rights and prosperity. If in the struggle the latter should fail, the right of conquest alone would destroy the institution of slavery. The North had no further authority but conquest, since the constitution shows clearly no power whatever to touch the subject. We had better, therefore, be free from further connection to frame our laws and institute our own national policy. It is all true that the constitution and laws of the U. S. were good enough for all our purposes, but what confidence had we in their proper administration, just construction, and faithful execution by a "higher law" party assuming the reins and possessing the power. Words alone are not binding enough where the popular will can do as it pleases—make, unmake, or change constitution and laws.

Cleburne met with so much opposition by others that I subsequently heard that he had given the matter up altogether, much to my regret.[4]

Hardee came from Tullahoma to see me one day, as he wished to visit our friend, old Mrs. Erwin. We walked together on the turnpike leading to her house, passing through my encampment which was on each side. Polite men met us on this thoroughfare of the camps. They kept the General continually returning their

4. Liddell privately expected another big fight as he stated in a letter to his friend Marcellin Gillis: "We have large opposing forces and there is no telling when a collision will occur. Both sides are disciplined and organized and confident of success. The shock of arms will be terrible and I pray the *God of our fathers* to protect us and give us victory." ". . . These are Western men not Yankees opposed to us." ". . . And it is well known that Rosecrans is the best of their commanders." Liddell to Marcellin Gillis, April 19, 1863, in Gillis Papers, SHC.

salutations. He was so much surprised at the unusual courtesy that he said, "Why, these men are very polite. Who are they?"

"Do you know them? They are our old Arkansas troops."

"Yes, yes, I see now. I instructed them."

"Yes, General, you made them," I said.

There had been quite a change in the same men of whom Hardee said to me in Arkansas in the first organization, "These men have no manners, and I am afraid we can't make much out of them." My experience with them was the reverse. They had uniformly behaved well, had obeyed orders implicitly and faithfully. In the whole course of my service with them, I never had occasion to prefer charges against a single individual for improper conduct. I always accomplished my purpose and preserved discipline by private reprimand and pledges on honor alone, which invariably elated the spirit of the soldiers. Who can say more for his command in our service?[5]

We had been at Mrs. Erwin's but a short time when Hardee told the company of the death of General Van Dorn, with the attendant circumstances.[6] I had already heard the facts, but had not thought it proper to mention them. The character of the general was discussed, and the common opinion was clearly expressive of condemnation. Little or no regret was felt for a man whose willful violation of social rights led him to such an inglorious end. He had started with the full confidence and favor of the people and President.

Hardee now recalled the opinion I had expressed at Corinth of Van Dorn's incapacity and ended by saying, "You were right, but I did not agree with you at the time." Van Dorn, after repeated failures with his corps (Price and others under him) had finally to acknowledge his incapacity for so large a command (for which he deserves credit). He fell back on two divisions of cavalry, but he again showed himself unequal to the task. In utter recklessness at his fallen state, Van Dorn gave way to passions that soon ruined him.

5. Liddell confided to Mary, "The soldiers call me 'the old man,' and hence I feel distressed to think that I must be getting to look old." Liddell to Mary M. Liddell, February 18, 1863, in Liddell Papers, LSU.

6. Dr. George Boddie Peters assassinated Van Dorn at his headquarters in Spring Hill, Tennessee, on May 7, 1863. Successfully fleeing Confederate officials, Peters turned up in West Tennessee after the war and died in 1889, a respected physician. A member of the "old army establishment," Van Dorn had not lived up to his military reputation, much to the disappointment of the commanders of the western armies of the Confederacy.

Just at this time, General Forrest succeeded in capturing Colonel Straight with his command, whilst pushing for a raid upon Rome in North Georgia. Mrs. Erwin told us that she had received a letter from her husband, who had gone further south to find an undisturbed home. Col. Erwin could not stop at Rome as he had desired, for my remark to him that "it would be raided on" turned out too quickly true. He would not go below Atlanta. I had long talks with the old Colonel and, finding him every way reliable, had imparted to him all my secret apprehensions of ultimate reverses to the South from the failure at Murfreesboro.

Sometime in May, my command was ordered up to Bell Buckle, six miles further to the front.[7] The rest of Hardee's Corps moved up to my old position at Wartrace, Cleburne taking possession of my old quarters opposite the depot building.

One day I had occasion to return to see Cleburne. Finding that he had ridden out with Hardee, I had to wait his return. Meanwhile, Dr. Johnson, chief surgeon of the division, a well-educated, thorough gentleman, full of good humor and witticism, amused me with comments on Cleburne's peculiarities and his bearish manners towards his staff.

In a short while, Cleburne came riding back alone, not very tidy in his appearance, no cravat on, and a shirt needing the washwoman's services. He came in grumbling something about Hardee's tardiness and running after women. While Cleburne was explaining, Hardee rode up to the gate calling out to us loudly, "Have you seen anything of my wild Irish general?" Cleburne, looking away in apparent brown study, tried not to notice the call. I could see his mouth stretch into a broad grin, though, when Dr. Johnson answered for him.

"Yes, General, he is here. Get down, come in."

As Hardee came in, he said to me, "Is it not proper for a subordinate officer invited to ride with his commander to come properly dressed?"

"Yes," I said, "That is the military rule, I believe, everywhere."

"Now here is Cleburne, coming out so badly dressed as to be frightened home at the sight of ladies whom we happen to meet on the road."

Cleburne grumbled out that he was not prepared to see ladies. He was not going to stand off waiting for Hardee to get through

7. Liddell's Brigade had been on outpost duty at Wartrace since early January. He moved to Bell Buckle on April 24. *O.R.* I, 23 (1), 587.

with his flatteries; therefore he came away. Dr. Johnson remarked by way of apology, "This may be all owing to where Cleburne was raised. I don't know whether Ireland or Arkansas."

"Stop. Allow me to correct you, Doctor," said Hardee. "Men are reared; horses, hogs, cattle, and sheep are raised."

"I thank you, General," said Dr. Johnson with a bow, "for the correction. I don't know which category you choose to place Cleburne in. I know that he is pretty rough with his staff and shows very slight respect sometimes for our feelings." At this sally, I laughed outright; the Doctor smiled sardonically. Cleburne grinned with all his might, as if he didn't care a "d - - n" for anybody. Hardee seemed smilingly concerned.

The trio evidently were concerned at having hit and having been hit all around, and after a momentary silence, the subject was changed. When I met Hardee again several days afterwards, he remarked with a laugh, "I didn't see the point in Dr. Johnson's remark regarding Cleburne at the time."

One of Cleburne's eccentricities was that he kept a pet coon whose antics amused him. He said that it would push its way under the cover of somebody's bed every night in the tent. Oftentimes it was kicked out, but would perseveringly hunt around for some friendly place, rarely failing to find one among the numerous staff. One night, however, everybody seemed unfriendly to him and kicked him away. After trying all the beds, the poor fellow stopped and set up a most pitiable cry or squall. This finally induced them to take him in, to the little animal's great relief. The coon deserted Cleburne when he retreated from the field to Murfreesboro. He ran up a tree, where he waited for the enemy and no inducements could bring him down to remain longer with the Confederates. He probably resented their indignities at this last moment and decided to join the other side. All this goes to prove the truth of the saying "wise as old coon."

In my circumscribed position at Bell Buckle, I was in utter ignorance of what was going on elsewhere in the world. Finding myself amongst good people, I gave cheerful permission to my men to aid the citizens in harvesting their crops of wheat and rye and afterwards planting their corn. The time was usefully and agreeably spent by the soldiers and citizens.[8] At the same

8. On June 1, Liddell's Brigade paraded. That day a visitor, Lt. Col. Arthur J. L. Fremantle, Coldstream Guards, observed:
   We all went to a review of General Liddell's brigade at Bell Buckle. . . .

time, I had the railroad from Bell Buckle repaired for public uses. We have the great satisfaction of knowing that we left no enemies behind us amongst the poor citizens.

One of the most distressing things to me was the appeal of the people, women and children, not to leave them to the hard mercies of the Yankees. With tears in my eyes I promised them that we would come back, but fate willed otherwise.[9] In truth, if I had been in command of the Army, I would have died before crossing the Southern boundary of Tennessee. He who is bold

There were three carriages full of ladies, and I rode an excellent horse, the gift of General John Morgan to General Hardee. The weather and the scenery were delightful. . . .

General Liddell's brigade was composed of Arkansas troops—five very weak regiments which have suffered severely in the different battles, and they cannot be easily recruited on account of the blockade of the Mississippi. The men were good-sized, healthy, and well clothed, though without any attempt at uniformity in color or cut, but nearly all were dressed in gray or brown coats and felt hats. . . .

Before the marching past of the brigade, many of the soldiers had taken off their coats and marched past the general in their shirt sleeves, on account of the warmth. Most of them were armed with Enfield rifles captured from the enemy. Many, however, had lost or thrown away their bayonets. . . .

Each regiment carried a "battle flag," blue, with a white border, on which were inscribed the names, "Belmont," "Shiloh," "Perryville," "Richmond, Kentucky," and "Murfreesboro." (The characteristic blue battle flag of Cleburne's Division, designed by Hardee.) They drilled tolerably well, and on advance in line were remarkably good; but General Liddell had invented several dodges of his own, for which he was reproved by General Hardee.

The review being over, the troops were harangued by Bishop Elliott. . . . He was followed by a Congressman of vulgar appearance, named Hanley, from Arkansas. . . . I imagine that the discipline in this army is the strictest in the Confederacy, and the men are much better workers than those I saw in Mississippi. *Fremantle Diary*, pp. 123-125.

9. Liddell worried about marauding Yankee gunboats coming up Black River and raiding. He worried about Mary and the trouble and expense of running Llanda without necessary manpower and supplies.

"I can't send Judge home to help you. He has joined Co. F, 1st Louisiana Cavalry, in Scott's (J. S.) Cavalry Brigade at Lenoir's Stat., E. Tenn."

"I would come if I could. I have thought of tendering my resignation because I am over age and would like to do what I can for my own state."

"I myself feel like I am amongst entire strangers, even with my own command. There is nobody but my servant Peter with me, whom I knew before. Wade Young is to all intents and purposes a stranger to me, hence I am alone and feel often times exceedingly solitary in a crowded camp of soldiers."

Liddell missed Hardee, but their positions now "cause us to be separated, and hence I feel the want of somebody to talk with *without reservations*. I am too plain spoken by nature to be a favorite."

What cavalry outfit has Willie joined. "Why did he not go to Gen. Kirby Smith direct and tell him the facts connected with his part in the battle of Richmond and the Kentucky campaign and in Battle of Murfreesboro with me and at Shiloh—all voluntary for a boy not 16. . . ." Liddell to Mary Liddell, June 2, 1863, in Liddell Papers, LSU.

124

enough to receive and assume command of an army ought, like the old Roman, to have died than give up the cause with which he was trusted.

It was about this period of our struggle that Mr. Vallandigham, of Ohio, passed through our lines for Richmond.[10] The circumstance seemed to create much excitement at the time, but I know too little about the matter to give any opinion and only state the fact of his coming into our lines, a refugee.

General Joseph E. Johnson had now arrived from Mississippi and was again expected to take command of the army in Bragg's place. The threatening movements of General Grant on Vicksburg, however, recalled him to that department. On his departure, Bragg was again stripped of 8,000 more effective troops, which reduced him at last to something like 25,000 effectives, totally insufficient for the operations then in his front and against an enemy every day improving in strength.

It would have been wise, I truly believe, to let Johnson stay with us in Tennessee, and Bragg go to Jackson and Vicksburg.

10. Clement Laird Vallandigham (1820-1871). Bitter political enemy of Lincoln and prominent Ohio politician, he was "banished to the Confederacy by Lincoln." In 1864, however, he delivered the keynote speech of the Democratic Convention. Vallandigham represented the "copperhead" movement then and has become its epitome historically.

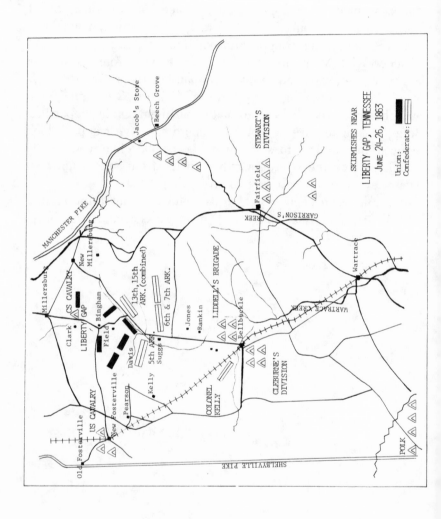

SKIRMISHES NEAR
LIBERTY GAP, TENNESSEE
JUNE 24-26, 1863

Union:
Confederate:

Jacob's Store

Beech Grove

STEWART'S DIVISION

Fairfield

GARRISON'S CREEK

Wartrace

MANCHESTER PIKE

Millersburg

New Millersburg

Clark

CS CAVALRY

LIBERTY GAP

Bingham

13th, 15th ARK. (combined)

6th & 7th ARK.

LIDDELL'S BRIGADE

Field

Davis

5th ARK.

Suggs

Jones

Rankin

Bellbuckle

WARTRACE CREEK

Kelly

Pearson

US CAVALRY

New Fosterville

Old Fosterville

COLONEL KELLY

CLEBURNE'S DIVISION

POLK

SHELBYVILLE PIKE

126

# CHAPTER XII

# RETREAT

Meanwhile, Rosecrans reinforced his force to 70,000 effectives. Finding everything ready, he began his movement on 24 June, 1862, attacking our right flank at Liberty and Hoover's Gaps. I had already moved up two regiments of my brigade to Liberty Gap to cover any approach through the knobs from that direction.[1]

On the morning of 25 June, information reached me at Bell Buckle of an attack upon that position by a division of the enemy. The enemy pushed so rapidly upon the place that I had no time to reinforce it from the camps which were some three miles in rear. After contending the ground as long as tenable with my small force, I withdrew to the next range of knobs, one mile further back, out in full view and hurried forward the rest of my brigade.

The next day the enemy renewed the attack and were repulsed, doubled up with heavy loss. Colonel Govan urged me not to fight any longer to maintain a position, which was of no avail in the general result. I told him, "No, hold on. I must obey the orders, whatever my own views or opinions are, and I will stay there until ordered or forced away." I soon afterwards withdrew from this knob to the next, where we held on with General Wood's assistance, inflicting heavy loss and suffering greatly until the night of the 26th.[2]

1. Liberty Gap was about three miles north of Liddell's camp at Bell Buckle.
2. Richard W. Johnson's Division of the XX Corps drove Liddell's 5th Arkansas and 13th and 15th (combined) Arkansas regiments through and out of Liberty Gap. Liddell personally directed the fighting here but his 530 men could not withstand Johnson's numbers, despite the advantage of terrain. Liddell and his two regiments fell back upon the rest of the brigade coming up through the mud from Bell Buckle.

On June 27th notice was sent me that Rosecrans had passed through Hoover's Gap four miles on our right. The enemy had driven General A. P. Stewart's Division back and was now getting close to Fairfield in our rear. I was directed to have my brigade cover the retreat of our division upon Tullahoma. Up to this time we kept the Federal Generals Miller and Willich locked in the Gap, unable to move out.[3]

General Wood retired soon after, transmitting to me the orders above mentioned. Accordingly, I marched my command steadily and unmolested back to my old camps to rest and prepare to obey orders. Here we remained all night and after breakfast next morning took up our line of march. The Texas cavalry brigade under Colonel Thomas Harrison took my place here to watch the enemy.

It rained terribly during the nights of June 27th and 28th. Nevertheless, we continued our line of march without molestation, getting to Tullahoma on the 28th. On arriving, I hastened to see General Bragg, whom I had not met with since Murfreesboro. Although unwell and suffering from chronic diarrhea, he told me that he had determined to fight at Tullahoma.

I expressed my disagreement with genuine candor as to the propriety of such a step. The country was so open and no natural advantages were offered for a weak force to contend with a strong one. After giving up the advantages of fighting in the gaps, we should fall back to the base of the mountains in the rear, where

June 25 Liddell probed Johnson's lines and a spirited affair between skirmish lines grew into a serious conflict late in the afternoon. Union Corps Commander Alexander McCook sent in Brigadier General Jefferson C. Davis with two brigades, and Liddell found his veterans fighting two enemy divisions. As predicted by McCook, these heavy numbers did "settle the thing decidedly."

To "the great mortification" of Liddell's Brigade, the color bearer of Govan's 2nd Arkansas when killed fell headlong down a steep hillside. The regiment did not discover the loss of their flag until it was too late.

Cleburne sent S. A. M. Wood's Brigade to help on the evening of the 25th. Together they beat off subsequent attacks. Liddell lost 120 men; McCook reported 239 killed and wounded.

Liddell curiously minimizes this engagement in his *Record*. He wrote one of his most detailed reports about it (*Official Record* 23 (1), 587-592), and his subordinates referred to the conflict with great pride. Perhaps because he lost his Liberty Gap notes, and because of the fluid, confused nature of Bragg's entire front in late June, his brigade's effort has been neglected.

3. John F. Miller and August Willich were hardly "locked in the Gap," but Willich and his German Brigade were wary. They had been surprised and mauled by the enveloping Confederate left at Murfreesboro. Willich was captured and had only recently returned to his command.

all these chances would favor us. But no, he was positive and fixed in his determination and would fight at Tullahoma. I then told him if so unalterably decided upon, that I would do my part honestly and to the best of my ability.

I added, however, "General, if you had only followed my advice at Murfreesboro, we would not now be here, but rather in Nashville or further North, perhaps on the Ohio River." He said to me in reply, I thought somewhat hurt, "General, it is too late now and cannot be helped."

After a moment's silent reflection, Bragg further said, "General, I depend on you to hold the bridges over the Duck River in my rear. If they are seized by the enemy, we are lost. Get ready to occupy them this evening." I told him that we would hold them under such circumstances to the last extremity.

Here I left him, and after arriving at my camp, told Colonel Govan of General Bragg's determination to fight at Tullahoma. He quietly said, "No, General, he will not fight here."

"But, Colonel, I have General Bragg's word for it."

"No matter."

"But Bragg would not so positively assert to me such a thing."

"No matter, General, I don't believe it, and I will go an oyster supper on it."

"Very well, the first time we shall be in New Orleans after the war."

"Agreed."

I owe the Colonel (now General Govan) for the lost wager yet (August 24th, 1866), but we have not met since the war ended.[4]

That night I moved with my command to the bridges on Duck River. So firmly did I believe in Bragg's assertions that I made every preparation for their defense. I posted the men in prepared stockades with instructions never to yield until they knew that I had gone up first. They told me quietly in reply that they would stand the test, "no matter what befell them."

I spent a watchful and anxious night and all the next day.

4. Daniel Chevilette Govan (1829-1911). Gold miner, planter, this transplanted North Carolinian joined near his Arkansas home and became the colonel of the 2nd Arkansas in 1861. He fought through all the battles with the Army of Tennessee until the desperate Carolina Campaign of 1865. Along with Lucius Polk and John C. Brown, his name is inseparable from that of Cleburne. Govan retired to Marianna, Arkansas, after the war. Liddell sent him at least one section of this manuscript to criticize.

Towards morning of the second day, what was my surprise to find myself suddenly interrupted in a few snatched moments of sleep by the presence of General Polk and others. They told me that Bragg had decided upon retreat, just the reverse of everything he had positively told me. I was so astonished that I could hardly be made to believe it. Yet it was true. What all this indecision of Bragg meant I could hardly understand. What the influence to bear upon him was, I found beyond my restricted range of information as a subordinate officer.

I felt it keenly, as I well knew that I had as much to lose as the rest, and it was hard that my poor voice could not be heard in my own behalf and interest.

No matter; it was the will of God. It was philosophy to bear all.

I had an hour or so discussion in friendly talk with Lieutenant General Polk and Major General Withers.[5] We reviewed some trifling but amusing incidents connected with the former in the Kentucky campaign. Then orders came to me to rejoin my division and give up my place to other troops.

5. Jones Mitchell Withers (1814-1890). This West Pointer (Class of 1835) succeeded. He prospered in business, won promotion to regimental command during the Mexican War, became mayor of Mobile before and after the Civil War, and won acclaim from Bragg and Polk for his work at Murfreesboro. The Army of Tennessee lost this veteran combat leader in July when he transferred for the duration to the quiet command of the reserve forces of Alabama.

# CHAPTER XIII

# AT CHATTANOOGA

We now took up the line of march for University Place,[1] with the remainder of the division. We continued our march to Chattanooga, where we arrived about the 4th July, 1863. On the 9th following, we heard of the fall of Vicksburg and the consequent complete occupation of the Mississippi River by the Federals.

It was clearly apparent now that we had receded until all chances of success had passed by. The turning points of the war had been fatally overlooked or were given up without sufficient effort and strategic concurrence. Henceforth, the war would slowly, but surely, wear out the Confederate States, which could only struggle on and abide their time.

So fully was I impressed with these opinions that I went to see Bragg in Chattanooga and proposed to him in my conversation to resign or otherwise be transferred to the Trans-Mississippi Department. This transfer would enable me to look after my family and secure something for their support from the wreck of my property in Louisiana. Bragg seemed very much depressed and said that we had backed to the last jumping-off place and could go back no further with any hope of success. He positively refused, however, to accept my withdrawal or transfer and urged me to hold on for another campaign. He would take my transfer to Louisiana under his favorable consideration at that time.

Knowing no alternative, I consented to stay that much longer. Bragg then said that he would give me command of a division with the object on his part of securing my promotion. I assured him that promotion had no weight with me, since I saw so many

1. Sewanee, where Polk and others launched a magnificent educational enterprise that turned to rubble as war destroyed their dreams.

131

unworthy men far above me in authority. I had not the slightest respect for their abilities and opinions.

We parted, as I thought, fully understanding each other in this matter. After the sad experience I had up to this time with men in office from President Davis to Sidney Johnston, Bragg and others, down to the very lowest in authority, I never saw one whose views impressed me with his absolute superiority so as to create profound respect. I saw clearly that plain practical ability was far better for Southern Interest and Safety than all this military fudge. Such pretense amounted to absolute folly, not perceptible to the uninitiated because of their not having the opportunity to look behind the scenes. Hence, there was but one office that I desired, viz., one directly from the President that would authorize me to look after the general interest of the Confederacy. I would set about stripping incompetent officials of their authority. Thereby I could aid the good officer, either in the field or in his administration. For the common good, I would depose these unworthy harpies, in the President's name.

I have seen so much abuse in office to the manifest injury of the cause that I could conceive of no other method of abating the public wrongs than by high-handed measures. These men had hardly gotten one office before they sought another still, so common was the political thirst for office in the military profession. Competency was disregarded.[2]

After the failures of Pemberton at Vicksburg, Hardee was transferred from the command of our corps to Meridian, Mississippi, where he was required to organize the troops exchanged since the surrender of the former place.

Lieutenant General Buckner assumed command of our Corps in Hardee's place. We were very sorry to lose Hardee. Long and faithful service had attached our Corps to him. I have more than once heard him say that he would like for once to know the feeling of holding possession of the battlefield by indisputable victory. I don't know that he ever once during the entire war enjoyed the wish. Whilst he was at Meridian, we won the Battle of Chickamauga, the greatest battle of the war. Hardee returned

2. On July 25, 1863, Liddell joined with seventeen other general officers in the Army of Tennessee in a letter imploring President Davis to stop the practice of employing substitutes. "Early and vigorous measures to recruit our wasted ranks may save us further loss of men and resources, and possibly the existence of the Southern Confederacy itself." OR, I, 4 (2), 670-71.

to us just in time to share the disaster of Mission Ridge. After Mission Ridge, if he had desired, he could have had permanent command of the Army and had his own way, but he declined. I believe his chief reason was that it was too late to remedy the defective system hitherto pursued, and reverses had become so overwhelming, as well as demoralizing, to the spirit of the Army. I inferred such to be Hardee's impression from many conversations with him at various times. If however my inferences are wrong, no harm has been done and some day I hope he will make known all the facts and motives.[3]

One thing I do not think that he ever knew the feelings of victory which he so much desired, but of all men, Hardee's record is clear for brave and faithful service to the end. If all his equals, as well as inferiors, in office had done as well, the fate of the South would have been different. There is no General whose escutcheon is brighter in my view.

Bragg had detached Walthall's Brigade from Polk's Corps and given it to me to be placed with my own in the reserve. Artillery was also ordered to be placed under my command. My camp was again moved to Chickamauga Station, in the same spot I had encamped just before the Kentucky Campaign, and I drilled my temporary division in the same fields.[4]

At General Buckner's desire, I gave up General J. H. Kelly of the 8th Arkansas to take command of a brigade in his division. As he was the best of my officers, I parted with him regretfully. At Chickamauga he handled his brigade with marked skill and bravery and fairly won his spurs. General Bragg soon promoted him to a cavalry command under Wheeler, to whom he well knew he was superior in ability in every respect. This young man, one of the most efficient officers in the Army, 22 or 23 years of age, was prematurely killed in one of Wheeler's miserable, useless

---

3. Hardee decided against explaining his actions and thoughts. After the war he wrote a short biographical article about his faithful friend, Patrick Cleburne, but otherwise remained above the thrust and counterthrust of quills. He died in 1873, soon after Liddell.

4. Liddell's Division consisted of Brigadier General Edward Cary Walthall's Brigade of five Mississippi regiments and Liddell's own brigade commanded by Brigadier General Daniel Chevilette Govan. The "Arkansas Brigade" of the Army of Tennessee was perhaps its finest brigade. Well drilled and disciplined, it formed the heart of Cleburne's commands and won success after success under Cleburne, Liddell, and Govan. In the fall of 1863 it consisted of the 8th Arkansas, six other Arkansas regiments consolidated into three, and the First Louisiana Infantry. Liddell's Division also contained two batteries of artillery.

133

plundering raids in Tennessee. More damage was done by his death than all that Wheeler's raids had accomplished for the Confederate side. I never knew anything good come of them. Brave Kelly—my heart leaned to the gallant palladin who waited for recognition of service rather than like the politician, thrust himself into notice without record. The office often made the record for the man.

My old friend, Mackall, who had been chief of staff for General Sidney Johnston and was afterwards captured while in command at Island No. 10, and had been exchanged and returned to the service, was now occupying the same position under Bragg (the two having been West Point classmates), that he held under Johnston.

At General Mackall's desire, I made with him a reconnaissance south and west of Chattanooga, over the grounds that afterwards became the scene of the desperate conflict of Chickamauga. We extended our observations from Lafayette across Lookout Mountain. We entered Wills Valley, which lies between Lookout Mountain and Raccoon Mountain. We crossed Running Water Creek, which comes out from between the two latter mountains into the valley of Wills Creek. Mackall and I followed its course northeast for seven or eight miles. Crossing the stream near the mouth, we moved around the base of the Lookout Point, close to the Tennessee River. Soon we emerged into the beautiful plain of Chattanooga.

General Mackall was partial to me and considered with friendly interest the opinions I expressed. He had been adjutant for General Worth in Mexico, for Sidney Johnston, J. E. Johnston, and Bragg. His association, therefore, had been with the best officers of the Old Army, as well as our own. I appreciated and valued his good opinion. We differed in some important points and he would frequently observe to me, "I can't think as you do." I found when he ended with this expression, it was only a waste of time to continue the conversation unless the subject was imperative for harmony as Chief of Staff.

I was ordered about the middle of August to attend a council to be held at Chattanooga. On going there, I found Lieutenant Generals Polk and D. H. Hill and Major Generals Hindman,[5]

5. Thomas Carmichael Hindman (1828-1868). Vigorous, outspoken politician, he led his men from Arkansas into the Army of Tennessee. He organized the 2nd Arkansas which subsequently became Govan's command. Hindman saw

Cheatham, Cleburne, W. H. T. Walker, and others present. Bragg informed us that Rosecrans had thrown two corps across the Tennessee River below Bridgeport. Two others were moving on the other side of the river upon Chattanooga and another corps under Burnside was at Knoxville.

Having never been called in council before, I went prepared only to listen. To my surprise, Bragg called on me first to give my views of the situation. I took a map and showed that Rosecrans' objective with the two corps that had crossed below Bridgeport was to move across the Lookout Mountain and gain our rear, with the view of causing the evacuation of Chattanooga. At the same time, he would threaten with the other two corps by direct attack. Our policy, on the other hand, was to be apparently ignorant of these movements. We even were extending our forces to protect his lines further to the right of the woods near Knoxville. The Army of Tennessee would continue to hold its position until Rosecrans had fairly made his position inextricable and had debouched the Bridgeport Corps beyond support in the valley south of us near Lafayette. With his force divided, we could strike with certainty one at a time. In short, Rosecrans was evidently making a hazardous movement, and we should not intercept him at this point. General Polk remarked, "You don't think Rosecrans so incautious as to take such a step?"

"Yes, I feel satisfied that he will, for he must have lost all caution after having flanked us so easily out of middle Tennessee. Rosecrans is stretched out in a long line of march which leaves him open by sudden concentrated attack upon his center, to be cut in two parts." General Polk, with a perceptible smile at my thoughtless hit at Bragg's policy, bowed assent. I quickly saw that I touched tender ground, but my earnestness cleared me of design.

General Hill[6] now said that his opinion was that we should cross the river and move back into middle Tennessee. I replied, "We have no transportation, in the first place, with which to cross

action at Shiloh under Hardee, took charge of the Trans-Mississippi Department after his appointment to major general in 1862, and ended his military service severely wounded at Chickamauga. Upon returning home to Helena from Mexico in 1868, he was murdered.

6. Daniel Harvey Hill (1821-1889). This professional soldier and teacher fought ably with the Army of Northern Virginia until 1863. He came to Bragg's army to command a corps and left bitterly criticizing his superior. The Chickamauga episode virtually ended his active service, as Jefferson Davis saw fit to shelve this quarrelsome lieutenant general.

the mountains. Furthermore, we have but a short time since left that section where the crops had been exhausted. It would render subsistence impossible for the season."

Bragg, who was listening up to this time, stood up and abruptly exclaimed that such a movement was absurd and under such circumstances not to be thought of for the present. I again urged that we remain in quiet preparation as we were and wait for Rosecrans to carry out all his plans. Bragg here expressed himself satisfied with the subject discussed and desired an expression of opinion upon another, viz., should he move to attack the two corps that had first crossed the Tennessee River below Bridgeport.

Since he was looking toward me, I asked if he wished my opinion first. He said, "Yes." I replied that I was opposed to such a step, that if we went there we would first have to evacuate Chattanooga. The enemy would immediately recross the river at Bridgeport, and his other corps would seize and occupy Chattanooga before we could retrace our steps. This was not to say anything of our difficulties of transportation across Lookout Mountain. Rosecrans was saving us all of this trouble if we would only wait upon him.

Bragg then asked the other officers, all of whom, after reticent hesitation, acquiesced in the views I had expressed. I noticed that General Wheeler was passed over, and I called Bragg's attention to the fact, as we were certainly entitled to the benefit of his council and experience.

Bragg said something privately to Wheeler and dropped the subject. I firmly believe Bragg designed to prevent the exposure of Wheeler's vague ideas. I honestly confess malice, in that I have not forgiven General Wheeler for the harm he had done us in the battle of Murfreesboro. As a man, I liked him for his simplicity and lack of self-presumption. As a public character, I felt that he was out of place and that our fortunes could not prosper under his guidance. Why cannot favor go hand-in-hand with merit?

The council now broke up, and for the first time I felt confident of success and freely expressed my belief in the certainty of winning the next battle.

Bragg now issued an order placing General W. H. T. Walker in command of the reserves and requiring me to report to him with my division. Reflecting on this sudden change in my status, I thought perhaps it must have been caused by my allusion in the council to Bragg's strategy. I asked General Mackall to explain it. He only said, "It was done contrary to my wishes." Be it so, but I could not get over the impression that Bragg had not acted in good faith. I understood his intentions voluntarily expressed to me. No matter, I would do my duty zealously and cheerfully without faltering.

General Walker was well-known to be a crackbrained fire-eater, always captious or cavilling about something whimsical and changeable and hardly reliable. I was very much annoyed by such a man in business relations, though otherwise I regarded him as honorable and high-strung in all engagements. We were very friendly but constantly differed in our views. It was my duty to obey his orders, regardless of consequences and they were often destitute of common sense. The only satisfaction that I had was that our official relations would end with the next battle.[7]

I busied myself with drilling and disciplining my command, and at the same time attending to the duty assigned me in looking after the preparation of the supply train for active operations.

---

7. Liddell neglects to mention that William Henry Talbot Walker (1816-1864) was another member of the Class of 1837. Distinguished action in the Seminole and Mexican wars had brought him acclaim from the War Department and from his native state of Georgia. He rose rapidly in rank and was held in high regard by Joseph Johnston. A quarrelsome officer, Walker at the Battle of Atlanta rode away from Hardee furious and bent on revenge. He never had the chance, however, for a Union private killed him soon after parting with Hardee.

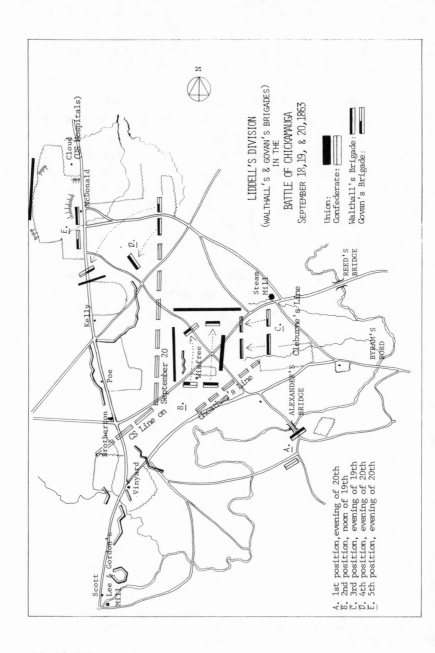

LIDDELL'S DIVISION
(WALTHALL'S & GOVAN'S BRIGADES)
IN THE
BATTLE OF CHICKAMAUGA
SEPTEMBER 18,19, & 20,1863

Union:
Confederate:
Walthall's Brigade:
Govan's Brigade:

A. 1st position, evening of 20th
B. 2nd position, noon of 19th
C. 3rd position, evening of 19th
D. 4th position, evening of 20th
E. 5th position, evening of 20th

# CHAPTER XIV

# THE BATTLE OF CHICKAMAUGA

Somewhere about the 10th of September, 1863, I was suddenly ordered to move at night toward Ringgold and Villanow. I had heard nothing of the enemy's movements since the council, but as the columns were directed southward, the inference was clear that Rosecrans was moving upon our rear. Nevertheless, I apprehended that we were premature in going after him. That is, going after him before he had fairly gotten into the pit he had prepared for himself. When riding along with General Walker, I so expressed my fears. I was afraid Bragg was pulling the string before the bird had entered the trap. Walker seemed to be of the same opinion.

We continued our march through Ringgold to Lafayette. There we were ordered to McLemore's Cove (a kind of pocket or valley formed by a spur of Lookout Mountain whence issued Lookout Creek, skirting the base and running north, emptying into the river at the foot of Lookout Point). There we found the enemy whose column was debouching into the plain of the valley.

Bragg impatiently urged attack by Hindman's Division from the north side or mouth of the cove, but it was somehow unaccountably delayed. Meanwhile, the enemy, finding himself in great danger and nearly enveloped, skillfully maneuvered with a bold front to gain time. Then, to the surprise of all, he suddenly withdrew from our front into Lookout Mountain, taking the road on the top directly for Chattanooga, which we had evacuated to no purpose by our precipitation. Thus was Bragg completely foiled, and these two enemy corps safely effected a junction with the balance of the army.

Bragg, now fully aroused, angry at the failure to accomplish the destruction of these two corps, was determined to give battle as soon as possible. He called forward all available resources and reinforcements. He knew well that he would now have to fight the united forces of Rosecrans, which he ought to have taken in detail whilst separated.

Bragg impatiently turned about and ordered Polk to meet Crittenden's Corps approaching from Ringgold. After the demonstration on our part, Crittenden fell back toward Chattanooga and joined the main body in their subsequent advance upon us. We immediately returned to Lafayette to await the denouement.

Whilst General Polk was at Rock Spring Church in command, General Walker and I were sent for in council. The positions were all arranged, the commands all waiting for orders, but Walker was not fully satisfied. He found fault with "Old Polk's" (as he called him) dispositions, one after another, until the General seemed greatly perplexed in trying to explain and alter them to suit Walker. Polk even laid aside important dispatches to settle the matter with him. Seeing no end to the dispute, one of Polk's staff officers appealed to me to get Walker off. I made the attempt and succeeded by persuasion so far as to get Walker to the door of the church. There, talking and looking about, something occurred to him. He went back to the General, determined to settle it or have the last word.

Walker continued the dispute with the old man, who seemed calm but good-naturedly perplexed. Seeing no way of ending Walker's pertinacious quibbles, I called on Cheatham to try his hand with him that we might go and take up our positions without delay. General Cheatham went to where they were and listened to Walker a moment. Suddenly, Cheatham turned around to me, saying with an oath that he would not serve two hours under Walker to save his life.

Walker stayed until he had pretty much exhausted rhetoric and expletives. He came grumblingly away, greatly to the relief of General Polk, who was completely badgered. This was the man Bragg had placed over me, with whom he was himself at loss, as he said to me, "worn out and disappointed."

We were now ordered to meet the enemy on the Lafayette Road across Chickamauga Creek, a little stream with a course slightly east of north. It lies between Mission and Graysville ridges, and winds around the head of the former, emptying into the Tennessee several miles above Chattanooga.

The head of the enemy's column had reached Lee and Gordon's Mill, where the Lafayette Road crossed the Chickamauga, and deployed at that point. Bragg confronted the column with General Longstreet, who was in command of the left wing. The right under Polk and D. H. Hill threatened Rosecrans' left flank by crossing the Chickamauga several miles lower down toward Chickamauga Station. These tactical changes caused our right wing to engage facing to the west.

Bragg's object, I believe, was to gain the enemy's rear. He hoped to cut him off from Chattanooga, only six miles distant from the rear of the enemy's column. I suppose that the opposing lines were hardly less than seven miles in length, that is from Lee and Gordon's Mill to a point six miles from Chattanooga.

On the evening of September 18, I was ordered by Walker to attack and drive the enemy away from Alexander's Bridge, which was done after a severe engagement in which many men (105) were killed and wounded, but the bridge was found broken up.[1] To avoid delay, we sought Byram's Ford, one and a half miles below where we waded the stream and, marching half a mile or more beyond, stopped to bivouac.

As dark was coming on, General Hood's Division, having disembarked from the trains at Ringgold during the day, reached the Chickamauga at a bridge some half a mile still below us and forced a crossing there at the same time we did. Soon after, his division marched across my front going towards Lee and Gordon's Mill to join General Longstreet on the left.

It was too dark to go so far, as he might stumble upon the enemy, who could not be more than half a mile west of us. We met at General Longstreet's campfire close at hand. Hood was above the general height and prepossessed me. I could not distinguish his features by firelight. His left arm, I think, was tied up in a sling caused from a wound received in Virginia. I found him affable, but his conversation was too short to enable me to form an estimate of his ability and military views. The next day

1. Liddell's men unfortunately encountered "Mr. Lincoln's gun" at Alexander's Bridge. John T. Wilder's Brigade, thanks to the imagination and persistence of their commander, had been armed recently with repeating Spencer rifles. The fire from these repeaters tore holes in Liddell's lines and led him to report sadly his heavy losses, "I can only account for this disproportion from the efficiency of this new weapon." Nevertheless, Liddell pushed aside Wilder's mounted infantry and captured a half dozen of the breech-loading rifles.

he was wounded in the leg, early in the fight. I never saw him again.

Major General Thomas commanded Rosecrans' left wing. He was one of the most indomitable generals in the Federal service. At Mill Springs he was said to have inflicted disaster on the Confederate Army. Thomas soon found out Bragg's design of gaining Rosecrans' rear. He prepared to prevent it the next day, 19th September, by driving back our right wing across the Chickamauga.

Early that morning Thomas drove Forrest's cavalry steadily upon us. Bragg ordered Walker to send two brigades to Forrest's assistance. They too were steadily forced back, both cavalry and infantry, vying with each other to hold their ground. The firing became hotter and nearer, when Walker called me to go with him to see what the force was opposed to Forrest.

It struck me at once, on getting to the scene of action, that Rosecrans had discovered his danger and was pushing a heavy force through the thick woods upon us. Unless we quickly met it in equal strength, we would soon be compelled to get out of the way. I told Walker so, and he communicated the facts to Bragg. I was now required to engage the enemy and check his advance until we could get up reinforcements.

Hood had gone to the left, and no other division of the right wing, other than Walker's and mine, now came up to meet this avalanche. No time was to be lost; we were quickly ready. All this occurred in the woods. The enemy now came on slowly and cautiously, but we could not see him from the underbrush.

Forward we went, and in a few minutes came into immediate close contact. My line pressed forward, giving and receiving heavy volleys. Loud shouts soon followed. We captured about 900 regulars and several batteries of artillery. Without stopping, on we went, driving back the second line and hotly engaging the third.

But General Thomas was prepared with far larger force than my little division of only two brigades in one line without support on flanks or in rear. He struck my flank with another division at an obtuse angle, which forced me back in turn, filing off as it were from the left to right.[2]

2. Liddell's Division fell back under the assault of Richard W. Johnson's Division. Johnson, however, ran into Cheatham's Tennesseans rushing to help Liddell and the fighting became furious and inconclusive. Both Thomas and Bragg

It was now about twelve o'clock, and the enemy was pushing up his lines when Cheatham luckily arrived on the ground with his division and was in position ready behind me. I told him what was coming, and that I would reform behind him. I had lost a great many men and officers, killed and wounded. We had captured Captain Van Pelt, with nearly all of his Loomis Michigan Battery, which, however, we had not time to remove, nearly all the horses being killed. We killed Major Coolidge of the regular Army in the conflict with the third line, which we had repulsed just as we were struck on the left flank by the fresh deploying line, but to no avail.

The enemy's force to our front had largely increased. Rosecrans had withdrawn units from his right (Longstreet's front) to maintain his ground on his left and to prevent our turning his rear. I was again forced back about 200 yards. All of our fighting had been done in thick oak and brush woodlands. We could not see each other until close at hand. Rosecrans, in supporting Thomas so heavily, so weakened his right wing that Longstreet's men had a comparatively easy time with the thin line opposed to them.

It was now getting late, almost sunset. We had been, I may say, constantly fighting since morning. Cleburne's Division arrived fresh, having up to this time been out of the fight. He now moved forward just in my rear, and seeing our condition, I rode hastily back to show him the enemy. They were halted in the woods, not far before us, probably to secure the ground gained and to rest for the night. I pressed Cleburne to move to the attack at once, with his fresh troops and drive the enemy back, as they must be greatly exhausted from our constant fighting. If Cleburne's attack was delayed till morning, the enemy would be found entrenched and fully prepared. I told him that no time was to be lost to give us room between our position and the Chickamauga, only some four hundred yards in rear. General Cleburne hesitated and said that he would await orders from General Hill.

Our opportunities were fast slipping away. Luckily, General Hill made his appearance, and I appealed to him, adding that Cheatham and I were too much exhausted and weakened to repeat the attempt, and all we could do until rested was to retard the enemy.

continued to send in reinforcements, and Liddell's attack turned out to be the pivot point for both armies.

General Hill finally told Cleburne to get ready. I then said to Cleburne, "General, I hope you will be quick, for a minute now will be worth an hour tomorrow."

He took his time, nevertheless, losing a half hour of daylight, at least. He moved just at dark over my lines, meeting the enemy unprepared and resting about two hundred yards from us. Cleburne's attack succeeded and the enemy entirely withdrew two miles to the Lafayette Road. There he threw up breastworks and awaited our approach the next day. After this, all was quiet for the night, excepting for the enemy felling trees for defense along his whole line. I felt satisfied now that he was put upon the defensive, a great point had been gained to us.

The attack was ordered by Bragg to commence early the next morning, the 20th, but through some unfortunate misunderstanding between Generals Polk and Hill, the execution of the order was delayed to 9 a.m.[3] After moving several miles to my right, I was directed by General Hill to make an attack upon the enemy's extreme left and rear at a place where General D. W. Adams' Brigade, in attempting to get in rear of the enemy's line, had been severely handled and driven back and Adams himself captured.[4]

General Hill had detached Walthall's Brigade to some other point, which upon my representations of the simple facts, highly incensed General Walker. Walker disliked Hill anyway.

I made the attack, but our brigade was altogether too weak in numbers to hold the ground gained against such odds with the concentrated fire of many batteries already prepared and in defensive positions. Govan was severely repulsed, although he had gained some distance in the enemy's rear.

Meanwhile, Generals Walker and Hill got into a high dispute about the detachment of Gist's brigade, as well as Walthall's.[5]

3. A costly delay, as the effectiveness of the subsequent attacks led Union General John M. Palmer to remark that if they had begun at daybreak as Bragg had ordered, "the battle would not have lasted an hour." "We would have gone to Chattanooga on the run."
4. Adams and Liddell would share a common cause again after the War. Both became involved in Confederate resettlement projects involving a number of Louisianans.
5. Edward Cary Walthall (1831-1898). A capable politician soldier, Walthall received command of 29th Mississippi after Shiloh. Chickamauga, Chattanooga, and the Atlanta Campaign gave proof of his effective leadership. As a major general and division commander, he anchored the Army of Tennessee in its final six months of agony.

Walker also severely criticized and loudly found fault with the propriety of Hill's plans of attack.

Whilst this miserable dispute was going on, reports reached us that the center under Cleburne had been repulsed with heavy loss. Amidst the excitement, General Polk rode up suddenly in cheerful spirits. Upon being asked by someone how goes it on the left, answered, "Oh merrily, merrily. Now let us arrange things for you."

Affairs were still discussed rather angrily. General Hill asserted that a gap in his line was not filled up. General Hill said to Polk, "Come with me and see." Polk declined, but ordered some staff officer to examine and make report to him. The dispute still continued. Walker joined in and complained to Polk of Hill's disposition of his command, that he now had no command.

I rode up to General Hill and told him I regretted these disputes. Something must be done, and I was ready to obey his orders, no matter what they were. Hill, however, walked off toward the skirmish line, apparently angry at something said by Walker. Walker saw this and remarked, "The man is mad, and in a mad fit will expose himself to the sharpshooters and will get killed." He then loudly called Hill to come back, apparently much troubled. Hill shortly afterwards returned, reserved and tired of discussion.

Having received new orders to move, Hill ordered me late in the evening to advance to the Lafayette Road. I was to pass beyond the enemy's left flank and attack him again.

I said, "General, support me, for I will be exposed front and flanks."

Hill assured me that he would do so, and I moved up to the position he had designated. I planted my battery of guns, which played down the lines of the enemy on his left and in his rear. I was between his left and Chattanooga. Upon my signal for the attack on the enemy's right, all of our forces simultaneously moved forward. The enemy left his works and escaped from the field. But in doing so, he struck my left flank and captured over one hundred men. His skirmishers at the same moment pressed on my left front and right from a position in the rear of our line. Meanwhile,

After the War this highly respected Mississippian served in the U. S. Senate from 1885 to 1898. The nation appreciated his attitude of conciliation. His soldiers remembered him, "besplattered with mud but looking every inch a soldier."

the enemy's batteries enfiladed my flanks down my lines, just as I was doing with his lines.

The thing was done so suddenly that it was incomprehensible. The enemy, passing my left flank in overwhelming numbers, took with him all of my men within reach. Our men coming up behind occupied their entrenchments, which were in my rear, bearing a little to my left a little later.

After the enemy had gained a safe distance in retreat, we heard him (9 p.m.) cheer loudly and repeatedly. This cheering was caused by their gratifications at the escape of Major General Thomas from the enveloped position in which he was placed when his indomitable resolution saved Rosecrans' Army.

It seems that by nightfall only a gap of half a mile intervened between our wings, through which Thomas managed adroitly to escape after holding on long enough to enable the rest to get away. This gap, unknown to us at the time, was, luckily for him, directly in his rear in the woods. He was the last of Rosecrans' officers who withdrew from the field. Thomas, therefore, deserves all the credit.

I don't know the facts, but I have heard it said, by what at the time appeared to be good authority, that General Thomas, a Virginian, had offered his services in the beginning to Mr. Davis. Davis, however, declined giving him a position corresponding with his character and rank in the Old Army. Undoubtedly Thomas would have been a host to the Confederate side. Mr. Davis, if the report be true, was a poor judge of ability and character to have overlooked him.

I saw in a newspaper after the battle that the officers of Rosecrans' right wing complained bitterly that Thomas drew so heavily from their flank in his fight against Polk. In consequence, they were unable to maintain their ground against Longstreet. One expression I saw stated was that the greedy man of the left had swallowed up all the reserves.

As I was in the advance on the extreme right closest to Chattanooga, my scouts reported to me at 9 p.m. after dark that the enemy had gone. Before day, I sought Polk's quarters to make known the fact. I found the old general in bed in his ambulance half asleep. I got his orders to move in pursuit.

At this point, Bragg and his staff rode up. I turned to Bragg and made known to him also these things, expecting confidently to receive my orders now directly from him to go forward. General

Polk quickly made his appearance from the ambulance and entered into conversation with the Commanding General. After delaying a little longer without getting instructions, I left him, in entire ignorance of the steps that had been determined upon.[6] Surely *now* was the time to push hard upon the traces of the enemy, not giving him one minute's rest. The men were ready and willing, and not a moment should be lost.

The fruits of the victory were before us if our General would only reach forth and grasp them. He had two ways to do so: one, to follow up immediately and untiringly. The other was to march with all rapidity across the Tennessee River near Stevenson. There he could cut all the communications of the demoralized enemy. By intercepting his reinforcements and supplies, Bragg would compel the enemy at Chattanooga either to escape or surrender.

I awaited the determination with great anxiety. General Cheatham's Division passed me to take the advance about 9 a.m., 21st September.

An hour later I received orders to march, but instead of going directly upon Chattanooga, we were directed to Missionary Mills, near Chickamauga Station, some seven miles from Chattanooga. Here we remained until next evening. What valuable time—irreparable to us—was now lost. For two days we were within seven miles of Chattanooga which we could have reached at any time in two hours at most (behind the enemy). How quickly the good sense of the Federals saw and improved the situation. This is all due to the brave General Thomas.

Alas, how few men with us knew how to improve victory, although taught again and again by the published maxims of the great French emperor. All this goes to prove that a great General is *born*, not made, and that Providence is very chary of such favors to man. Amongst our enemies, not one had displayed any great strategic ability, but good sense had taught them, with their preponderance of numbers and resources, to cut us into sectional parts was the proper course to ensure success.

After the unpardonable loss of two days' time since the battle,

6. Bragg reported, "on my arrival about sunrise near Lieutenant General Polk's bivouac, I met the ever vigilant Brigadier General Liddell commanding a division in our front line, who was awaiting the general to report that his picket this morning discovered the enemy had retreated during the night from his immediate front. Instructions were promptly given to push our whole line of skirmishers to the front, and I moved to the left and extended these orders." *OR*, I, 30 (2), 34-35.

we moved up to Missionary Ridge with the intention, it was supposed, to assault the enemy. He was now in possession of our own works around Chattanooga, which he had passed through in his flight. After finding our hesitation to follow him, he had returned and occupied our old works.

It became now apparent to Bragg that the enemy had improved the works and lines and was securely lodged. To force things at this late date would cause the sacrifice of more men than he felt justified in losing for the mere possession of that place. He hesitated, delayed, and finally sat down on the ridge overlooking the place, apparently undecided what to do. He devised plans, and every now and then set on foot some fruitless expedition.

Bragg had been successful up to this time and asked nobody's advice now. No council was held that I ever heard tell of. He was wrapped up in his own self-opinion, and at present was unapproachable. I gave it up for the time, at least until his pride and elation had subsided.

My loss in my two brigades in the battle was 1,404 killed, wounded, and missing, out of an effective total 3,175 in action, nearly half of the whole, which shows the severity of the struggle and how dearly this victory was purchased. Bragg's total loss, killed and wounded, was 15,017. This was out of a force of 40,000 each day of the fight, over one-third of the whole. Reinforcements arrived on the trains making up closely for each day's loss. This was the largest army Bragg ever had together under his command —that of Rosecrans' I have conjectured to be 70,000 effectives or more.[7]

7. Livermore's studies show that Confederate losses totalled 18,454 (28%) and that Union losses were 16,170 (28%). Glen Tucker reveals, "Indiana alone lost more in killed and wounded than were lost by American land and sea forces in the Spanish war. The Indiana casualties at Chickamauga, 3,926 killed and wounded, were one eighth of the state's losses in the entire four years of war." Glen Tucker, *Chickamauga*, p. 388.

# CHAPTER XV

# MISSION RIDGE

Bragg now broke up General Walker's reserve command, reducing him to his division of three brigades. He deprived me also of Walthall's Brigade, which was ordered back to Polk's Corps, and I was placed in Cleburne's Division, Hill's Corps. Stripped of my troops without any cause being assigned, I sought an explanation from Bragg. He told me that Polk complained so much of being deprived of Walthall's Brigade and Walker had annoyed him so greatly, that he had no other course to pursue.

I then reminded him of his promise in good faith to approve and recommend my transfer to the Trans-Mississippi Department after the campaign. I desired him now to fulfill the agreement. To my great surprise and astonishment, he declined again! He said that he could not spare me and would give me promotion with another and larger division. I told him that I was not seeking such honors and only wished to go where I could be useful in some respect. At the same time, I wished to be near enough to aid my family, now exposed to the plundering operations of Jayhawkers[1] and deserters. All to no purpose. He finally said that Mr. Davis would be here in a few days and he would enable me to lay the matter before him for his decision.

1. To underscore the reality of Liddell's concern, one need only read accounts of life during the war in Catahoula Parish. A standing Catahoula joke concerned a Union soldier who married after the war the widow of the owner of Eutaw Plantation. One day while plowing, this newcomer uncovered a group of skeletons. Disturbed, he rushed into Jonesville, where he met blank expressions and sly half-smiles. "Local citizens knew that the bones belonged to the eleven Jayhawkers who had been killed on the stairway in the main house on Eutaw. . . . These neighbors thought it fitting that the bones should be plowed up by a Yankee."

Of course I gladly availed myself of this opportunity, there being no alternative. Nevertheless, my faith in Bragg's word and promises was now badly shaken, not to say gone. He had no friendship for anybody except to serve his own purposes or to maintain his reputation. His social and personal relations were, in consequence, affected by his ambition. I had seen enough to satisfy me that, able as he was, he was better fitted for high official place in the Government than in the field of active, offensive operations. He was routine in intellect rather than operative.

One morning soon after we had taken possession of Mission Ridge, I found Bragg walking about in his room in ill humor, saying,

> "I have not a single general officer of cavalry fit for command. Look at Forrest! I sent him with express orders to cross the Tennessee above and get around in the rear of the enemy to destroy his provision trains coming to Chattanooga through Sequatchie Valley, and the man instead of attending to this has allowed himself to be drawn off toward Knoxville on a general *rampage*, capturing villages and towns that are of no use whatever to me in the result. I have sent courier after courier with instructions that such was not my object and to attend to his orders; but he sends word back to me that he is driving the enemy's skirmishers and outposts towards Knoxville and has captured certain villages, etc. The man is ignorant and does not know anything of *cooperation*. He is nothing more than a good raider. I have sent General Wheeler to relieve him. Chattanooga is short of supplies, and if Forrest had executed my orders, the place would have by this time surrendered."

General Wheeler did make the attempt, but it was too late. Sufficient supplies had been received in Chattanooga to enable the enemy to hold on until reinforcements could come with more.

About the middle of October, Mr. Davis visited the lines on Mission Ridge. When the chance offered, I laid my case before him, at the same time requesting Bragg to be present. In truth, I feared Bragg might privately undo any point I gained. I saw plainly that Bragg would not let me leave if he could help it and save his credit at the same time.

I had a long interview with President Davis, and I assigned all

150

the reasons I had already given to Bragg and now urged further the promotion of Colonel D. C. Govan to my position. Govan was from Arkansas and justly entitled to the command of the troops of his own State. I was from the State of Louisiana, and although put in place at the special desire of the officers of the Brigade, I had now held it long enough. I should give way to one of them at a time too when I might properly be transferred without injury to the service. Mr. Davis said that he could not deprive General Bragg of any valuable officer.

Turning to Bragg, he said if at any time he could spare me from his army without detriment to the service, he could give me an order to the Trans-Mississippi Department. Bragg replied to Mr. Davis that he had use for me and could not spare me, but he had promised to assist me some time back in approving such a transfer. The matter now rested with Bragg, who said nothing more to me about it, nor did I to him, for I knew that he would continually put me off. I had to rest contented until something favorable turned up.

Just before Mr. Davis's visit, a petition to relieve Bragg of the command of the army had been sent around for signatures among the general officers. I declined to sign on the ground that "indifferent as Bragg was, I did not know of any better general to take his place." General Lucius Polk, nephew of the Lieutenant General, said that "anybody would do better." I asked him to name one, which he declined doing. I then said, "Perhaps Pemberton (who was here with Mr. Davis and much favored by him) might be substituted."

He remarked, "Surely not him."

"You don't know then who? The President won't select General Joe Johnston; who then now *could* be named?" Cleburne was of Polk's opinion but was very reticent of expression.

My refusal to join in this matter after my free spoken opinions of General Bragg's lack of strategic ability and unflinching determination of purpose, so necessary to a Commanding General, led some probably to think me inconsistent and to have a superficial view of things. Perhaps in a few thoughtless instances, my position created some feelings of dislike. They suspected perhaps that I had some object to gain. All this was emphatically wrong. I had no influence with him, *known to me*, for which I was sorry on account of the public service. I had already repeatedly refused promotion and will yet again have to do it, as will be seen in the sequel. Suspecting some doubt of my sincerity, I mentioned the fact of my application to Bragg to be relieved and transferred, which was hardly credited by Polk and Cleburne. Thus the matter passed on.

Alas, my mind did not run in this vein—in these petty, miserable, political jealousies. I could ask nothing better than that they would finish this wretched war without my instrumentality. Nothing would please me more. I had other interests at stake, and the failure to maintain Southern rights involved their destruction. There being discontents, I saw, would ruin the best general in the world. What arbitrary authority was there to stop them? I at once sought the opportunity to see Bragg and talk with him upon the propriety of making friends and quieting this dissatisfaction among his general officers. But to my distress, *his* mettle was also up and beyond the control of dispassionate reason. He said with emphasis, "General, I want to get rid of all such generals. I have better men now in subordinate stations to fill their places. Let them send in their resignations. I shall accept every one without hesitation."

Finding that I could do nothing now effecting reconciliation between him and his dissatisfied generals, I ceased to listen or talk upon the subject, letting the thing take its course. I truly regret that Longstreet, Buckner, D. H. Hill, Cleburne, Cheatham, and many subordinate officers had joined either directly or indirectly in this thing. At such a critical period, too, when every means was necessary to keep alive the animus of the Army and the unity and harmony of action. I have no doubt but that this deplorable affair will be explained by each of the officers taking part in it, in their respective records.

Here I will leave the subject with the remark that Mr. Davis not only sustained Bragg, but (as I was told by the latter) fully authorized him to relieve any and every officer who did not cheerfully and zealously sustain him. I myself heard Mr. Davis speak most feelingly of the dissatisfaction of the officers with Bragg. Mr. Davis knew that it was wholly wrong and that it would eventually be the cause of disaster to that army. His words were prophetic and so struck me at the time. I saw that his previous elation at first coming to us was completely neutralized by this (almost) mutiny of high officers, which would extend its influence to the ranks.

I well recollect saying, "Mr. Davis, your orders in this matter will bring everybody back to his place."

"No," said he, "there is something more needed, that orders will not reach. It is zealous, unreserved cooperation with the Commander."

This was true. There was no gainsaying it. He said that he wished every good officer friendly to the Commanding General should remain steadfast for the public good. I firmly believe that he left us disheartened, though he came to us in the highest spirit of elation.

Really, as much as I had found fault with him, I felt his distresses. He had never done anything or shown anything partial for me beyond kind treatment and generous consideration. Still I felt he was the President of the Confederacy and demanded our respect and support throughout. I had found him passionate, but kindhearted. He felt deeply for those injured by the calamities of war. He never expressed the slightest vindictiveness toward his enemies, though he never seemed to forgive opposition. I have now formed my opinion from three different interviews and conversations. Its correctness perhaps *may* not be exact, yet I believe it will tally with the common opinion of the Country and possibly with the opinion of those who knew him better.

General Pemberton was with the President on the occasion of this visit, I think with the desire on the part of Mr. Davis to place him in command of Polk's Corps. Polk and D. H. Hill had been relieved by Bragg's orders, but some objection being manifested, Pemberton, in the lofty spirit of chivalry, declined being put in command. I knew Pemberton at West Point many years since; we had been in the same class. I was satisfied that he was honest and true, let others say what they please.

We talked together of the Vicksburg affair. Pemberton said frankly, "I had provisions to hold Vicksburg two weeks longer—but I could not see the utility since General Johnston either could not or would not relieve me. *My* regret was that the surrender was on the 4th of July, but this was of no consequence except with the masses."

I saw in this conversation but too clearly that there was some misunderstanding between Pemberton and Johnston which could only result in mutual recrimination. It was also evident that the President was prepossessed in favor of Pemberton and therefore could hardly do justice to Johnston.

The President, having sustained Bragg in the difficulties with his generals, gave him carte blanche to do that which he deemed best for the public interest. It only remained for Bragg now to pursue his own course and relieve from command those whom he thought proper to relieve or to be in his way. But, notwithstanding all his anger, Bragg took no further steps. He seemed satisfied to let the disaffected generals grumble to their hearts' content, since he himself was secure beyond peradventure in his position with the President.

Here, all this trouble ended to the satisfaction of nobody. Everything remained just as in the beginning. Nobody was pleased but Bragg.

Grant now approached with Hooker's and Sherman's corps to relieve Chattanooga. Bragg was well advised of what was going on. I used to visit him almost daily (as our quarters were close together). Apprehending Grant's overwhelming numbers, I endeavored to impress Bragg with the necessity of being well prepared in a secure position. I approached the delicate subject with caution and felt hopeful when he agreed with me.

Our lines extended along the north base of Mission Ridge to about opposite Lookout Point, thence across the intervening (Lookout) valley and across Lookout Mountain into Wills Valley beyond. These encircled Chattanooga on the south side, leaving the whole north side of the river open in the enemy's possession, with the Chattanooga bend on the south side. Both lines threw up earthworks, which doubtless will remain in all future time as historical marks of the great Civil War.

General Breckinridge now commanded Hardee's or Hill's Corps on the ridge in the center. Cheatham commanded Polk's Corps on the right and Longstreet commanded the left wing. Cleburne one day expressed some concern to me at the appointment of Breckinridge to the command of our Corps. He said that Breckinridge "was an unlucky man and inspired no confidence in success." I was of the same opinion, but there was no help for it unless Hardee returned, which was talked of. Cleburne went on to say, "I would rather that the command was given to you." At this I laughed and said, "You would resign were I appointed over you." Nevertheless he earnestly, to all appearance, reasserted the preference for me. Hardee soon afterwards came to Mission Ridge and relieved Breckinridge.

Perceiving the dangers now surrounding our Army from the great accumulation of forces approaching under Grant, I hesitated no longer to urge Bragg to withdraw his lines in time to Taylor's

Ridge at Ringgold, Georgia. From this position eleven miles away, he would be secure from any sudden attack in great force and could meantime reorganize his Army for future usefulness. By all means, he should not lose the prestige of the victory of Chickamauga by any disaster. He agreed with me as to the wisdom of such a step, but had now other things in view, which he would try first.

Some short time previous to this, he had relieved General Mackall, Chief of Staff, at his own request. Being now in want of one to replace Mackall, Bragg mentioned my name along with three others. I declined at once in favor of the others, as I had no turn for such a responsible place. The fact was I did not believe we could get along smoothly together, or I would have tried it. I heard no more of this matter, nor did Bragg select anyone. This led me to suspect afterwards that he was only adroitly feeling my inclination. Probably one cause of his deferring the new command he had spoken of was the desire to give me this place next to him.

It was clearly impossible for me to get along with him, for we too widely differed on many important points. I was willing and ever ready to help him to success, but not for office. When office was put upon me or taken away, it made no impression upon the sincerity of my motives, since I was satisfied with the hope that good service was rendered the cause. I believe that those who knew me best in the army will conscientiously say that my acts accorded faithfully with my professions.

Feeling restless and disturbed one night, I was very wakeful. About the middle of the night, a bright moonlight night, I heard heavy volleys of musketry in the Moccasin Bend, near the foot of Lookout Point. My camp was on the top of Mission Ridge, and everything was still near me. Listening attentively, I knew a contest for some object was going on, and my apprehensions led to the quick conclusion that it was injurious to our lagging efforts. I waited impatiently for the morning that I might visit the scene and solve the mystery.

The next morning, passing Bragg's quarters, I saw him talking to someone at the gate, and he called to me inquiring where I was going. When I told him, he expressed great surprise. He said that he had heard nothing from General Longstreet, who was in command there with his corps and requested me to report the facts, should anything wrong be going on.

On getting to the top of Lookout Point, I had to wait some time for the heavy clouds floating over the plains below, like a sea when seen from this high place, to clear off before I could distinguish any object beneath. When this occurred, I could see that the enemy had seized and now occupied a position on our side of the river, having driven away Longstreet's men. The enemy was now busily engaged in throwing a pontoon bridge from the Moccasin Bend across to the lower part of Wills Valley. All this quietly progressing, undisturbed by any firing from Longstreet's pickets.

I could not understand the indifference on our part at this unmistakable lodgment of the enemy. On my return, I informed Bragg of all the facts. He was very incensed and sent for Longstreet, whom he said he would direct to reoccupy his lost ground immediately. He complained that Longstreet had boasted to the President that "he could whip the whole Yankee Army with his Corps alone." Mr. Davis, commenting on this absurdity, had instructed Bragg "to put him at the work." Afterwards when Bragg wanted Longstreet to cross the river at Bridgeport, improvise log pontoons, and drive the enemy from that place, Longstreet, notwithstanding his boast, shrunk from the attempt. Such was one of the plans proposed by the officers who were dissatisfied with Bragg's course. After this Bragg thought Longstreet ought to *hold* Wills Valley.

I left Bragg and waited in suspense all that day and the following night to hear the sound of guns, indicating the struggle. None were heard, and I went early the next morning to Lookout Point again, where I found Bragg had arrived before me. The enemy was busy and stirring. On our side, everything was stationary, except that a battery of Longstreet's was planted on top of Lookout. The range, however, was too great to do much damage to the enemy in the Moccasin Bend. The fire was returned from the bend, at an elevation of the guns hardly less than 45°, and I noticed that all their projectiles drifted a short distance, 25 to 30 paces, to our left. They were at least 1,500 feet below us, and at point-blank distance, about 1,700 yards (apparently). Firing downwards at them with the same calibre rifle guns required an elevation of 6 and 7°. The pontoon bridge was entirely beyond range, lower down the river.

I was observing the effect and accuracy of this artillery duel, when Longstreet came hastily up on foot. Just then a shell exploded above us, causing Longstreet to duck his head considerably. After witnessing a shot from his battery, he went on to see Bragg, who was reconnoitering a little further on, among the rocks at the point. Apprehensive that Bragg would have an outbreak of words with Longstreet and unwilling to be a witness, I went away to the left side of the mountain. There I could have a distinct view of Wills Valley and the Memphis and Charleston Railroad.

I had been there but a few moments when I discovered a Federal column debouching from Raccoon Mountain and moving down the valley to connect with the forces at the pontoon bridge. I sent back the information to Colonel Alexander, Chief of Artillery for Longstreet's Corps.[2] Alexander immediately afterwards made his appearance with several of his rifle pieces and tried their range upon the column, at least 1,400 feet below and one mile, apparently on an air line, distant. I could not perceive that much damage was done, though the shells caused the enemy to hesitate. They swerved aside into the woods out of aim and emerged at a lower point beyond range. Soon afterwards they passed along the front of Longstreet's position at the foot of the mountain and drove aside his line of skirmishers.

Bragg and Longstreet had just before this come up to the place I was standing and witnessed the proceedings. Bragg was very restless and complained with bitterness of Longstreet's inactivity and lack of ability, asserting him to be greatly overrated. He said that Longstreet asked his permission to make the attack by moonlight tonight, which he assented—anything to accomplish the purpose. We returned to our quarters, and that night, sure enough, the attempt was made, but unfortunately without success. Longstreet was compelled to withdraw to the mountain. They had learned now to respect the valor of these Western men, whom with overwhelming confidence they had previously underestimated.

Shortly after this affair, Bragg ordered Longstreet with 12,000 men to Knoxville, as he said to me, to get rid of him and see what he could do on his own resources. It was folly for Bragg to do this. He thereby reduced his own strength to such extent that there was left hardly 25,000 at Mission Ridge to meet the accumulation of all the Western Armies against him, at least 4 to 1 odds. But Bragg was headstrong and too often unreasonable.

2. Edward Porter Alexander (1835-1910), outstanding artillery officer and author of one of the most readable if not significant Civil War works.

Longstreet even took with him a part of Bragg's old forces to Knoxville. As his actions there are unknown to me, except the grand result (a signal failure), I can recount nothing of his plans of operations. I never saw him again until after the close of the War.

This affair of Longstreet's on our left extremity was the opening point of operations of the enemy. He gradually moved up to the base of Lookout Point, which we had entrenched on the slopes to keep him back. Hardee now took command of the left wing and strained every point to maintain himself. Danger was thickening fast around Bragg. But he seemed singularly indifferent. When I called his attention to the wretched condition of the roads and bridges in his rear, which might be needed for a retreat, he merely assented to the facts and wished me to examine them and report to him. I complied at once, taking two days, but my report had no weight with him. I thought he was infatuated with the hopeless anxiety to take Chattanooga. This caused him to overlook the gathering storm.

Thinking the enemy had rebuilt the railroad between Bridgeport and Wills Valley, Bragg now wanted me to burn the Running Water Bridge in a deep narrow valley of the Sand Mountain and to be ready by 10:00 a.m. tomorrow. Bragg said he would have a division of cavalry for me at his quarters. I was there before the appointed time, but instead of the division, he offered me a fraction of the 1st Louisiana Cavalry, about 120 men and officers. I was not much astonished. It tallied precisely with almost all other promises he had made me. But how was I to do this work with so few men and the enemy moving on the roads over this mountain and guarding all threatened points with brigades and divisions of infantry? He explained to me that he could not get all the cavalry up in time. He now only wished me to make the reconnaissance with this escort to see what could be done. If practicable, he would let me have two brigades of infantry. I saw it was all absurd, but it was my duty not to discuss orders, but to do my best with all possible zeal.[3]

3. Hardee, Liddell's superior, was not privy to the secret plans of Bragg and Liddell. He let his feelings be known to Bragg in a message which borders uncharacteristically on the impertinent.
   "I have received your order to send 2,000 men to report to General Liddell at Trenton tomorrow night, which order will be complied with, but I desire to say that whenever you order troops on special service it is proper to state the amount of rations to be taken. This is indispensable to avoid delay. I am

158

Dispatch was now the word. I went to the base of Lookout Mountain near Trenton until 11:00 at night, when I started on the reconnaissance across the valley, up the side of the Sand Mountain, then by the roads known to guides with me, to a place near enough to ascertain that I could get to the bridge without my object being discovered and then return by a mountain trail. The enemy discovered the reconnaissancing party and attempted to capture it, but were too late.

Whatever was done, I knew, had to be done quickly, for the enemy was all around and approaching almost on every road. I sent a report to Bragg, and after some delay, he sent me Generals J. C. Brown's and Cumming's brigades. I ordered Cumming and Brown to post several regiments in advantageous places to cover our return on the next day. While we were meeting, firing was heard not far before us, and it soon became known that enemy infantry, with cavalry and artillery, had entered the valley from the opposite mountainside and had interposed themselves between me and the bridge. I could see the force plainly, just equal to us in strength.[4] I telegraphed by signal the circumstances to Bragg that I should attack them by daylight. The reply was practical. He directed the immediate withdrawal of the two brigades—and then sent me orders, *direct*, "not to make the attack."

My business here was at an end, but I had use for all my philosophy to endure the disappointment. The enemy in ignorance of my proximity had put himself, as it were, into our hands. Bragg now regretted his haste, saying,

"I thought you were going to attack a corps with only two brigades."

"You should have given me more credit for common sense."

"Why did not you do it, irrespective of orders?"

"I tried that, with the generals who had reported to me, asking them to pocket the orders for the time, but they declined. General Brown, the senior officer, gave for reason that he did not 'stand too well to disobey an order.' I offered to stand him and you,

not presumed to know what orders have been given by the commanding general to General Liddell and what amounts of rations are needed." W. J. Hardee to G. W. Brent, November 16, 1863. *OR*, I, 31 (3), 702.

4. Sherman intended to make a show of force. He lit camp fires in great long lines "representing an army corps at least and made a fine show in the valley." He felt Hugh Ewing's division was in danger, however, and intended to withdraw if Liddell attacked.

all to no purpose; hence, I had no recourse but to return to my command."

I was now tired of Bragg's purposeless plans and objects and requested a short leave of absence to visit an old friend not far from Atlanta. Being subject to recall, this leave would not put me beyond reach over 24 hours. He gave it with reluctance, and in three days I received a dispatch to return immediately.

I jumped into the first train to get to Ringgold, just in time to find the whole army in retreat from Mission Ridge. Hardee and Bragg came along and stopped a while to talk with me. The latter was so much depressed that I had not an unkind word at hand to reproach him for his unmitigated follies. He had been simply infatuated. As to Hardee, a soldier by education and nature, he was hardened to disasters. He bore them all with this cheerful philosophy. Calling me aside, he said, "I want to tell you a secret. I am engaged to be married to a most estimable young lady." I looked incredulous. "I am in earnest—goodby," and went away.[5]

The troops were now passing, but Hardee had told me before that Cleburne was in the rear, and I would have to wait until night. At last, the command made its appearance after daylight the next morning. I joined it and took position with the division in Ringgold Gap to check the enemy's pursuit.

We were soon on Taylor's Ridge, the place where I wanted Bragg to withdraw *in time* to fail Grant in his expectation of an overwhelming attack upon us. Our position was a fine one, and we held the enemy in check until Cleburne ordered us to fall back further. I thought there was no necessity just then for falling back. So long as we were doing damage to the enemy, let us hold on and thereto give ample time for all our trains to get beyond reach. But Cleburne thought otherwise and ordered further retreat.

After we had left, the enemy, feeling his way cautiously, came a mile or so within the Gap—then withdrew to Chattanooga. Cleburne did not wait to see this, but knew it shortly afterwards.

5. He was in earnest. Hardee and Mary Foreman Lewis were married January 13, 1864. They had met the previous September while Hardee was on detached service in Mississippi. A typical show of lightheartedness in the face of gloom characterized this man whom Liddell so admired. Even as his only son lay in his grave less than three weeks and his soldiers desolate in final defeat, Hardee treated his captors in 1865 with warmth and humor. He was at his best when the times were worst.

I had said nothing to him whatever on the subject after withdrawing from the Gap, but he voluntarily sought occasion to justify the step, saying that the enemy would have gotten around him it he had delayed longer.

This was clearly aimed at me, for what cause I could not discover. I was unconscious of being in his way. Some meddlesome persons had probably influenced him and I truly felt sorry, as we had never any cause for difference. I was more than anxious to aid him to do well. Perhaps my *supposed* friendship for Bragg had operated with him. He was evidently averse to my suggestions, even when he might add thereby to his own military reputation. His reticence and coolness were now unmistakable. It became necessary for me to put an end to all absurd wrangling by being perfectly indifferent to all that might be said.

Cleburne was resentful, exceedingly ambitious, friendly to those useful to him, until they stood in the way of his advancement. Then he did not hesitate to shake them off. He was brave and considerate in danger, but slow to conception. He was ever ready, however, to learn by the experience of others and closely applied the lessons he had received in actual service in the field. He studied well the business he had on hand always and applied his resources well. In his younger days, he had been a noncommissioned officer in the British Army. He was a southern Palladin and sacrificed his life in a later part of the struggle for the cause of his adoption. We have lost many such men in our unfortunate struggle.

Soon after getting to Tunnel Hill, I went to see Cleburne. He said to me that he had just had a quarrel with a citizen about some forage which his quartermaster had purchased from the man, who now demanded its restitution. He said, "I threatened to blow a hole thro' the fellow as big as a Barn Door before I could get rid of him."

To laugh at the absurdity of the threat was irresistible with me, at which Cleburne looked surprised and reiterated, "D--d, if I would not have done it."

I then observed, "You would have to *stretch* the man to accommodate him to so large a hole." He saw at once the bull he had made and relaxing the sternness of his features, joined in the laugh, fully restored to good humor.[6]

6. Patrick Cleburne, as was his habit, shared the success his division achieved at Missionary Ridge and Ringgold Gap. "General Liddell was absent on leave,

161

Of all men in this great Civil War, the greatest honor and consideration are due to the brave private. He had to endure *all* the hardships, all the digging, all the labor, without favor or affection. He served, for the greatest part of the time, without even the slightest allowance of pay. As an officer endeavoring to do my duty honorably, the hardship to *me* was nothing. Exposure with warm clothing never injured me, and personal discomfort never troubled me. In fact, the life of a soldier was so exciting and agreeable that it often recalled to mind the campaigns and acts of great warriors and made me think that war had too many *natural* charms for the peace of man.

At Tunnel Hill we halted. All the rest of the troops had passed on to Dalton and below there, my brigade the last—weary and hungry. I stopped at the door of a house which seemed to be still occupied to ask for something to eat. A lady came to the door and informed me with a mournful countenance that she could give me nothing and asked in return if "Liddell's Brigade had passed."

"No madam, it will stop here."

"Are you sure? For all the others passing by told me to look for the Yankees after that Brigade had passed."

I assured her that it had orders to stop here, that the enemy had come no further than Ringgold. "Well then," she said, "I am delighted. You shall have dinner—something—the best we have, since you will stay and defend us."

What mortal dread the poor people had of being insulted and stripped of everything by the Yankees and of their houses being burnt over their heads for having been Southern people vindicating their own inalienable rights, "life, liberty, and the pursuit of happiness." I have seen on the Red River in Louisiana and in Florida the houses of citizens, where women and children only lived, burned by the retreating forces of the enemy, and have been lighted on my march in pursuit by the blazing roofs. Thank the great God I have never seen one solitary instance of incendiarism committed by Confederate Soldiers. Inhuman Civil War! Who should seek such savage methods to injure those whose *only* harm was refusal to submit to the arbitrary rule of other states. The sins of the South were great, it is true. It is

but hearing of the fight returned and rendered me all the assistance in his power. He selected and reformed the new line after we withdrew from our first position."

now to be hoped that they have been all wiped out in the blood of her people so freely poured out in defense of her rights, now gone forever.

The enemy having ceased operations and withdrawn to Chattanooga, the army of Bragg was at last seated within "Taylor's Ridge" for the winter, to reorganize and prepare for another campaign the coming spring. Thus had occurred the outrageous disaster at Mission Ridge, which I had so often tried to get Bragg to avert, to save the *morale* of his men and to preserve the prestige of Chickamauga for more favorable chances.

The failure to push up without a moment's loss of time after the battle of Chickamauga, the subsequent quarrel with his officers causing apathy and demoralization among the men, the diversion of Longstreet with 12,000 men to Knoxville, the magnitude of the enemy's reinforcements, all combined to warn Bragg of his temerity in remaining so exposed at Mission Ridge. If only he had not been so infatuated with his projects.

The truth is that an expert commander of the Federals could have driven Bragg away from his position with less than half that number brought forward by Grant. Grant wanted, I suppose, to make a *sure* thing of it. I was told by either Hardee or Cleburne that Bragg called a council of war when he saw the attack coming, in which all the officers advised immediate retreat, except Breckinridge. He said that if they couldn't fight here with such advantage of position, they couldn't fight anywhere.

Unlucky advice from Breckinridge, who had forgotten that the enemy could easily flank the position by Rossville and that the enemy numbers were appalling to the men, looking on in excited suspense from the elevation of Mission Ridge. The odds of more than 4 to 1 were too unmistakable. Hence, the disinclination to fight was quite general. Hardee and Cleburne were on our right opposite to Sherman, who was repeatedly repulsed. But the left wing and center gave way precipitately and in the greatest confusion. In fact, from Cleburne's reports, there was very little fighting except where he and Sherman met near the railroad tunnel. Our total loss was but 4,000, at least four-fifths of which were prisoners taken while straggling away from Mission Ridge that night and the following day.

# CHAPTER XVI

## Transfer to Louisiana

Bragg sent for me to come to Dalton and informed me that the President had relieved him at his own request. The Army of Tennessee had generally behaved badly at Mission Ridge and he wanted someone to take the command who would inspire more confidence and afford better satisfaction to the officers.

"Here now," said he, "is Cheatham, drinking in Dalton and going around shaking his head when speaking of me, saying, 'I told you so.' But what more could be expected from a man whose occupation in Nashville before the war was to keep a drinking saloon and a stallion? I am disgusted with politicians for generals and executive officers. I have no dependence upon them. I shall retire to private station. I feel deeply distressed for our poor failing cause."

"I have sent for you in reference to your transfer to Louisiana.[1] I shall turn over the army to Hardee, and I don't like to deprive him of your services just as I am going away, without consent. See him, will you, and get it."

I answered, "Hardee will not give his consent. If you place this obstacle in the way, the matter ends here, for to you only had Mr. Davis given authority to make the transfer. Hence, it will never be done unless you choose to do it."

"At all events, go and see Hardee."

I did so and was most positively refused. Then I returned with the answer to Bragg.

---

1. Back in Louisiana, Liddell's slaves were on their way to Texas. Major General John B. Magruder issued a special order protecting Liddell's slaves, wagons and teams. While in Texas, Liddell's slaves would be used by the Confederate government feeding cattle at depots in Houston County. Special Orders No. 350, Headquarters, District of Texas, New Mexico, and Arizona, December 22, 1863, in Liddell Papers, LSU.

Bragg said, "General, you are needed in this army. I have respected your views and opinions more than any other officer in it."

I assured him that I was not aware of it. If my ordinary conversations with him elicited my views and opinions, I could not see that he was ever governed by them. I had never been, but once, called in his councils.

"I don't follow any views but my own. There are more ways than the council to obtain the views and opinions of those whom I respect, though I may not see proper to be governed by them. I want you, General, to stay and receive promotion."

"To show you, General, how little I regard promotion, I tell you now that if you were to offer me a Lieutenant General's commission with one hand and my transfer with the other, I shall quickly take the latter and go on my way satisfied."

"Well, I will have to gratify you and shall give you the order."

When the papers were furnished me, I called on Hardee and reported the fact.[2] He observed that it was all right. He did not blame me for wishing to go home, and he knew that my family was dear to me. We had poor encouragement for success with the army in Louisiana, but he was sorry to lose me.[3]

I returned late to my quarters at Tunnel Hill and made known the facts to some of my officers, purposing to leave the next evening. I soon disposed of my limited effects amongst my staff. I gave my special friend, Dr. McFadden, a buffalo robe given me by Dr. White of Louisiana, and divided the balance as far as they would go amongst the rest. None of them seemed pleased at my leaving.

It got rumored in the camps, and some officers and privates,

2. Bragg relieved Brigadier General Liddell from duty with the Army of Tennessee on December 2, 1863, and directed that he report to the Trans-Mississippi Department. As sometimes happened, someone forgot to inform the proper parties. On December 26 Adjutant General Samuel Cooper wrote Hardee (who succeeded Bragg in command of the Army of Tennessee) in some heat, that he had not been informed. "By whose order was this done?"

3. Another factor adding to Liddell's concern about home was the death of Willie. Although the circumstances are not known to the editor, Willie died in late December or early January. Marcellin Gillis paid for the "coffin and trimmings." Willie had been in Louisiana since the spring of 1863 and had visited his relatives at their plantation while recuperating.

Moses had headed home by this time, probably to transport the Negroes to Texas. Wade Young had been sent by Liddell, it appears, to Llanda to protect Mary and the children. Liddell's letters are full of warnings to be careful of deserters, stragglers, and robbers. "Tell Wade to lookout and take care of himself."

wishing to know the truth, visited me. I told them all the facts and that the command of the brigade now devolved upon Colonel D. C. Govan. He would soon be promoted, for he well deserved to have been long since for his services. My withdrawal was partly to pave the way. I had no heart to visit the camps or to call the men together to bid them God speed. I would go quietly, as I had come. Some expressed regrets, some were apparently incensed, many indifferent. I don't know the prevailing sentiment.

I do know, however, that I left the brigade unconscious of having made an enemy in it during the entire period of my service. I never had a dispute with anybody, nor was ever a private punished or court-martialed at my hands, for any offense whatever. What commander can say more than this? I had been treated with uniform respect, not only by my own men, but by the whole army. I often rode a mule through the camps and was permitted to pass without jeering or commenting upon my appearance, such was the general respect shown me. Yet I regret that I might have shown more energy and industry in looking after the comforts and wants of the men and exerting myself more laboriously for the good of the cause.

Cleburne had given a dinner for the officers of his command and of many of the other commands. Although our quarters were close by, he was careful not to invite me. I disregarded it so entirely that I went there to bid adieu to my brother officers and arranged with Hardee to stay with him overnight in Dalton on my way to Louisiana.

In Dalton, we had a long talk over the past and the future. I could see that Hardee was touched about something. Perhaps I had not shown him enough attention of late. At all events, I was unconscious of the slightest wrong or injustice, either to himself, Cleburne his friend, or anyone whatever. I could not understand what the matter was. I hoped, however, that some remark would explain or give some clue. I don't know to this day, and I expect that they themselves knew it to be all *smoke*.

Hardee was loath to part with me and offered me the place of Chief of Staff. I objected to the confinement of the office. He said that I should not be restricted to that business part of the office, which his Adjutant General would attend to. He wanted me with him as a friend to assist him with the army and that I should be free to follow my own suggestions.

At the same time, he informed me that he had telegraphed

to the President declining the command of the army. I then told him if he still held the command and I had failed to get across the Mississippi, or even before crossing could hear that my family were *not in want*, I would return and embrace the offer. I knew that I could get along with him, as a reasonable man, and I regarded him sincerely for his many kindnesses to me in the past.

We continued to converse upon the future prospects of the South, in the success of which his faith was on the wane. I remarked that if we could but keep up supplies we might prolong the war for forty years. This last vital want *was the difficulty*, and the Federals knew it well. They, therefore, bent all their energy and power to destroy Southern resources of subsistence and supplies of all kinds. They did not hesitate to seize or destroy the last hope of supply to the already destitute widow or orphan. This barbarous method of conducting war had been overlooked as obsolete or only a relic of barbarism. Otherwise, I cannot but believe that stronger efforts would have been made, by concentration of forces, to keep the war in the border states.

Both Bragg and Hardee gave me friendly and complimentary letters to General E. Kirby Smith. Upon parting with Hardee, I took occasion to congratulate him upon his approaching marriage with Miss Mary Foreman Lewis of Alabama, wishing him happiness, etc. But imagine my surprise when he assured me it was all a joke, notwithstanding his positive assurance to me, voluntary at that, at Ringgold. But *he did* marry the lady, that winter!

Leaving Dalton early in the morning for Rome, I had to pass through the camps and was recognized by Colonel Brantley of Walthall's Brigade, afterwards promoted to general.[4] Brantley rapidly rode forward to meet me, with pleasure expressed in his open, generous face. He invited me to go to his camp. I told him I was on my way to Louisiana, transferred to the West. "Good God, I am sorry for it. Are you correct?" I assured him of the fact. His countenance fell at once. He seemed disappointed and expressed his regrets pointedly.

---

4. William Felix Brantley (1830-1870). This Mississippi brigadier inspired respect in the ranks. A young enlisted man in the Army of Tennessee reported, "We have discipline now with a vengeance. Col. Brantley is the tightest man I ever saw. He enforces the law in every instance. Gen. Bragg is a lenient man to him, but it suits me very well and the beauty of it is that he comes down on the officers first." J. W. Ward to Father, March 28, 1863. Ward Letters, Emory University Library.

I was sensitively struck at the evidence of feeling. I had not known him before his brigade served under me. We parted with the silent thoughts of friends who cannot penetrate the gloom of the future and with the sad foreboding that evil days will befall our country ere we meet again.

Further on, I came to the camp of W. H. T. Walker. He manifested great delight at seeing me. Upon dismounting to stay a few moments with him, I told him where I was going. He seemed shocked, expressed his regret most feelingly, not sparing emphatic oaths. He commented severely upon the sad state of affairs that caused the invasion of his state (Georgia). I had never before appreciated Walker's kindly feelings. Under a rough exterior and brusque mannerism, there was a large heart. A truer man and brave, existed not in the army. He loved his state and died by its cause. He was the military teacher of those leaders who now invaded his country and impoverished his family and his people. I knew the man more thoroughly in these few moments of feeling than I had ever been able to learn in all my former associations.

I was at Rome before nightfall and the next night at Jacksonville, Alabama, where I took the railroad to Talladega and Selma. Riding all this time in silence (my servant only following), my thoughts naturally fell into the usual train of thought obtaining with me for the past three years: *What can we do in our existing condition to improve public affairs?*

The terminus of the railroad at Jacksonville was intended to have been at Ringgold or Dalton. The distance was not exceeding, I think, sixty miles. Why could we not have our base of operations supported by both these roads, enabling us to shift to either one at pleasure, as the movements of an enemy moving between these points indicated the proper course for us? At the same time, if the enemy should attempt a march directly southward from Chattanooga, we could strike him nearly at right angles from the east or the west, on whichever side we might happen to be in position. The practical utility of the tactical movement was very clear. The chances and means of procuring supplies, available from Talladega and Selma, were certainly equal to those from Marietta and Atlanta.

Then why not use both railroads and avail ourselves of all chances for success? With our line of operations being nearly at right angles to the enemy's line, we could retard and confuse his offensive plans. If we compelled him to divide to occupy both roads, a happy concentration against one of the fractions might result to our great advantage. If, however, the enemy refused to divide, he could not march southward. Our forces would be always threatening his communications. This was so plain and feasible that I was astonished no effort was ever made to put it to practical effect.

As soon as it occurred to me, at Jacksonville, I deliberated upon the propriety of calling it to Hardee's attention. But then it was so plain as to be unmistakable. A general's business is to know all the topographical features and railroad communications of the country in which he operates. Hence, it was superfluous on my part and was dismissed from further thought until the following spring. Then the marches of Sherman southward proved to me that this matter was either rejected if known or overlooked entirely. Somehow I understood that General Polk wanted to establish himself and his immediate command on the Jacksonville base, while Johnson took the Dalton Base. This would not do, as separation on our part (so fatal heretofore) would be again involved, whereas concentration meant success for our army.

On getting to Meridian, Mississippi, I went to see General J. E. Johnston whom I found to be very affable and communicative. He probably knew me by the friendly representations of my old classmate, General Mackall, who, however, was not with him at this time. General Johnston was exceedingly bitter about the President in reference to the turn of affairs between himself and General John C. Pemberton. The latter he seemed to regard with no other feeling than that of an instrument of the President to strike at him. He spoke of the willful disobedience of his orders by Pemberton, as to lead me to the inference that it was premeditated.

I may be possibly at fault in this inference, but such from the tenor of his remarks were my impressions. He was evidently fortifying his actions from the turn that events had taken *after* the facts. I thought General Johnston showed a good deal of adroitness in putting the best construction upon his own views, stretching them naturally to suit results. I was sorry to see it in a man for whom I had formed so high an opinion. I suggested the probability of his being required to take the command of the Tennessee army at Dalton, since Hardee had declined it. He quickly replied, "No, Mr. Davis will not place me in any position where there is any chance or possibility of success."

I had never conceived before the extent of the breach between them until hearing this expression from him. I afterwards mentioned it to one of his staff, who said that he hoped the General would not get this command if he entertained such feeling.

In my allusion to Hardee being retained in command, he said, "Hardee likes the show of war, but dislikes its labors and responsibilities." I thought there was truthfulness in this remark, as Hardee, who was not self-confident, seemed to shun the weight of responsibility. I believe he was not intended by nature to be a great leader. I alluded to Hardee's wish to make me Chief of Staff. The General said that I did well not to take it, inasmuch as it was a thankless office and one very convenient to attach blame for failure, whilst no credit was allowed for success. My answer was that I cared nothing for that if I could only serve the cause.

We parted very friendly; my impression of him was that he was an able, but shrewd man. He was cautious in everything, in action and expression, until this virtue which had been tried to its full stretch lost its weight. Then he at once became bold and uncompromising. This was the moment that he seemed to watch and wait for. It was the Yankee part of his character mixed with a southern chivalry.

I cannot help the impression if he had been allowed to take his *own* time and method, he would have either been successful or he would at least have kept up his army in condition to strike any time. He certainly would have retarded and disconcerted Sherman's plans. Then Johnston may have assumed the other phase of his character and fought with the obstinacy that good sense sometimes justified for good results. He was clearly Fabian in strategic policy—wary but determined. But the impatience of the President and of the times interfered to prevent the exercise of this man's faculties. His untimely removal from command brought on disaster and ruin.

When I reached Jackson, Mississippi, I was astonished at the change. It was at least half burnt up by Grant's forces. In many places, the chimneys alone indicated the locality of habitations, both in town and country. The following winter, Sherman's raid nearly finished what remained, leaving behind him the mark of his traces that a century will hardly efface. Sherman assuredly determined to fix his name in the memory of the people.

At Port Gibson, I found the crossing of the Mississippi River obstructed by the presence and plundering operations of what was called the Marine Brigade of Federal licensed thieves. This obstacle turned my steps to Woodville, further south, and thence to Tunica. There at midnight I succeeded in swimming my horse and mule by the side of a small ferryboat. The water was so cold that my horse was chilled. I attempted to relieve him by keeping him on the move the remainder of the night. It took him nearly six months to get over this cold bath and exertion of swimming.

Near the Atchafalaya crossing I met with a division of Major General John G. Walker's infantry. A pontoon had been thrown across that outlet of the Mississippi River, which enabled the troops to operate against the Federal forces near Morganza.

My road now lay in the river track of Bank's Army on its return from Alexandria on the Red River. The marks and ravages of war were plainly visible on every side. The standing chimneys and wasted plantations were so many evidences of the energy of this miserable apology of a Federal general. In preservation of the union which he once so detested he originated the expression "Let the Union slide" than remain longer in connection with the South—notwithstanding the constitution and laws.

This is the wretch of Yankee Puritanical proclivities, who gloated, like Butler, over the desolation he could cause amongst an honorable people to whose moral standard he well knew God never intended him to reach. So debased at the close of the war was he in New Orleans, that his brother officers felt contaminated by even official association.

In my youthful days (1836), I had traveled through the Bayou De Glaize section while it was yet a cane brake, almost impenetrable, having here and there at wide intervals small improvements. It had been subsequently all opened and improved with large cotton plantations—level and beautiful for their order and regularity of cultivation.

How changed the scene now! Who could have imagined then that the desolation of war would ever reach this secluded corner?

The next day, after passing Avoyelles Parish, I reached Fort De Russy, where I saw the colonel of that name superintending the works. Colonel Lewis G. De Russy had been elected colonel of the 2nd Louisiana Regiment, had served a short time in Virginia, but finding his brother directly opposed to him there on the Federal side, resigned and returned to Louisiana, taking charge of the works named for him.

171

The following evening I succeeded in getting to my home on the Black River. It is a tributary of the Red River from Arkansas, changing its name to Ouachita, flowing almost directly southward and navigable for many hundred miles above its mouth.

I had not seen my family for two years and had not heard from them for over a year. I was, therefore, agreeably surprised to find them at home and doing well in health. The place was badly dilapidated from visits of Yankees and plunderers, and most of the Negroes had been sent to Texas for security. Enough remained to support the plantation if the products of their labor could only be secured from seizure by both sides in the war.

Our own side were equally eager to plunder people living on the borders. They disregarded the helpless condition of women and children, whose male protectors were among the first to go to the front in Virginia and Tennessee. These *vile* men remained behind to avoid the dangers of war. To have things made easy, they sought this opportunity to destroy the property and break up the families of those whose interests they should have felt every sense of honor to protect. Nothing better was looked for from the enemy than injury, but from soldiers pretending to be friends, to out-Herod the Yankees in doing injury was shocking beyond measure.[5]

I remained with my family but a few days, in which time I learned that one Lieutenant Thomas O. Selridge, U. S. Navy, had visited the place the preceding spring with his gunboat fleet, but had refrained from doing injury to it. He, however, had burnt up the mill of a poor citizen (Captain Skinner) at Trinity.

On the first of January, 1864, I got to Shreveport and reported to Lieutenant General E. Kirby Smith. He received me very cordially but declined to allow me to return to Hardee in Georgia, which, upon realizing the sad state of affairs in Louisiana, I was particularly anxious to do. Demoralization pervaded everybody, and confusion generally prevailed in the administration, both civil and military.

General Smith ordered me to report to General Richard Taylor at Alexandria, Louisiana, for assignment to duty in the subdistrict

5. Major General Richard Taylor, commanding the District of West Louisiana, desperately wanted to protect citizens against the savagery of the outlaws roaming the countryside. (Quantrill's men, Jayhawkers, and mixed groups of criminals). He dispatched cavalry against them whenever possible. When they took to the swamps he had units pursue with dogs. Liddell himself would be busy fighting the outlaws when time and men could be spared.

of North Louisiana, and I went there a few days afterwards to receive his instructions. I found Taylor very self-important and self-opinionated in his general expression of men and things. He required me to establish myself at Monroe on the Ouachita in North Louisiana, and told me, somewhat sneeringly, that he would give me a small regiment of cavalry, commanded by one Colonel W. H. Harrison. I could add to the same two battalions in process of organization, and raise this command to a small brigade. There was a brigade of infantry belonging to H. W. Allen, now governor of the state, which when exchanged would be placed under my authority. As this was quite uncertain, it would not do to depend upon for the present, at least. Small business, I thought truly. Nevertheless, there was no help for it. I went to Monroe about the 25th of January to take command of whatever I might find.[6]

I found certainly demoralization on every side, but went to work patiently and increased my little cavalry concern to about seven hundred men.[7] They were chiefly deserters from the armies of Virginia and Tennessee, now dodging conscription by entering the cavalry. They regarded lightly the honor of serving in our great armies in the East where danger added to reputation. Now these men were desirous of legalized plunder, with the smallest possible amount of service or danger to themselves. A small battery of two light pieces belonged to this command. With all of this, I was required to guard and protect a line extending from the mouth of Red River to the Arkansas Line—something like 120 miles, at least.[8]

6. Brig. Gen. Alfred Mouton's infantry division operated in North Louisiana, but did not fall under Liddell's command. Taylor hoped that Liddell would swell his command to brigade size by forcing paroled Confederate soldiers into camp.
7. Edmund Kirby Smith sent Liddell to Taylor armed with complimentary letters from Bragg and Hardee. ". . . So gallant a soldier in that region might be of great service at this time, and also lessen to some extent your own responsibilities." OR, I, 34 (2), 829.

To fulfill these responsibilities, Richard Taylor had dispersed his tiny army across upper Louisiana. Alfred Mouton's division held the area near Monroe; Polignac occupied Harrisonburg with his brigade, while Liddell recruited a force to operate further north.

The nucleus of Liddell's command was Col. Harrison's cavalry regiment. Taylor hoped Liddell would quickly fatten up this unit. Taylor probed everywhere for more men and horses. North Louisiana, infested with draft dodgers and deserters, remained only nominally under the control of the Confederate government.
8. Lawlessness prevailed in northeastern Louisiana, where the Jayhawkers were particularly active. Liddell sent his men to clear them out. "Bob Taliaferro, leading a company of desperadoes, was intercepted near Black River, and

Constant orders were received by me from Taylor to seize property in horses and mules on the Mississippi plantations. Not satisfied with the supply obtained from this source, orders were also received to impress horses from citizens on the west side of the Ouachita and within our lines.[9] All these abitrary proceedings depressed the people greatly and created unmistakable dissatisfaction. I saw that the military restrictions on this side of the Mississippi exceeded those of the other greatly, and hence greater demoralization and discontent prevailed. It was a sort of "much or nothing" business—and want must follow so many exactions, before long. I heard new reports of Major General Taylor's tyranny described with horror. They could see no hope of redress for wrong or immunity from his arbitrary will.

It was not long before I received a letter from a Colonel W. A. Broadwell of General Smith's staff to know my opinion as to the disposition of the cotton on the Ouachita. I replied in substance,

Tax it twenty cents per pound. Let it go to parties authorized to come in the lines for the purpose—parties known to be hostile—who would manage to carry it through the Yankee lines in some way. Then the people should have something to live by. It was hard to strip them of everything. The Confederate Government would be benefited by the proceeds of the tax, in procuring all necessary supplies, which had *at last* to come through Yankee sources. Why wantonly throw away that which serves both people and Government?

These views did not meet the cupidity of the Cotton Bureau, which seemed inclined to the absorption of all this interest for selfish purposes, though suspected and condemned by all others. The matter therefore was passed over, and I heard no more in reference to the disposition of the cotton except to *burn it*. This bureau had the contract for all the cotton in Louisiana, Arkansas, and Texas. What wisdom could there be in destroying that which was useful to us, without being of decided advantage to the enemy.

after a running fight and loss of eleven men, Taliaferro's gang scattered into the swamp." Taliaferro had plundered Llanda itself in January. Winter, C. W., *Civil War in Louisiana*, p. 387.
9. Taylor urged Liddell to break up the enemy's "Government plantations." (Abandoned plantations rented to agents of the U. S. Treasury Department.) "Secure the negroes and teams for our own use." *OR*, I, 34 (2), 953-956.

About the 20th of February, I went with Major H. T. Douglas of the Engineer Corps to Trinity (near my home) where it was proposed to construct some isolated parks for heavy artillery.[10] The place is about thirty miles from Natchez, directly west, and is accessible at ordinary stages of water, by the Black River which is a continuation of the Ouachita River, flowing south from Arkansas. The position so convenient for approach both by land and water rendered the construction of the proposed works open to interruption and extremely hazardous.

Major Douglas was instructed to consult with me but not to be governed by me. I used every argument and persuasion with him, and reduced it all to the point, "Are these positions expected to be isolated and unsupported." He agreed to leave the question to Major General Taylor.

Major Douglas, finding his own views sustained by Taylor, began and pushed forward the construction without further reference or notice of my opinions or wishes. My recourse now was to General E. Kirby Smith. I candidly stated that such works could not be held long enough to do any good. I represented that the engineer who insisted upon putting them up ought to be required to stay in them like Tattleben,[11] and prove their usefulness. I also told Major Douglas himself that I would not give him more than two hours to hold the place when attacked.

I was overruled in the whole thing. Major General Taylor sent Brigadier General Polignac's Brigade[12] of General Alfred Mou-

10. Trinity was within shouting distance of Mary M. Liddell and the family at Llanda. Liddell, however, made his headquarters at Columbia. There he worried about his family and urged Mary to leave. Marcellin Gillis, with Liddell, observed, ". . . but I hardly think that Mrs. Liddell will consent to it."

    By early March, Judge had returned from Texas, but the news was bad. Even there property and lives were endangered. "Probably it is best for you to remain at Llanda. Remain closely at home," "seek no cause and create no trouble," "be very circumspect in language that might give excuse to our enemies." "If we lose I shall be in exile. Be cheerful, though. Others suffer worse than we. Keep stores in the main house. Keep someone close by. Congregate for safety. Don't let Judge stay in Llanda. It's dangerous for him if arrested." St. John R. Liddell to Mary M. Liddell, March 7, 1864. Liddell Papers, LSU; Marcellin Gillis to Carolina Gillis, February 25, 1864, Gillis Papers, SHC.

11. This editor ruined an otherwise delightful evening at a major library trying to discover the meaning of Tattleben. In the process of failing, he wore out two feverish reference librarians.

12. Camille Armand Jules Marie, Prince de Polignac (1832-1913). This prominent and well-educated Frenchman joined the Confederacy in July, 1861. Because of his extensive military background and his impressive intelligence, he rose

175

ton's command to cover the working party of Negroes and to protect the government property, which would certainly be exposed. All haste possible was used. The guns were brought down on steamboats from Fort Beauregard to Harrisonburg and landed close at hand for mounting with dispatch.

It so happened at that time, March 2nd, I visited my family living a short distance below the site of this proposed fortification. Previously at the desire of Polignac I had given him three or four companies of cavalry to scout for him, to assist in picketing the approaches from Natchez, and to watch the movement of the gunboats in the river below. I was at home but a few hours when some reliable scouts gave me the information that six gunboats were coming up the river and would soon be at Trinity.[13]

I went at once to see Polignac. He was not under my control, having been specially excepted by Taylor in his instructions to me. Therefore I could only assist by voluntary council and advice. I met him, luckily, coming to see me, but he altogether discredited the report of the cavalry scouts, who had deceived him so often. But whilst talking with me, he was interrupted by the unmistakable sound of heavy artillery from the gunboat fleet in the bend below.

Polignac was now convinced, but unprepared for their reception. He hastened back to make up for lost time. Meanwhile the fleet of six gunboats and some tenders soon appeared off the village. They drove him from the place, and then proceeded up the river. This was late in the evening. Nevertheless, Polignac pushed to meet them with his brigade at Harrisonburg fifteen miles distant. The gunboats had anchored, however, for the night about halfway between the villages to wait for morning. This gave Polignac ample time to make all his dispositions.

The next morning early I proposed to him to visit his position in good time to have everything ready, but he delayed from one

to major general by April 1864. He is remembered principally for his service in the Trans-Mississippi. The Franco-Prussian War gave Polignac a second chance and he succeeded, commanding a French division.

13. When Federal gunboats prowled near the plantation of Francis D. Richardson, he took action.

"He provided Northern soldiers with what they called 'one of their best laughs' when he piled his pontoon bridge high with hay, set it afire and let it drift down the bayou in the hope that it would ignite the advancing Federal gunboats. But the Yankees merely fended the burning bridge away from their vessel with long poles, until the bridge itself had been consumed by the flames."

cause and another. When we arrived on the ground, the boats were just rounding the bend in sight and in full range—leaving him only a few hasty moments to arrange his lines. This compelled him to withdraw under cover of the ravines in his rear.

Polignac's movement was seen by the officer (Captain Ramsey) commanding the Union fleet and induced him to land a party. They burned up part of the town next to the river. It is useless to deny this fact, for there were other eyewitnesses than myself.

The gunboats now pretended to go up the river further still, but finding the Catahoula shoals impassable, returned. I proposed to Polignac now to send immediately back to Trinity and remove the heavy ordinance and material before the fleet could get there by morning, but he declined doing so, saying with a shrug of his shoulders, "The cavalry will have to attend to that." At the same time, he complained of their inefficiency, which I thought was so much the greater reason for his sending a working party from his own command. Nothing was done, and by daylight on March 4 the gunboats returned to Trinity. They took the guns on their boats, burned all the carriages, etc., and then proceeded down the river unmolested.

Thus had Polignac utterly failed in the special object he had been sent to do, that is the protection of the works and guns. To my utter astonishment, a short time afterwards, Major General Taylor came out in a glowing, laudatory address to the troops under Polignac's command, for effectually driving away this fleet from Trinity and Harrisonburg. He said nothing, however, about the loss sustained in government war material.

This shows how easy it was for a designing commander to put the best construction upon that for which he himself is open to censure for not opposing, if not approving. Taylor knew that he had to bear some portion of blame in this matter, hence he took this course to ignore everything but the bravery of his own troops in the transaction. I heard, however, that he sought at last to cast censure upon Major Douglas, the engineer of the works. If so, why did he not sustain me in my opposition to these works? Was not his reticence of opinion direct acquiescence? When he stated or replied to the engineer that the works would have to be *isolated*, did he not perceive that he supported their construction and must share the blame with him of failure or loss? But Taylor was brother-in-law to the President. He could take responsibilities with impunity to advance his own interests and reputation.

A week later reports reached us of Major General W. T. Sherman's raid upon Jackson and Meridian, Mississippi. Directly upon the heels of this trouble followed reports of the intended raid of Major General Nathaniel P. Banks up the Red River Country. For greater convenience I moved my quarters to Columbia, and on the 13th received reports of the enemy's intention to move upon Shreveport in two columns. One from Little Rock, Arkansas, would be under Major General Frederick Steele and the other up the Red River under Major General Banks. Simultaneously, they were to converge upon Shreveport.

Opportunity to concentrate upon these detachments was now presented. General Smith wrote me in cypher that all of General Sterling Price's command except Fagan's brigade was ordered to join Taylor at Natchitoches, to burn all the cotton east of the Ouachita and then cooperate with the general movement of his troops.

On the first of April I moved my command consisting of Harrison's little brigade of cavalry. They numbered about six hundred effective at the outset, but a portion deserted on the way and returned to their homes for the purposes of plundering and marauding. I had no time, or spare men to send after them. Therefore I was compelled to put off the arrest and punishment that these men deserved. Besides this small force, I had two sections of six-pounders that were available for field service.

I had a slight engagement with the enemy at Campti on Red River on April 6, 1864, with a part of this command. From this point up to the mouth of Loggy Bayou I damaged the gunboats and transports at every opportunity with the sharpshooters of two sections of artillery.

When the fleet reached Loggy Bayou they found their further progress barred by a sunken boat in the channel. While waiting and working to remove it, information reached them from Banks, who had moved some distance out from the river on the south side with the main body of his army, to return to Grand Ecore, as he had met with repulses at Mansfield and Pleasant Hill.

Banks now withdrew to Natchitoches and Grand Ecore, on the banks of the Red River, with all his forces. There, although fortifying his position, he seemed undecided what further steps to take. In fact, the check he had met with had greatly demoralized him. He contemplated (as reported to me by spies) leaving the fleet to take care of itself and retreating directly across the country from Grand Ecore to the Ouachita River. Pontoons were thrown across the Red River, as if such was his purpose. He was now some seventy-five or eighty miles above Alexandria by land and one hundred miles by water. The Red River was very low and still falling, and the gunboats and transports were grounding at all the shoals.

My little force again kept up a constant fire upon the boats now going back to Grand Ecore. At Bordelon's Point my two sections of artillery stopped the whole fleet for a half a day. Little damage, however, could be done with small arms and four small pieces against ironclads. They protected the transports at regular intervals the whole way descending the river. Citizens' houses were burned wherever they could land.

Perceiving the condition, it occurred to me that Taylor could force Banks to retreat in the way most advantageous for our purposes. Taylor should move rapidly to Alexandria, and occupy that place with his whole infantry force, leaving his large cavalry force for outside work. Such action would give us all of Banks' supplies at Alexandria. It would cut off all Banks' reinforcements coming up the river. All must end in our capturing or destroying the fleet and disintegrating Banks' army. The plan was so simple, and safe, that I expected every moment to receive orders indicating it. I so spoke to the officers of my staff.

Time was valuable. Four days had elapsed; perhaps Taylor had overlooked it. I hesitated to write to him, fearing that he would prove to be another Van Dorn in self-consequence. My duty and the officers to whom I had mentioned the movement urged me not to hesitate to make it known, and having occasion to write to him on other matters, I sought the opportunity to put the idea in his head. On the 20th of April, by way of suggestion in a separate paragraph, I dispatched it. Much time had already been lost. Before this we might have been already in possession of Alexandria.

I received orders to bring two twenty-pounders from the Ouachita to be drawn by oxen a distance of at least 100 miles over the only practicable road, and to send my two six-pounders to Arkansas. Thus I had now nothing but the small cavalry command, not a full regiment by any means in strength. The transports had been protected on the sides by barricades of

179

thick planks and other material. Swivels and small howitzers were mounted on the hurricane decks, which brought the range of their guns just above the level of the banks, allowing free sweep to cannister and grape.

Receiving no reply from General Taylor to my suggestions, after the lapse of several days, I gave up the matter and determined to make a sudden raid from Pineville opposite to Alexandria. Riding day and night for thirty-six hours, I reached the place just at 7:00 a.m., April 24th. I captured it, killing and wounding the enemy found there, driving some across the river. Then my command was fired at with a few rounds of artillery from the Alexandria side. But this battery was suddenly withdrawn to the rear of the town as it was imagined that there must be a cooperating force from Taylor's side of the river. The gunboats and transports were all tied up on the Alexandria side out of reach, where also were the stores of the enemy. The confusion and panic was great. We could do nothing more, however, having no means of crossing. In an hour or so, I withdrew the command, unmolested. I had done all or more than expected, besides ascertaining the fact of how easily Taylor could have taken and secured the place while Banks was above.[14] Coming away, I received a letter from Taylor, dated April 25th, that he was going to *drive* the enemy *into* Alexandria and expected to drive *him out* of it.

This I suppose was intended as an answer to my suggestions, and might be considered cool contempt for a man who was trying his best to help him. Taylor had bitterly complained to the world that General Smith had taken away his troops, or a portion of them, at a critical period. Enough still remained to him, however, as he wrote me, to drive the enemy *into* and *out* of Alexandria. If he could *drive the enemy before him*, what need had he for more? Then why not by a fortunate stroke of strategy confuse Banks and force him to cross the country to the Ouachita, destroy his gunboats and leave them to our capture?

In conversation with General E. Kirby Smith, at the close of the war, he said that some step of the kind I mentioned was intended, in which case the result would have been very disastrous to the Federal Army and Navy. But Taylor's wisdom led him to drive them, and afforded them time to reach their supplies

14. Taylor complimented Liddell on his good work. He considered Liddell's command "raw levies," and their success was all the more gratifying.

and get reinforcements from below by the river. All might have been prevented by timely seizure of Alexandria and holding the falls. When Taylor came to his senses it was too late, and his attempts to invest them from below Alexandria amounted to nothing. As soon as Banks was ready he moved, brushing Taylor aside, and safely withdrawing to the mouth of Red River, with very little loss.

In all military operations, if the proper moment to execute plans is not seized, the attempt becomes hardly short of folly. General Smith's design was to draw Banks near enough to him at Shreveport that he might be enabled to concentrate upon him, and ruin his chances for safe retreat. Generals Mouton and Thomas Green, I have been credibly informed, precipitated the fight at Mansfield, drawing Taylor into it when it became unavoidable. The success was simply a lucky *accident*. Price's troops now joined Taylor and his elation induced him to try it again the next day. The attempt met with less success and would have proven disastrous, but for the lucky timidity and *demoralization* of Banks, who ordered his forces to withdraw too soon. Thus, chance governed everything here.

General Smith, it is clear, should have kept his forces together and pushed these successes, and will always be censured for this neglect. But this does not clear Taylor, who now with a smaller force had a splendid opportunity to exercise his strategy and accomplish incredible results. The capture of the gunboat fleet, and all the transports in Red River, would have immortalized him. What might not have been the consequence? The Mississippi River would have again reverted to us, while Taylor's army could have crossed and united with Johnson to repel Sherman. The reflecting and intelligent reader, acquainted with the geography and topography of the Red River country where Banks' operations occurred, must see at a glance the feasibility of that which I have written.

Unfortunately for the Confederates, General Taylor was carried away by childish elation and vain glory. As he was incapable of definite plans, he would give way to paroxysms of passionate abuse of his officers for not repairing faults which he himself had committed. It was soon made apparent that my temerity in presuming to send him a suggestion had incurred his enmity. From this time, he never ceased to find fault with everything I did. Regardless of my reports of facts, he preferred the reports of the ignorant couriers between us, picked up by the way from stragglers.

I was now constantly receiving offensive communications from him. No statement would satisfy him, but I had determined to bear with his malice and frenzy until the conclusion of the campaign.

The raid on Pineville had annoyed Banks to such extent that he sent one of his Adjutant Generals, with Brigadier General Kilby Smith in command of a brigade of infantry and one of cavalry, having a full battery to each, to effect my capture, or destruction. I had but five hundred seventy men which were necessarily scattered in detachments: scouting, skirmishing, picketing, or guarding innumerable roads. Hence I could scarcely keep more than two hundred fifty men with me at a time. The enemy came out at nightfall, and the enemy brigade of cavalry with its battery made a wide circuit (a thing very easily done with the pine woods guides who had deserted to them), and succeeded in getting in my rear, about four miles distant, and then halted for daylight.

I found out the facts through a courier who had accidently discovered them without being himself perceived. I was satisfied that they would attempt my capture in my camp by daylight. I therefore moved quietly off after midnight with my command and gained their rear just about the time they had reached my camp in the morning. I attacked them instead of being attacked. This so confused them that after slight resistance they gave way in haste, and left us the field. The infantry was some four miles nearer Alexandria. The design was to enclose me between them, each brigade numbering probably four times my force. This little affair occurred on Hadnot's branch of the Rigolets De Baudeau.[15]

If they had boldly pushed on me, I am satisfied they could have run over me and have broken up my command. It was simply a matter *chance,* as were all the fights on Red River during this whole campaign. Banks' Adjutant General, alluded to above, was

15. Rigolets De Baudeau caused quite a "little affair" for Liddell's poor editor. Leaving two disillusioned and exhausted reference librarians behind him, the editor abandoned the Troy Middleton Library at closing hour one Saturday, declaring that two hours' work by three people for one footnote is enough. His best guess is that, by repeatedly transcribing, Rigolets De Baudeau popped up in place of Rigolet de Bon Dieu. The latter, an arm of the Red River, extends from a point about two miles below Grand Ecore to Colfax, where it rejoins the Red.

captured during the night while making the necessary dispositions to bring up the infantry. He told me all the plans, in which he said but for his unlucky capture they would have succeeded. Banks' army and fleet had all arrived at Alexandria—*driven!* by Taylor!, possibly, before the 1st of May. They were busily engaged in building a dam, or rather a series of jutting dams on opposite sides of the river at the falls. The effect of this would concentrate the water into a narrow channel, thus enabling them to raise the water and float all the boats over the shoals.

Banks' whole army was well in hand at Alexandria. A large working party of soldiers (over four thousand men) were engaged in constructing these dams, with arms at hand. These workers were guarded by troops on both sides of the river, all were under cover of the gunboats.

Taylor sent me an order that my failure to "harass the enemy at Pineville and their works on the falls" "would necessitate a change in the command." I had already attempted this business with my handful of men, but now thought it would avail very little to sacrifice them. Taylor himself had signally failed on his side of the river. He was equally, if not more convenient to the enemy's works, with his whole force of six thousand infantry and some fifteen thousand cavalry, and at least fifty pieces of artillery.

I had no available artillery whatever. That which I started with, Taylor had himself sent to Price in Arkansas. The battery of two twenty-four pounders drawn by oxen from the Ouachita had not yet come up. I think that Taylor was at last convinced that he had foolishly thrown away, for lack of good common sense, all his chances. He now had to exercise all his cunning to find some one to bear the blame, since all further efforts by himself were about to prove futile.

Our correspondence became unpleasant and I requested to be relieved. He, meantime, again changed his orders without reference to the previous one which conveyed an insulting threat and was imperative and conflicted with the one last sent, and ordered me to go below Alexandria. I however, obeyed the last, wholly unable to reconcile these contradictions. Fortunately, soon after, I was relieved from the command, as I had requested. I was pleased at the prospect of getting rid of this wretchedly mismanaged business under the guidance of a foolish man. I had long foreseen that no good would come of it, while not much credit would be attached to those who figured in it.

Shortly after this, I reported to General E. K. Smith at Shreveport for orders, and submitted to him for inspection all of Taylor's contradictory orders, in many instances exhibiting childishness and absurdities unbecoming an officer who pretended to be a leader of an army. He looked over several of the papers carefully, then threw them down abruptly on the table before him, saying, "General Taylor's mind is affected from the paralysis he had some years since, and is hardly responsible."

"Then, General, he should not be in such a place, when so much is at stake for others. I will serve no more under such a man. He has not even ability enough to make one bear with, or overlook, his intolerable conduct."

General Smith still continued to apologize for and mitigate Taylor's follies, evidently influenced by the kindest feelings. He never gave me the slightest intimation of difference between them, though it had not only been common rumor but I had indications of misunderstandings from official endorsements of papers forwarded by me.[16]

However, be this as it may, Taylor's paralysis made his conduct and arrogance become at last so intolerable to General Smith that he ordered him under arrest to Natchitoches to await the action of the President, his brother-in-law.[17] The fact is, Taylor never would have reached his position, except by the favor and determination of Mr. Davis. Mr. Davis gave him the Louisiana Brigade in Virginia, notwithstanding their outspoken objections. They preferred General W. H. T. Walker of Georgia for their commander. Mr. Davis persisted, however, and the brigade submitted reluctantly. Taylor pocketed all sense of honor in taking the command, under the circumstances. He took the brigade over men who were *his superiors* in good sense, and in true patriotism. They had preceded him in the field, and were more highly regarded at home.

16. Richard Taylor in his memoirs admits Liddell lacked artillery and sufficient force to inflict serious damage, and manages to treat Liddell evenly. The larger blame for the failure of the Taylor campaign must be placed squarely on Edmund Kirby Smith. "In all ages since the establishment of the Assyrian monarchy, no commander has possessed equal power to destroy a cause. . . . The opportunity of striking a blow decisive of the war was afforded." *Destruction and Reconstruction*, pp. 229-230. Red River historians have tended to support Taylor.
17. Smith relieved Taylor on June 10, 1864, and ordered him to remain at Natchitoches until President Davis could learn about the situation. Davis reassigned Taylor in the middle of July. Liddell could not escape Taylor, as we shall see.

General Smith now gave me thirty days to look after the affairs of my family. Upon the expiration of this time, he told me that he would place me in command of all West Louisiana (Taylor's district), to which I demurred, but he overruled all my objections and had determined upon it.[18] In the meantime, he left Shreveport to look after affairs in the interior of Texas.

At Shreveport I met with my old friend, Dr. D. W. Yandell, who had been banished from General Johnston's staff for his letter to Dr. Johnson of General Hardee's staff. He had not lost any of his good spirits, was now Medical Director of the Department, and spoke unreservedly of men and affairs. He told me that he had never met with a purer or more conscientious man than E. Kirby Smith, or a more ambitious and self-important one than R. Taylor. Dr. Smith, Chief Surgeon on Kirby Smith's staff, told me that Taylor, so far from being opposed to the troops being taken away from him after the Pleasant Hill affair, wanted to take the command of the troops going to attack Steele, in Arkansas. He only "cut up" when General Smith, refused to give him the command.

He also said that when Kirby Smith and staff got to Pleasant Hill in the evening, Taylor's army was in miserably confused retreat. General Smith saw the condition of affairs, and rode to Polignac whose division had not yet left the field, and instructed him to "maintain his place and tomorrow his should be the post of honor." Polignac responded that he had been ordered by Taylor to withdraw and cover the retreat, but General Smith, as Taylor's superior, directed him now to stand fast. I think this matter gave rise to an insulting letter from Taylor to General Smith, which was passed over quietly for its scandalousness.

I went to see Governor H. W. Allen. I hardly know in what way to express my regard and respect for this man. Will it be sufficient to say that he was a man—every inch a man—brave, chivalrous, thoughtful and comprehensive in his views, undismayed at reverses, and always hopeful, and assured of ultimate success. I wish to God we had many such characters, whose purity of motive was far above all personal considerations, and who thought only of southern independence. We might then have succeeded. Yet this man was lightly appreciated by Mr. Davis, while on the other hand, the people of Louisiana gave him their confidence and the most responsible state trust.

18. The West Louisiana command went to Major General John G. Walker.

Governor Allen told me that he and Taylor could not get along in the state, and that he had informed General Smith if Taylor was not removed from command in his state, the issue would be between themselves (Smith and himself). Governor Allen sent back one of Taylor's insulting letters to him, but retained the copy for future uses. I have stated these things just as I heard them.

It seems that Taylor's senselessness kept the whole department stirred up. His insults had no other effect than to gain the ill will of everyone and to injure greatly the public service. His indiscriminate orders to drive out of the lines whole families of women and children, who happened to have had some members that had deserted to the enemy, was partially carried into effect before Governor Allen could get it revoked.

I have now given my experience of affairs in the Trans-Mississippi Department during my four months service there; enough in all conscience.

# CHAPTER XVII

# Spanish Fort

About July 10, 1864, I received a telegram to return to the east side of the Mississippi and report for duty to General S. D. Lee at Meridian, Mississippi. I succeeded in crossing the Mississippi above the mouth of the Homochitto River, about the 21st of July.[1] I was placed in command of East Louisiana and South Mississippi, but only for a few days.[2] New orders reached me from Richmond to report first at Mobile and, if no suitable command was found there, to report for duty to General J. B. Hood, now in command of the Tennessee army.[3]

These repeated changes involved changes in my staff, for general orders from the War Department required the staff to remain attached to their commands, unless by special permission. Exceptions in certain instances were allowed. This was difficult for an officer of my inferior rank, and I had therefore to take any favorite that my superiors chose to send me. I was, however, very lucky to get very good young men who proved to be zealous and energetic.[4]

---

1. Liddell, at Woodville, Mississippi, on July 23, wrote Mary that he was "too pleasantly situated for a soldier." The people here are getting along very well when contrasted to "disturbed and dilapidated Louisiana." Liddell to Mary Liddell, July 23, 1864, Liddell Papers, LSU.
2. Liddell's command consisted of the brigade of Col. John S. Scott and the territory between the Mississippi and Pearl River south of Natchez. His chief responsibility seems to have been facilitating the crossing of Dick Taylor's infantry from the Trans-Mississippi Department.
   Liddell wrote Mary on July 27, "I hope dear wife that *God* will be a friend to me and enable me to do my duty to Him, to my country, and you and my children." Liddell to Mary Liddell, July 27, 1864, Liddell Papers, LSU.
3. Jefferson Davis, "deeply humiliated" by the loss of Fort Gaines, told Dabney Maury that he was ordering Liddell to Mobile. Liddell should fill Maury's request for veteran infantry leadership.
4. Some of these staff officers were George Williams, Wade Ross Young, Moses ("Judge") Liddell, and Andrew Metcalfe. Judge, meanwhile, had come to the attention of General S. B. Buckner, who recommended him for promotion, August 31. Booth, III, 757.

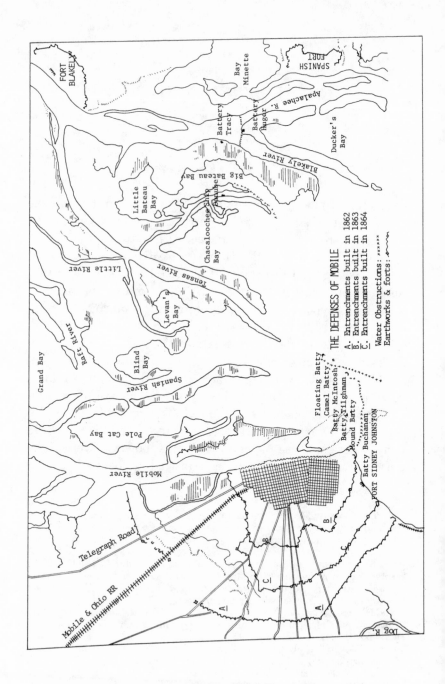

THE DEFENSES OF MOBILE

A. Entrenchments built in 1862
B. Entrenchments built in 1863
C. Entrenchments built in 1864

Water Obstructions: xxxxxx
Earthworks & forts: ‿‿‿

General Dabney H. Maury, who was in command of the defense of Mobile, gave me the command of the Eastern Division, all east of the Mobile Bay. I established my quarters at Blakely, just above the separation of the Blakely and Tensas Rivers, which were separate arms of the Alabama River. After reaching the flat country at the head of Mobile Bay, I assumed the direction of affairs here on the 19th of September, and remained until the closing hours of the Confederacy. Fort Morgan, at the entrance to the Bay of Mobile, fell in a few days after my getting to Blakely. Everything now on the seacoast was in the enemy's possession.[5]

Enemy ships anchored in sight in the Bay and guarded all egress by blockade runners. Pensacola Bay was also in his possession.[6] We could now only bide the time when he was ready to move inland. This was deferred until the following spring. Meanwhile, we on our part busied ourselves in throwing up works and otherwise preparing for his warm reception.[7] I found General Maury to be a good man, kind and generous, and using every means to secure his position. My position and social relations with him were very pleasant.

General Taylor, recently promoted for his great services on Red River, was called to this side and, to my disgust, placed in command of the Department over General Maury and of course over me again. I at once wrote to General Bragg and asked his interposition to relieve me from his detested authority. At the same time, I received a letter from Kirby Smith who wrote that, if he had been at Shreveport when the dispatch came for me to return to the east, he would not have allowed my going. He wished me again to make application to Bragg for my return to

5. Serving with the 1st Louisiana Cavalry under Col. John S. Scott, Judge had been captured October 8, at Woodville. Liddell, downcast over this and his assignment under Maury, wrote, "If I can't do any better I shall resign. I find there is no reliance to be placed upon Bragg to stick to his promises." Liddell to Mary Liddell, October 25, 1864. Liddell Papers, LSU.

6. Mobile had been stripped of troops and weapons. These had been sent to strengthen the Army of Tennessee, but at the cost of decisively weakening the seaports defenses. Maury, aided by Liddell, assumed the task of resisting with token resources a large, effective Union expeditionary force.

7. By November 1, Liddell's command consisted of a division in name: Alpheus Baker's Brigade (the 22nd Louisiana, four Alabama regiments, and two battalions of reserves); Col. Henry Maury's 15 CSA Cavalry; a company of the 7th Mississippi Cavalry; three artillery batteries; and Col. Robert Mc-Cullough's Mississippi cavalry brigade operating in West Florida. Present for duty were about 2,700 men. Maury reported about 6,500 present for the defense of Mobile.

the Trans-Mississippi Department. I forwarded Smith's letter with my application, which Bragg approved. It was never acted on, however, except to refer the matter to General Maury. Thus my Confederate career ended under this man's authority.

I had correspondence with Bragg relative to Taylor's Red River Campaign, but it was all taken by some Yankee, with my baggage, when Blakeley subsequently fell. Probably it will some day or other find the way to the public in some Yankee newspaper. Bragg wrote that one of the reasons for ordering me back to this side was that General Smith had not appreciated me, and had not given me an adequate command. I wrote in reply that I had no trouble with Smith, that Taylor was the man. Bragg favored Taylor, and I don't know that he had ever found out to this day all the facts connected with that man's conduct in Louisiana.

Fort Huger was built in the marsh, in the fork where the Blakely River separates from the Appalachee, on raised earthworks. Fort Tracy was constructed in a similar way, diagonally opposite. A short distance above Huger on the west side of the Blakely River, Tracy's works were intended to command the channel of the river. After a while it was discovered that the heights of the eastern side of the Bay commanded Huger and Tracy, therefore it became necessary to construct a work there (Spanish Fort). Soon afterward someone discovered Spanish Fort to be commanded by the higher points inland. Hence other works were put up one by one, until the whole being connected formed an extensive line over 1800 yards in length, requiring 4,000 men to defend.

Meanwhile, it again became apparent that the communication with these places was jeopardized by the position at Blakely rendering it necessary to construct works there, which also were extended to over 2600 yards, requiring for defense at least 5,000 men. Spanish Fort had five batteries and Blakely, nine. The distance between Huger and Tracy was about 300 yards, thence to Spanish Fort 1700 yards, and from the latter to Blakely above and separated by the Bay Minette, about five miles on an air line. Each work therefore was isolated.

I used every effort to make possible and practical infantry connections, but had much trouble and very little time to effect my object. Obstacles were often designedly thrown in my way, as the work considered by General Maury to be superfluous.

The time did come, however, when he was glad to avail himself of what I had accomplished. It eventually saved the garrison of Spanish Fort.

About the end of November, General John W. Davidson made a raid with several thousand cavalry from Baton Rouge in the direction of Mobile.[8] General Maury reacted by ordering all the cavalry on my side across the Bay to meet this raid. The cavalry were collected at Blakely and were being carried over in transports. Information reached me that the enemy at Pensacola, commanded by some Colonel, now fully apprised of this movement and the perfect depletion of my force in consequence, had taken this opportunity to make a raid upon the Mobile and Montgomery Railroad. His force, consisting of 3,000 Negro troops[9] and 250 cavalry, struck the railroad at Pollard Station. They devastated the country, burning houses and stripping the people, women and children, of every means of subsistence. They often ravished the women, who offered their concealed valuables without avail to these diabolical scoundrels for immunity from outrage.

The facts were made known to General Maury at Mobile, who sent back the cavalry in fractions as fast as he could, but the distance was at least seventy miles, and valuable time was already lost. Davidson's raid had luckily gone back and General Maury was relieved in that quarter.

I started off with the first detachment and met the enemy with one hundred fifty men some six miles from Pollard. I did all I could to detain them. The Negroes fought well, obstinately, and pressed us back steadily. I was aware that some troops had been sent by railroad, but I had not been able to reach them, as they were above the enemy. I therefore sent couriers and detachments around to find and bring them up. Then burning all the bridges over the streams, I moved to the rear of the enemy, and brought up what I could find to attack the Negroes at the bridges. We engaged them hotly at each bridge. At the second bridge, late in the evening, we pressed so hard upon them that they fled in great panic. The houses of the people were burned by the road-

8. Liddell sent the happy news home November 20 that Judge had escaped. Mary had been keeping sick and wounded Confederate soldiers at Llanda, but recently had had an unfortunate incident with Charles Jones. Sallie Chapman to Mary M. Liddell, Nov. 20, 1864. Liddell Papers, LSU.
9. Col. George D. Robinson's 97th U. S. Colored Infantry consisted of some 800 Negro troops sent up from their base in Barrancas, Florida, to shatter the railroad at Pollard.

side, and we pursued the enemy by the light of his fires. Not a Negro surrendered or was taken prisoner.

Night now coming on, they took advantage of it to give us the slip by taking a road through the woods known to their guides, and to gain distance upon us, at least; but I persisted in the pursuit, giving no rest either to enemy or to my own men. We came upon them at a difficult ford on the Pine Barren Creek, and there captured many of their wagons, besides killing and wounding a large number of the Negroes and some of the whites.[10] My men and horses, after traveling without stopping one hundred miles since leaving Blakely, were incapable of going farther. The pursuit ceased. I lost my own horse from the strain upon his system.[11]

I had occasion, about the end of December, to write to Edward Sparrow, Senator from Louisiana and Chairman of the Military Committee. I took some pains to express my firm conviction that the war was going against us unless we could get foreign assistance or we could unite with the people to emanicipate the slaves and put all the men in the army that were willing to join our side.[12] Though I must confess, from the lateness of the hour in the struggle, the latter was doubtful. We ought to have done this for effect at the time of Mr. Lincoln's Emanicipation Proclamation. If nothing else could be done, we must make terms of some kind, for General Lee would be hard-pressed in the interior of Virginia by spring, and Sherman would attempt to cooperate with and probably join Grant in pressing Lee. I understood from Major Starke, who carried the letter, that Sparrow exhibited it to General Lee. Lee agreed with me on these points and desired to get Negro soldiers, saying that he could make soldiers out of any human being that had arms and legs.

Toward the end of January, the Monroe Conference[13] with

10. Liddell's light command, composed primarily of men from Alpheus Baker's infantry and Charles G. Armstead's cavalry brigades, inflicted upward of 80 casualties and prevented the Union column from destroying the railroad. Within a month traffic was as usual.
11. Brig. Gen. James H. Clanton reported, "We pursued the enemy thirty miles, capturing a portion of his transportation, baggage, and supplies. The road for miles is strewn with his dead. . . . General Liddell, our commander, acted with great spirit and energy, as did his entire command."
     Gen. Beauregard reported the action to President Davis, adding, "Our forces, commanded by General Liddell, acted with spirit and gallantry." OR, I, 45 (2), 709; OR, I, 40, 449.
12. Patrick Cleburne's ill-fated plan of the winter of 1863-1864.
13. The Hampton Roads Conference was held February 3, 1865.

Lincoln occurred, but Messrs. A. H. Stephens and J. A. Campbell were restricted to such extent by Mr. Davis as rendered any terms of settlement without independence impossible. The war continued. Hood had met with disaster in Tennessee, and Sherman had made his grand raid of plunder and incendiarism through Georgia to Savannah, whence he was preparing to move into the Carolinas toward Grant.[14] Our affairs were approaching rapidly final solution, perceptible now even to the chief actors or rather directors of affairs.

I was in Mobile one day and, meeting on the street General George Maney of Tennessee, was accosted by him rather feelingly.

"Why did you leave us; what did you quit the Army of Tennessee for?"

I saw at once that the question was intended for reproach, mingled probably with regret. I only stammered out some excuse that there were enough general officers without me, but that I now regretted not having taken up Hardee's offer as chief of staff. Maney was somewhat dejected and had not gotten entirely well from the wound he received at Mission Ridge. He was on his way, however, to join his command.[15]

Major General E. R. S. Canby left New Orleans with about 60,000 men to attack Mobile in March. He had a large fleet and innumerable transports. After collecting all his men and equipment on Dauphin Island, he determined to attack our eastern defenses first. This would enable him to flank Mobile both by land and water.

Canby sent a corps under General A. J. Smith (I think) up Fish River to Dannelly's Mills to gain footing for a starting point. General Maury sent me the commands of Generals Francis M.

14. The Tennessee (Hood's) Army has nearly all gone to the Carolinas. Taylor has been allowed to retain enough for the defense of his district or department so that he (Taylor) is no better off than he was before, which must be a sad disappointment to him. I have met with him *once* and I have never seen a man more polite and desirous of my goodwill, at which, after what happened, I felt naturally very much astonished. *Let him go,* I thought, and I have felt disposed ever since not to bother myself with the man, or his duplicity. There are plenty such people in this world."
"I wish for more active service rather than being confined to fortifications in their vicinity." ". . . But at all counts, dear wife, you must move away from such neighborhoods as Cataboula until the whole thing (war) is settled." Liddell to Mary M. Liddell, February 13, 1865, in Liddell Papers, LSU.

15. George Maney commanded his Tennesseans until the day of surrender. Unknown to Liddell, Generals S. B. Buckner and Edmund Kirby Smith both requested that the War Department promote Liddell and assign him to command of Polignac's Division in the Trans-Mississippi. General Maury, however, would not permit. *OR*, I, 48 (1), 1387, 1430.

Cockrell of Missouri, Randall L. Gibson[16] of Louisiana, and Bryan M. Thomas and James T. Holtzclaw of Alabama, in all about four thousand men, effective.[17] I was fully satisfied that this small force should not be demoralized by defeat in the field against such odds.

Before entering the works, which were in a very incomplete state, I demanded labor before the enemy came up. I directed Generals Gibson and Holtzclaw to occupy Spanish Fort, which in addition to the garrison in the batteries there, comprised about 2,600 men. I placed Generals Cockrell and Thomas in Blakely, about 2,500 men, including the artillerists of the batteries. Forts Huger and Tracy, lying in the marsh between these two first named places, could not be attacked until Spanish Fort or Blakely fell. I had also sent to me four gunboats of Confederate States construction, which carried armaments of heavy guns.[18] Each of the forts had also heavy guns, both rifled and smooth, as well as I can call to mind, my data being all lost. There were between eighty and ninety pieces of all kinds in all the works.

General Canby moved up and began the attack first on Spanish Fort about the last week in March.[19] Meanwhile, General Steele's Corps moving from Pensacola struck the railroad above Blakely, and on the first of April invested Blakely, thus by the last week of March, 1864, both places were fairly invested.

A gentleman accompanied a friend from Mobile in a boat to see me, at night. While we were talking a bullet fell on a table by us, close to the light. He was astonished and asked how that happened. I explained to him that the sharpshooters in the rifle

16. This Yale man and diplomat led the 13th Louisiana at Shiloh. He saw heavy action, earning brigade command before the Atlanta campaign. After the war Gibson served in the U. S. House and Senate from 1875 until his death. In Congress his broad committee assignments showed the range of the unusual interest and abilities.

   He had already proven his competence taking combat command of D. W. Adams' brigade *three* times when Adams was wounded.

   The paths of Gibson and Liddell crossed after the war as well as at Spanish Fort.
17. This committed all of Maury's infantry. Quite a show of confidence in Liddell, and quite a willingness to concentrate on the part of Maury.
18. Coordination between Liddell and the gunboats proved effective until Canby concentrated his artillery against them and drove them off. Liddell's artillery implacements and his quick movements to exploit good firing positions impressed Union officers.
19. Liddell aggressively set out to attack Canby, but he had underestimated the strength opposing him. Canby quickly moved to outflank Liddell, who realized his peril and withdrew toward Blakely.

pits were firing all night long and balls frequently fell near, glancing from trees sometimes, and that shells exploded sometimes near. Just before he came, one fell without exploding in front of my tent. He said that he had no idea of such doings at night, and that he would leave forthwith. My friend remarked, "You are bound to go up. I feel sorry for you. Good-bye. I hope you live through all this."

The bombardment of Spanish Fort was exceedingly heavy, and by the evening of the 8th of April the approaches of the enemy were close enough to enable him at dark to make a lodgment on the left of the lines, next to the Bay Minette. An evacuation must now be effected. If not, a Union assault, with every reasonable probability of the works being carried, must take place by morning. Use was now found at night for the causeway and bridge I had made. By a tedious and toilsome march through the marsh, all of the garrison escaped except some six hunded men, who were unable to find their way out.[20] Fort Huger now had some use for her heavy guns to turn upon Spanish Fort, occupied by the enemy.

Meanwhile Canby turned his attention and his united force upon Blakely. Exasperated by the escape of the forces from Spanish Fort, he determined to assault Blakely, which he had not tried with the former. Our lines at Blakely could not be filled by one half, except by placing the men about one yard apart which gave no volume to the fire from the lines. General Maury, however, declined to allow me to retain the troops that had escaped from Spanish Fort.[21] He sent them all in transports and blockade runners to Mobile in sight of the enemy's boats from the Bay, who could not fail to perceive the weakness of the remaining forces in the works. In fact, they thought that we were evacuating the places in toto.[22]

20. Liddell's force totaled about 2,700 effectives; Holtzclaw's Brigade, Thomas' Alabama Reserve Brigade, Sears' Brigade, and Cockrell's Brigade, plus artillery men. The defense of Spanish Fort became primarily the responsibility of Gibson. Both Maury and Liddell were impressed by his work. Gibson's April 16, 1865, report (OR, I, 49, 313-319) is full and dependable.
21. Liddell's causeway saved them, but the withdrawal was tedious and alarming, as several thousand men threaded their way over a two-foot-wide "treadway." One thousand of Gibson's men cut across the swamp directly to Blakely. Maury miffed Liddell when he sent these tired bodies on to Mobile.
22. Liddell understates his role at Spanish Fort and Blakely. In the closing days of March and during the first week in April, he moved his troops carefully and skillfully. This advantageous use of terrain and their line of men were augmented by sharp, effective sorties led by Gibson and Cockrell. A Union

Toward evening of April 9th, Negro troops under Steele assaulted our left, next to the river, but were driven back with heavy loss. Later the enemy fire heavily increased from all the batteries, and the discharges were incessant. Just at sunset they suddenly ceased, and the plain around our front swarmed with assaulting lines. The enemy scrambled over brush, abatis, stretched wires, through subterra explosions, added to our fire of grape, cannister, and musketry. It was well and quickly done. The works were entered. Some of my men were shot from the rear, while at their guns firing to the front. Thus Blakely fell at the point of the bayonet. No flag was ever lowered. Some men escaped by swimming to the gunboats, some on rafts hastily improvised, some through the marshes; many were drowned, and many killed or wounded.

I was taken prisoner by a Captain Julian and treated with some show of respect. Some officers of my staff were captured with me, others at points where they were on duty at the time the enemy entered the works. Generals Cockrell and Thomas were captured unhurt, with most of their staffs.[23]

I believe if General Maury had permitted me to keep the Spanish Fort garrison, I could have repelled this assault. The weight or volume of fire would have been sufficiently heavy and deadly to have driven back the assaulting columns. As it was, my line was nothing more than a good skirmish line, whose fire was entirely too weak. I know that General Maury did all in his power, but it was impossible to hold the defenses with such inadequate forces.[24]

It was a wonder to me that Canby did not attempt to capture Mobile without the fire of a gun. How? By moving up the Alabama to its junction with the Tombigbee. The place would have been evacuated at the demonstration. But I suppose Canby

commander reported, ". . . whereupon that indefatigable officer (Liddell) went out and selected a good position on the north bank of the Minette Bayou, for a light battery, which would give Wimmer and Cox a reverse and ranking fire." Andrews, p. 91.

23. On the Prisoner of War Register, it is noted that Liddell was 49 years old, gray eyes, dark hair, and five feet, nine inches in height.

24. Maury intended to evacuate Liddell and all his men, but felt certain Liddell could hold a little longer, and thus delayed fatally for the Blakely force. Liddell did pretty well holding back Canby for nine days and then yielding to one of the most magnificently timed and executed assaults in the Civil War (35 regiments, 16,000 actual attackers, along a three-mile front). Andrews in his *History of the Campaign of Mobile* and others commented on Liddell's effective coordination with the C.S. Navy see *O.R.*, I, 44 (1), 319-322.

wanted to make sure of the river for the transportation of his supplies which were very heavy for so large an army.

The next morning I was sent to Canby, who treated me with consideration and courtesy. He told me that he had captured 623 in Spanish Fort, and I think he succeeded in getting nearly 2,000 in Blakely all told, Negroes, etc. I asked him if he knew his losses in the assault the last evening. He said that he did not know. Just then General C. C. Andrews came up and, hearing the question and reply, remarked that he had lost for his share alone about 500 men.[25] Conversing with Canby, I remarked, "I suppose now slavery is gone, and with it goes the cotton interest in our country." "No," he said, "not so, for more cotton under free labor will be made in three years than ever before."

At the time of my writing this, two years have elapsed since this conversation, and the showing has not improved. I told the general that I might now consider myself as ruined, but if he would make a bet with me on three years it might be the means of reinstating my fortune. He declined, likely from principle. I felt surer of winning such a bet than of holding Blakely with one-half of the men that the works required against fifty thousand men.

General Canby sent me in his ambulance with my staff to the village on the eastern shore, about six miles below Spanish Fort. I remained there until the next morning and then was sent to Dauphin Island to remain a prisoner until further instructions. He had, however, said to me that we would soon be paroled.

We were there but a few days when news came by New Orleans, I think, of the surrender of General Lee and his army, on the 9th of April. The same day that Blakely was carried by assault at dark, also the 9th, came news of the assassination of Mr. Lincoln. Now the South had given up her cause without stipulating or being able to exact terms. This miserable business was attributed to her policy, thus adding disgrace to her load of troubles, and piling on the agony.

The South fought the battle fairly and in full compliance with the strictest rules of modern warfare. She had no outside assistance, no friendly nation to help her, or to hold out to her the right hand of fellowship. No crowds of foreigners, with no homes in this country, enlisted from mercenary motives under her banners. The Anglo-Saxon of the Southern States was overpowered

25. Candy did lose 500 in the assault, but he captured some 3,300.

and put down by the Puritans of the same race, aided, abetted, and encouraged by all other peoples. They did this for the freedom of the African, whom their own inherent love of gold first introduced here in *slavery*. The South owes no thanks or favors to any people on earth. Her hands are henceforth untied, to act when she deems best for her own interest.

I remained a prisoner six weeks on Dauphin Island, under General T. Kilby Smith, who treated me with much respect and kindness. General Smith gave me the limits of the entire island without hesitation, for which courtesy I acknowledge my indebtedness to this day. I was paroled on the 16th of May, 1865, and sent to New Orleans. There I returned to my home, a sadder if not a wiser man, than I started out four years since.

I found everyone, men, women, and children, sadly disappointed at the adverse termination of the war. Even those who had basely deserted their cause were now bitterly complaining and bewailing their misfortunes and suicidal conduct. Hope still lingers, such that it is.

# CHAPTER XVIII

# AFTER THE WAR

During May, 1865, St. John Liddell remained a prisoner at Fort Gaines on Dauphin Island. Carolina Gillis carried food and clothing to him from New Orleans and went to see Major General Edward Canby in his behalf. Liddell, fortunately, made a friend of his captor Canby. He would need him in the future.[1]

When released, Liddell tried to head back home, but the flood covered everything near Llanda. It ". . . is now over the face of the earth." The mud and water of the Mississippi and its tributaries ruined crops, fields, roads, and homes. The cotton that miraculously had been saved through the war was damaged.[2]

Cotton factor D. B. Penn told Liddell that the market for his cotton was dropping fast. He had tried to get $0.34 a pound earlier, but now he would settle for $0.29 if he could find a buyer. The money Liddell did realize, he used to purchase $2,700 in gold. To do this cost him $3,908.25 in greenbacks. All of it, however, was applied against the debts run up at Llanda during the war by Mary Liddell.[3]

Mary, in a rare existing letter to St. John, tried to set the mood for what was to come.

1. Major General Edward R. S. Canby, U.S.A. (1817-1873). A West Point cadet at the same time with Liddell, Canby later pursued a career in the regular army. He distinguished himself in the Mexican War and received rapid promotions for his achievements on the Pacific Coast in the late 1850's. Canby fought efficiently against Sibley in Texas early in the War, and then returned Banks' disorganized Red River expeditionary force to the combat effectiveness that resulted in the capture of Mobile and Liddell. Canby represented military rule in Louisiana following the surrender, then he headed west to die at the hands of Captain Jack during a negotiating session in 1872. Carolina Gillis to St. John R. Liddell, May 14, 1865, in Gillis Papers, SHC.
2. Carolina Gillis to St. John R. Liddell, May 14, 1865, in Gillis Papers, SHC.
3. D. B. Penn to St. John R. Liddell, August 29, 1865, in Liddell Papers, LSU.

I know you must at times feel very much discouraged at the wreck of things, but let us begin again a life of industry and economy and try to provide for those who are dependent on us and at the same time divert our minds from the calamities which have befallen us.[4]

St. John Liddell's condition mirrored that of Louisiana. From 1865 until 1870, Liddell's world was one of high inflation, scarcity of goods and money, and exorbitant interest rates. Louisiana, led by 26-year-old embezzler Henry C. Warmoth, could not meet its obligations. The state, therefore, could not pay interest on its debts, so it borrowed more. By 1868 State bonds were being sold in the market for $0.47 on the dollar. They would drop as low as $0.25.

"The Mississippi exacted the penalty of neglected, broken levees by devastating floods." A blight in 1866 was followed in 1867 by another failure. Not until 1868 did an average crop come along. That year short-handed Liddell experienced a severe drought.[5]

At Bayou Goula Plantation, John H. Randolph reported that he had ". . . 40 or 50 acres in cane, 75 acres in corn, the remainder in mud." As for Liddell, instead of the total of 500-800 bales he produced annually in the late 1850's, Liddell's land yielded "only 76 bales made in all and this had to be split."[6]

Aggravating all of these dangerous economic conditions was an acute labor shortage. The Freedman's Bureau required that contracts be negotiated with the former slaves and approved by the Bureau. In the meantime, Bureau personnel and policies kept changing.

Liddell sent Judge to Texas to get his former slaves to return. In December, 1865, Judge and most of the Negroes started back to Llanda. Judge reported, however, that they had not signed their contracts. They would wait until the Liddells transported them back to Louisiana, and ". . . then they may. I don't believe the Negroes will sign a contract with you."

In desperation Liddell went into partnership with P. S. Kennard. Kennard would procure 100 good workers east of the

4. Mary M. Liddell to St. John R. Liddell, July 15, 1865, in Liddell Papers, LSU.
5. Ella Lonn, *Reconstruction in Louisiana after 1868* (New York, 1918), pp. 5ff; Plantation Diary No. 39, in Liddell Papers, LSU.
6. John H. Randolph to St. John R. Liddell, August 25, 1865, in Liddell Papers, LSU.

Mississippi and bring them back to Black River. The partnership proved disastrous. Kennard, who produced only a handful of workers, made off with the $5,000 Liddell gave him, plus unauthorized drafts on Marcellin Gillis for $3,500 more. Liddell sued futilely.[7]

The Freedman's Bureau surprised Liddell when it declared his Boeuff River property "an abandoned estate," and leased it to tenants of the Bureau's choosing. Liddell managed to get these tenants off his property although he allowed them to remain until their crops were sold. Friends interceded with the Freedman's Bureau and Liddell regained his Boeuff River tract, but how was he to find the money to operate it?

The slim profit on the stored 1865 cotton had been eaten up by debts and "sharp insurance costs for shipping." Marcellin Gillis demanded payment of the $2,000 Mary had borrowed in 1863. "This is due immediately." Liddell's old cotton was being confiscated by the Federal authorities. Doctor bills had to be paid.

All of this proved too much for General Liddell. He planned to salvage what he could, gather his youngest children, and go to Brazil. He corresponded throughout the fall of 1865 with W. H. Johnson about joining General Wirt Adams'[8] group. His friends begged him not to go. Brazil meant escape, however, and Liddell clung to this hope as late as 1867. The General and his boys ". . . began to turn our eyes toward Brazil—the land of promise. He seems pretty determined to leave the U. S. and I too am almost tempted to leave in the fall with him."[9]

The desperation inherent in the Brazilian venture underlines how poorly Liddell adapted to postwar conditions. The terms "despair, disillusion, disgust, distraught" take on fuller meaning when one reads Liddell's correspondence. Prior to 1861, the Liddells had seen adversity at first hand. During the war they suffered loss of property, dislocation, and death. All that went before, however, pales when compared to the misfortunes of 1865-70.

---

7. Moses J. Liddell to St. John R. Liddell, December 15, 1865; (first name unknown) Baldwin to St. John R. Liddell, August 14, 1865; D. B. Penn to St. John R. Liddell, July 18, 1865; in Liddell Papers, LSU.
8. William Wirt Adams (1819-1888). This brother of the colonel of the 1st Louisiana became colonel of the 1st Mississippi Cavalry Regiment. He served mostly in Tennessee and along the Mississippi River. He won distinction as one of Forrest's subordinates. A planter and politician before the war, he returned to Mississippi and died there in Jackson at the hands of a newspaper editor.
9. Moses J. Liddell to Andrew Liddell, May 28, 1867, Liddell Papers, LSU.

Liddell thought of Brazil; he turned in his depression to writing his *Record*, but the hounds of indebtedness continued to pursue.

Mary kept going. The Llanda journals show an increasing number of entries in her hand. She kept careful books and notes, paying some 30-75 workers. She managed, with the General putting property and funds in her name, to keep balanced on the tightrope.

The young managed to cope, too. Francis Richardson wrote, "The only ones that do not seem to feel the ruin that has fallen upon our country are the young folks. Their spirits are too buoyant to be crushed by such small matters. They laugh as loud, frolic and dance. . . ."[10]

Bethia Liddell represented this attitude. She and Wade Ross Young married at Llanda in the fall of 1865. Young (1842-1911), formerly an energetic Confederate officer, admired his father-in-law, and worked well with Judge. The other children, including Judge, returned to Llanda reluctantly. Life as a refugee in 1865 had been more exciting. "Loulie" Liddell wrote in the fall of 1866, "Vollie cannot become accustomed to living in the Swamp, but I do hope by degrees that he will accustom himself to it. He finds it extremely dull; so did I at first."[11]

Liddell gave top priority to his children's education and managed to send them all off to school. With his desperate shortage of funds, he was embarrassed repeatedly by school officials. He did succeed in placing Volney in Edmund Kirby Smith's school in Kentucky, although at great sacrifice. "I hope you will be able to send me to school for three or four years. *Try Pa and do so. That is all I ask.* Write to me in Kentucky."[12]

Widespread violence prevailed in Louisiana, as it had since late 1863. To combat disorder, the governor of Louisiana organized a regiment of militia for Catahoula Parish in the fall of 1865, naming Liddell as colonel. Liddell issued a passionate proclamation appealing for the preservation of peace and good order, but nothing came of it. It was the day of disenfranchisement and carpetbaggers and Republicans. Judge Taliaferro, however, had

10. Francis D. Richardson to St. John R. Liddell, December 4, 1965, in Liddell Papers, LSU.
11. Loulie Liddell to Moses J. Liddell, September 18, 1866, in Liddell Papers, LSU.
12. In one of the terrible ironies that wracked Liddell's life, the last letter he would receive from Volney, in January, 1870, requested permission to quit school and to come home. Volney M. Liddell to St. John R. Liddell, January 16, 1869, January 2, 1870, in Liddell Papers, LSU.

power and influence, as did Lt. Col. Charles Jones, recent Republican convert. Upon urging by his friends, Liddell did seek amnesty. His application was accompanied by strong endorsements from Louisiana Democratic political figures and General Canby.[13]

In 1866 Liddell mortgaged Llanda for $18,114.52. By 1868 the principal of this debt had risen to $25,000.00. The Citizens Bank of New Orleans held the major note. Liddell tried to pay the interest, but the demands of his other debts, $72,408.31, plus two of unknown amounts, crushed him. The bank foreclosed on two-thirds of his property.

At the advice of Richardson, Randolph, and others, Liddell petitioned for bankruptcy in December of 1868. Twenty-eight creditors were listed with a total indebtedness of $86,808.31. Richardson's reasoning tells a good deal about Liddell's plight:

1. You owe at least $35,000 which has been at interest for several years.
2. Your plantation on Black River is subject to overflow, dilapidated and out of repair, upon which for the last three years you have been attempting to raise crops that would pay expenses, but without success.
3. Balance of your real estate is wild unimproved land, also subject to overflow.
4. Your farming stock is old and worn out.
5. You have a large family to educate and support.[14]

Mary Liddell's appeal to lease Llanda "upon which I have been living for 27 years, and which my husband has given up in bankruptcy" was successful. She did put into the agreement a stipulation about overflows, "since such disasters in the past have chiefly helped to ruin my husband and will ruin anyone."[15]

Bankruptcy and the humiliation of having to deal with friends, strangers, and enemies on terms of helplessness drove Liddell to write his children,

Study every word and sentence (in a volume containing Liddell land holdings and transactions) for you will be

13. Louisiana State Military Commission of St. John R. Liddell, October 28, 1865; Proclamation of Col. St. John R. Liddell, November 23, 1865; T. L. Bayne to St. John R. Liddell, September 20, 1865, in Liddell Papers, LSU.
14. Francis D. Richardson to St. John R. Liddell, December 1, 1868; St. John R. Liddell to Dr. Miller, March 24, 1869; R. W. Richardson to C. W. Cammack, November 17, 1869, in Liddell Papers, LSU.
15. Mary M. Liddell to J. S. Scott, December 21, 1868, in Liddell Papers, LSU.

preyed upon by covetous and designing men who profess to be more or less connected with my affairs, and who will strip you of the last cent if *they can.*[16]

To his Plantation Diary Liddell had confided early in 1868, Everything seems to work against me and ruin stares me full in the face. I am indifferent to all things, but subsistence and clothing for my family. I am ready for any change in government.

Most discouraging prospect for Southern people. Negroes refusing to do anything but idle. Radicals ruining any hope with a chance of confidence in stability by partisan, selfish, ruinous, and revolutionary legislation.[17]

The ultimate blow to St. John R. Liddell came on February 17, 1869, when Mary Metcalfe Roper Liddell died. With her went the ability even to lease Llanda; with her went all hope.

The Liddell family disintegrated. Friends stepped in and paid for the children's schooling. Volney went back to Kentucky, two of the girls entered a Catholic convent, and Louis drifted off to Texas to visit Judge. Liddell thought about joining his friend, Col. J. S. Scott, in business in New Orleans.

In a series of events of which tragedies are made, the bank put Llanda on the auction block. It was sold to Charles Cammack, who intended to resell it to Charles Jones and his partner, Elijah Cotton. Liddell faced eviction and his work of a lifetime falling into the hands of his mortal enemy. General Liddell warned Jones ". . . that it would not be healthy for the Colonel to purchase the graves of his family."

Cammack, however, decided not to sell. Jones, furious, brought suit. There matters stood with Cammack frustrating Jones and pressing Liddell for $6,000 of additional debt.[18] Then on January 8, 1870, Cammack and Jones' cotton factor, John Nixon, Jr., clashed in New Orleans. Cammack killed Nixon, who had allegedly charged Cammack with violation of his contract to sell Liddell's plantation to Jones and Cotton.[19]

16. April 24, 1868, entry in Plantation Notebook No. 22, in Liddell Papers, LSU.
17. January 31, 1868, entry in Plantation Diary No. 39, in Liddell Papers, LSU.
18. Volney M. Liddell to St. John R. Liddell, January 16, 1869, January 2, 1870, Miscellaneous Liddell family letters, Spring, 1869; St. John R. Liddell to Maj. D. F. Boyd, July 30, 1869, in Liddell Papers, LSU.
19. Michael L. Lanza, "The Jones-Liddell Feud," *Red River Valley Historical Review, II* (Winter, 1975), 467 ff.; New Orleans *Daily Picayune*, March 23, 25, 1870; J. S. Scott to St. John R. Liddell, December 23, 1869, J. H. Boatner

On February 14, 1870, Liddell, deep in depression, disgraced and full of fury, set out down the Black River on the steamer *St. Mary*. It soon stopped to pick up cotton at Garrett's Landing. The two Jones boys, William and Cuthbert, came on board and saw Liddell. They got off immediately, and rode off toward their home.

After the steamer left Garrett's she next stopped at Jones' to take on cotton. At this juncture Col. Jones and his two sons came on board fully armed and went up into the cabin.

General Liddell was sitting at the table eating dinner as they entered, but attempted to rise from his seat as they approached. At this instant two shots were discharged at him, one by Col. Jones and the other by one of the sons, both supposed to have taken effect in his breast. He fell, but while in the act of falling, drew his revolver and shot once at Col. Jones, who was retreating out of the pantry gangway, the ball from Gen. Liddell's pistol lodging in the ceiling over his head.

The sons of Jones fired several shots at Gen. Liddell after he had fallen, some of which took effect. Gen. Liddell did not speak, and expired almost immediately.

The passengers all fled from the cabin. . . . After the shooting, Col. Jones and his sons went on shore, and the steamer returned to Gen. Liddell's plantation with the body of the deceased.[20]

The *Picayune* account omitted some pertinent details. Liddell told the steamer's clerk "when he saw and heard the sons" to let Jones know he was on board and that "Jones had better not come on." The doctor, W. A. White, who examined Liddell's body "found seven gunshot wounds, three of which could have caused death." Cuthbert Jones claimed that Liddell provoked the fight and drew first. Col. Charles H. Morrison, who was dining with Liddell, said Jones and Liddell "eyed each other sternly," then Jones advanced. Liddell rose though Morrison tried to hold him to his seat. Liddell ". . . had partially drawn a pistol from his breast" as he rose.

to St. John R. Liddell, November 9, 16, 23, 1869, in Liddell Papers, LSU; W. M. Crawford, "The Jones-Liddell Feud, Cataboula Parish, 1852-1870." Catahoula Parish Library, Harrisonburg, Louisiana.
20. New Orleans *Daily Picayune*, February 16, 1870.

The Jones gave themselves up to the custody of friendly Sheriff Oliver G. Ballard in Harrisonburg and were kept in his house. A few days after Liddell's murder, Judge passed Harrisonburg on a steamer and spotted Charles Jones on the Ballard porch. He fired a shotgun from the steamer and slightly wounded Jones.

About 2:00 a.m. the night of February 27, a group of about 30 men surrounded the Ballard house. In the mob were Judge and Volney, Wade Young, and Andrew and Volney Metcalfe. The Jones (Charles, William, and Cuthbert) were inside, along with Sheriff Ballard, Elijah Cotton, and several women of the Ballard family. The mob allowed all to leave but the Jones. They then shot and killed Charles and William, but Cuthbert eluded them, miraculously hanging from a window ledge for eight to ten minutes.[21] Then he escaped to New Orleans and was never tried. Volney Liddell and Wade Young were arrested but the case was dismissed.[22]

For a while after the killings, even the steamboats would not land near Trinity. These tense times caused a woman to remember the prophecy of old Mrs. Glenn, ". . . that Liddell's and Jones' bodies would contain as many shots as her son's did and that neither of them would die a natural death."[23]

"It was one of those fierce feuds which time had no power to abate, and would yield to no pacific influence. Surviving the excitement of conflict in which these minor passions might well be absorbed or lost, nor forgotten even during the bitter years of reconstruction, mutual resentment at length culminated in desperate and bloody issue."[24]

21. Lanza, "Jones-Liddell Feud"; Charles Brashear to Moses J. Liddell, February 16, 1870, in Liddell Papers, LSU; New Orleans *Daily Picayune*, March 11, 18, 1870.
22. Cuthbert Jones conveniently became Consul to Tripoli. Judge became Chief Justice of the Territory of Montana in 1888 and died there at age 47. Col. Wade R. Young, Bethia's husband, became the law partner of General Zebulon York at Vidalia, Louisiana in 1880.

    Laura Stewart Jones moved to Troy Plantation where she built a nice home. She also secured title to Llanda. Laura lived in seclusion and, since she was ". . . noted for brutality with the slaves before the war, she was not a person with whom folks would trifle. . . ." In 1871 Laura took her land and carefully laid out a town. She erected a post office and gave that dark land between the two rivers a new name. She called it "Jonesville." "Welcome to Jonesville," pamphlet published in Jonesville in 1949; New Orleans *Daily Picayune*, February 20, March 20, 1870, Liddell Papers, LSU; Lanza, "Jones-Liddell Feud."
23. L. B. A. to J. G. Taliaferro, March 12, 1870, in Taliaferro Papers, LSU.
24. *Southern Bivouac I* (December, 1885), 411.

# BIBLIOGRAPHY
## MANUSCRIPTS

Department of Archives, Louisiana State University, Baton Rouge
  Caffery Papers (Donaldson and Family)
  Francis C. Richardson Manuscript
  James G. Taliaferro Family Papers
  John H. Randolph Papers
  Liddell Papers (Moses, St. John, and Family)
  Walter Lynnwood Fleming Collection
National Archives, Confederate Records Division, Washington D.C.
  Department of the Gulf, Letters Sent, 1864-1865
  Department of the Gulf, Telegram Received, 1865
  General St. John R. Liddell Papers
Southern Historical Collection, University of North Carolina, Chapel Hill
  Caffery Family Papers
  Daniel C. Govan Papers
  Francis D. Richardson Memoirs
  Frank Liddell Richardson Papers
  Franklin A. Hudson Diary
  Irving A. Buck Papers
  Marcellin Gillis Papers
  St. John R. Liddell Papers
  William S. Hamilton Papers
Miscellaneous
  Cadet Record and Correspondence of St. John R. Liddell in United States
    Military Academy Archives, West Point, New York
  George A. Williams Speech, "St. John R. Liddell," in Howard-Tilton Memorial
    Library, Tulane University, New Orleans
  Marriage Books, in Adams County Courthouse, Natchez, Mississippi
  Probate Court Records, in Catahoula Parish Court House, Harrisonburg,
    Louisiana
  Eleventh Judicial District Records, in Catahoula Parish Courthouse, Harrison-
    burg, Louisiana
  Dabney H. Maury Papers, Henry S. Huntington Library, San Marino, Calif.

## CENSUSES

1830, 1840, 1850 - Adams County, Mississippi
1840, 1850, 1860, 1870 - Catahoula Parish, Louisiana
1850 - St. Mary Parish, Louisiana
1840, 1850 - Wilkinson County, Mississippi

## NEWSPAPERS

Alexandria, Louisiana, *Louisiana Democrat*
Harrisonburg, Louisiana, *The Independent*
Harrisonburg, Louisiana, *Southern Advocate*
New Orleans, Louisiana, *Daily Picayune*
New Orleans, Louisiana, *Evening Delta*
Vidalia, Louisiana, *Concordia Intelligencer*
Washington, D.C., *Southern Advocate*

## PRINTED PRIMARY SOURCES, PUBLIC DOCUMENTS, AND REMINISCENCES

Andrews, C. C. *History of the Campaign of Mobile.* New York, 1867.
Liddell, St. John R. "Liddell's Record." *Southern Bivouac I* (December 1885
  and February 1886), 411-419, 529-535.
Lord, Walter (ed.). *Fremantle Diary, Being the Journal of the Lieutenant Colonel
  James Arthur Lyon Fremantle, Coldstream Guards, on His Three Months in
  the Southern States.* Boston, 1954.
Maury, Dabney H. *Recollections of a Virginian.* New York, 1894.

Prichard, Walter (ed.). "A Tourist's Description of Louisiana in 1860," *Louisiana Historical Quarterly, XXI* (October, 1938), 1203-1207.
Richardson, Frank Liddell. "The War as I Saw It, 1861-1865," *Louisiana Historical Quarterly, VI* (January, April, 1923), 86-106, 223ff.
Ridley, Bromfield (ed.). *Battles and Sketches of the Army of Tennessee.* Mexico, Missouri, 1906.
Rowland, Dunbar. *Jefferson Davis, Constitutionalist: His Letters, Papers, and Speeches.* 10 vols. Jackson, Mississippi, 1923.
Tarrant, Edward W. "Siege and Capture of Fort Blakely." *Confederate Veteran, XXIII* (1915), 457-458.
Taylor, Richard. *Destruction and Reconstruction; Personal Experiences of the Late War.* New York, 1879.
*War of the Rebellion: A Compilation of the Official Records of the Union and Confederate Armies.* 73 vols. Washington, D.C., 1880-1901.
Woodward, C. Vann (ed.). *Mary Chestnut's Civil War.* New Haven, 1981.

## SECONDARY SOURCES

Anonymous. "Jones-Liddell Feud." Unpublished Manuscript. Catahoula Parish Library, Harrisonburg, La.
Anonymous. "The Jones-Liddell Feud." Unpublished Manuscript. Catahoula Parish Court House, Harrisonburg, La.
Avery, Sue C., Alice B. McL. Winegeart, and Alma McC. Womack, *Jonesville Through the Mirror of Time.* 3 vols. Jonesville, Louisiana, 1978.
Bergeron, Arthur W., Jr. "The Confederate Defense of Mobile, 1861-1865." Unpublished Ph.D. Thesis. Louisiana State University, 1980.
Booth, Andrew B. *Records of Louisiana Confederate Soldiers and Louisiana Confederate Commands.* 3 vols. New Orleans, 1920.
Bragg, Jefferson D. *Louisiana in the Confederacy.* Baton Rouge, 1941.
Bridges, Hal. *Lee's Maverick General.* New York, 1961.
Buck, Irving A. *Cleburne and His Command.* Ed. T. R. Hay. 2nd ed. Jackson, Tennessee, 1959.
Caskey, Willie M. *Secession and Restoration in Louisiana.* Baton Rouge, 1938.
Castel, Albert. *General Sterling Price and the Civil War in the West.* Baton Rouge, 1968.
Connelly, Thomas L. *Army of the Heartland: The Army of Tennessee, 1861-1862.* Baton Rouge, 1967.
————, *Autumn of Glory: The Army of Tennessee, 1862-1865.* Baton Rouge, 1971.
Crawford, W. M. "The Jones-Liddell Feud, Catahoula Parish, 1852-1870." Unpublished manuscript in Catahoula Parish Library, Harrisonburg, La.
Davis, William. *The Orphan Brigade.* New York, 1980.
Eliot, Ellsworth, Jr. *West Point in the Confederacy.* New York, 1941.
Evans, Clement (ed.). *Confederate Military History.* 12 vols. Atlanta, 1899.
Ficklen, John R. *History of Reconstruction in Louisiana Through 1868.* Baltimore, 1910.
Fortier, Alcee. *Louisiana.* 3 vols. New Orleans, 1914.
Freeman, Douglas Southall. *Lee's Lieutenants, A Study in Command.* 3 vols., New York, 1942-1944.
Goodspeed, Weston A. *The Province and the State: A History of the Province of Louisiana.* Madison, 1904.
Hay, Thomas Robson. "Braxton Bragg and the Southern Confederacy," *Georgia Historical Quarterly, IX* (December, 1925), 267-316.
Hartje, Robert. *Van Dorn: The Life and Times of a Confederate General.* Nashville, 1967.
Heck, Frank H. *Proud Kentuckian: John C. Breckinridge, 1821-1875.* Lexington, 1976.
Hepworth, George H. *Whip, Hoe and Sword or the Gulf Department in 1863-1864.*
Horn, Stanley F. *Army of Tennessee.* 2nd ed., Norman, Oklahoma, 1955.
Hughes, Nathaniel C., Jr. *General William J. Hardee: Old Reliable.* Baton Rouge, 1965.
Johnson, Ludwell H. *Red River Campaign.* Baltimore, 1958.
Jonesville, Louisiana, "Welcome to Jonesville," pamphlet published in 1949.

Kane, Harnett T. *The Bayous of Louisiana.* New York, 1943.

Kerby, Robert L. *Kirby Smith's Confederacy. The Trans-Mississippi South, 1863-1865.* New York, 1972.

Lanza, Michael L. "The Jones-Liddell Feud." *Red River Valley Historical Review, II* (Winter, 1975), 467ff.

Livermore, Thomas L. *Numbers and Losses in the Civil War.* 2nd ed. Bloomington, 1957.

Lonn, Ella. *Reconstruction in Louisiana after 1868.* New York, 1918.

*Louisiana Geneological Register.* XIV (1967), p. 64.

McLamore, Thomas M. "The Civil War Campaign in Louisiana." Unpublished M. A. Thesis. Louisiana State University, 1916.

McWhiney, Grady. *Braxton Bragg and Confederate Defeat.* New York, 1969.

Meade, Robert Douthat. *Judah P. Benjamin: Confederate Statesman.* London, 1943.

Oates, Stephen B. *Confederate Cavalry West of the Mississippi.* Austin, 1961.

Parks, Joseph Howard. *General Edmund Kirby Smith, C.S.A.* Baton Rouge, 1954.

-----, Joseph Howard. *General Leonidas Polk, C.S.A., The Fighting Bishop.* Baton Rouge, 1962.

Postell, Paul. "John Hampton Randolph, A Louisiana Planter." *Louisiana Historical Quarterly, XXV* (January, 1942), 149-223.

Purdue, Howell and Elizabeth. *Pat Cleburne: Confederate General.* Hillsboro, Texas, 1973.

Raphael, Morris. *The Battle in the Bayou Country.* Detroit, 1975.

Roland, Charles P. *Albert Sidney Johnston: Soldier of Three Republics.* Austin, 1964.

Stickles, Arndt M. *Simon Bolivar Buckner, Borderland Knight.* Chapel Hill, 1940.

Strode, Hudson. *Jefferson Davis.* 3 vols. New York, 1955-1964.

Taylor, Joe Gray. *Louisiana Reconstructed, 1863-1877.* Baton Rouge, 1974.

Tucker, Glenn. *Chickamauga: Bloody Battle in the West.* Indianapolis, 1963.

Warner, Ezra J. *Generals in Gray: Lives of the Confederate Commanders.* Baton Rouge, 1959.

Warner, Ezra J. and W. Buck Yearns. *Biographical Register of the Confederate Congress.* Baton Rouge, 1975.

Williams, Samuel Cole, *General John T. Wilder, Commander of the Lightning Brigade.* Bloomington, 1936.

Williams, T. Harry. *P. G. T. Beauregard, Napoleon in Gray.* Baton Rouge, 1955.

Winters, John D. *The Civil War in Louisiana.* Baton Rouge, 1963.

# INDEX

211

# N

217

Walker, William H. T., 12, 135-142, 144, 145, 149, 168, 184
Walthall, Edward C., 144n, 145n
Walthall's Brigade, 133, 133n, 144, 149, 167
Warmouth, Henry C., 200
Wartrace Station, Tenn., 118-120, 122, 122n
Washington, D. C., 13
Wharton, John A., 108, 108n, 110, 111n
Wheat, Chatham Roberdeau "Rob," 32, 32n
Wheeler, Joseph, 87, 88, 115, 133, 134, 136, 150
White, Dr., W. A., 165, 205
Wiggins, Moses, 25
Wilder, John T., 82, 82n
Wilder's Brigade, 141n
Wilkinson Academy, 45n
Wilkinson County, Miss., 11
Wilkinson Turnpike, 109, 110
Williams, George A., 10, 79, 101n, 103n, 106, 187n

Willich, August, 128, 128n
Willis, Bugler, 103
Wills Creek, 134
Wills Valley, 134, 154, 156, 157, 158
Wimmer, ------, 196n
Withers Division, 91
Withers, Jones M., 82, 118, 119, 130, 130n
Wood, Sterling A. M., 37, 81, 103, 103n, 108n, 127, 128, 128n
Woodville, Miss., 11, 13, 45n, 171, 187n, 189n
Worth, William J., 134

## Y

Yandell, Dr. D. W., 185
York, Zebulon, 206n
Young, Wade, 165n, 187n, 206, 206n

## Z

Zollicoffer, Felix K., 48, 48n